D1594338

LEWIS EGERTON SMOOT MEMORIAL LIBRARY
9533 Kings Highway
General Delivery
King George, Virginia 22485

The World of Camelot

LEWIS EGERTON SMOOT MEMORIAL LIBRARY
9533 Kings Highway
General Delivery
King George, Virginia 22485

The World of Camelot

King Arthur and the Knights of the Round Table

Michael Foss

Sterling Publishing Co., Inc. New York

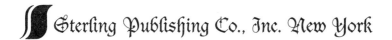
LEWIS EGERTON SMOOT MEMORIAL LIBRARY
9533 Kings Highway
General Delivery
King George, Virginia 22485

Library of Congress Cataloging-in-Publication Data Available

10 9 8 7 6 5 4 3 2 1

Published 1995 by Sterling Publishing Group, Inc.
387 Park Avenue South, New York, N.Y. 10016
First published in Great Britain by
Michael O'Mara Books Limited

© 1995 by Michael Foss

Distributed in Canada by Sterling Publishing
c/o Canadian Manda Group, One Atlantic Avenue, Suite 105
Toronto, Ontario, Canada M6K 3E7
Printed and bound in Great Britain
All rights reserved

Sterling ISBN 0-8069-1314-2

✟ Contents ✟

✤ Prologue: The Prisoner ✤

If he could find a dry place for the table, between the drips from the ceiling, he would get the work under way.

The room was large, but low, dank and foul. The air was fetid with odours of rot. Outside, a curtain of November drizzle drifted by the small, barred window. What did he expect? This was Newgate prison, at the start of a London winter, and a cell was no lady's chamber. But he had seen worse places, and a long career as a soldier had taught him to endure. From his youth he had taken the chances that life threw at him and had gone on resolutely.

Now that he was brought to rest he had time to reconsider. He remembered his early days, raised as a man of property in the county of Warwickshire. Eager for all adventure in the entourage of his liege lord, the famous Earl of Warwick, he had fought at the siege of Calais in 1436. Who better to teach chivalry than the earl, descendant of the legendary hero Guy of Warwick, of whom even the Saracens had heard? In the long-drawn-out French wars the earl had fought many resplendent and glorious jousts, on foot and on horseback, with broadsword and lance. In Jerusalem he had charmed even the infidel Turks. At the Council of Constance, the Holy Roman Emperor himself had declared that this English knight, Richard of Warwick, was the flower of courtesy and honour. Under the patronage and example of Warwick, the prisoner had fared well. By 1445 he sat in Parliament: Sir Thomas Malory, knight of chivalry and representative at the seat of government for the county of Warwickshire.

But his life began to go wrong. In the Wars of the Roses, which shattered his land for so many bitter years, he had taken the unlucky side. On behalf of the Lancastrians he had plundered and looted, been cruel and brave, wily and treacherous. He had done all those things a soldier must do in the agony of a civil war. Few chances for chivalry lay there. Slowly, the party he supported sank. Malory grew desperate with the times. He was deep in debt, ruining his inheritance with the expenses of war. He was accused of brigandage and cattle-stealing. Twice he was charged with rape. On successive days he tried to plunder the Abbey of Combe. Most shamefully, he attempted to murder the Duke of Buckingham.

In retrospect, Malory thought with wonder, 'How did I step so far from the path of honour? Truly, passion and party feeling, when they ride together, soon force chivalry from the field.'

Indicted for these and other offences, Malory saw the inside of several prisons after 1450. Indicted but not convicted, he benefited from the privileges of his class. The law was easy on knights. His imprisonment was quite gentlemanly, without the brutality and dire execution that so often awaited common criminals. Loosely guarded, he twice escaped: once he swam the moat in the night and fled; another time, he organized a break-out of armed desperadoes. But this boldness and enterprise made him a danger to the Yorkists. When Edward IV gave a general pardon to the Lancastrians, Malory was excluded. He was sent to Newgate, in London, where the authorities could keep an eye on him. Time lay on his hands. As long as a king of the House of York reigned, he could expect no release.

Sir Thomas Malory was that odd thing in the fifteenth century – a bookish knight. The poems of the troubadours, singing of courtly love, had beguiled his early years; later, he read the tales and romances of chivalry. He himself had stories to tell. In his riotous and unreflective way he too had been a knight errant, doing mighty deeds in France and England until poverty and weariness and the cruel polity of civil war had overwhelmed his ideals. He did not regret his life. No, he had tried in the main to live in the great tradition that noble men and gentle ladies ought to follow. But what did they know about it now? The world of heroism and knightly courtesy was dying. Warfare had become filth and butchery. The world forgot. But he had the inclination, and chance had given him the time, to set out once more the old tales of love and gallantry before they were finally blotted out by the raw torrent of blood.

Locked up in Newgate, he set to his task. Whittington, lord mayor of London, had founded a famous library in the house of the Grey Friars, no more than a hundred paces from Newgate. As a knight and a political prisoner, Malory was permitted the indulgence of books. A soldier caged and preoccupied with old volumes was no further danger to the state. Lucas the jailer would fetch them. That simpleton could just be relied on to make the short walk between Newgate and Grey Friars.

Impatiently, Malory waited for his messenger's return. With many grumbles Lucas dumped heavy volumes on the cell table. Malory blew off the dust. He turned many stained and scuffed pages, smelling the old leather of the bindings. Words, so many words. Dust got in his nose and made him sneeze; faint ink and the vagaries of the handwritten script tested his eyes in the poor prison light. Often his heart sank. What, he wondered, had these artifices of chivalry got to do with present reality – with the locked door and the creeping damp, with the insolence of the Yorkist victory and the pain of Lancastrian defeat? Then he began to read once more, and his resolve returned. 'All that is written here,' he told himself, 'is for our doctrine, so that we fall not into vice or sin, but exercise and follow virtue.'

With renewed energy he plunged into the books. On the cell table lay the old Latin stories of Arthur of Britain, more fiction than history. And there, at another time, were piled long French romances in verse and prose. With slow deliberation, Malory read and noted. He read the English *Sir Percyvell*, the French *Perlesvaus*, the German *Parzival*. He knew tales from many lands of Merlin, Gawain, Tristan and Galahad. He studied the *Mort Artu* and the alliterative *Morte Arthur*. Malory read them all in joy and wonder. His head rang with the blows of chivalry. Knights with blazoned shields jousted in fields of wild flowers. He saw in his imagination noble ladies, as pale as their white mules, ride to the lists dressed in marten and ermine and watered silk. Gloves and ribbons fell at the feet of the combatants. Stern cries rang out: 'Be worthy of your ancestors' and 'Remember whose son you are'.

All at once the stench of Newgate had vanished. Drizzling London beyond the cell window was no more. Released from the cell, his spirit entered another world of light and love, of grace and valour.

After some years of steady application, he had read enough. Now he must make this world known before it was too late. He must start writing. He would begin at the beginning.

✦ The Coming of Arthur ✦

In the days when Uther Pendragon was king of all England, the Duke of Cornwall, a bold and mighty man, made war against him for a long time. Worn down by the expense and misery of battle, King Uther at last sent for this duke, charging him also to bring his wife. She was known to be a beautiful lady, with wisdom that matched her looks, and her name was Igraine.

Now, when the king saw Igraine he liked her very well and desired to lie with her. But she was a good woman and would not consent. Uther pressed her. What is a king but a lord of all his people? Look at my person, he said, my riches, my castles, my power. But Igraine cast her eyes down to the floor and went into another room.

'Why were we sent for?' she asked the duke. 'Was it so that I should be dishonoured? Husband, fly away. Come, let us ride through the night to our own lands.'

When the king learnt that they had fled, he was angry and summoned them again, with the threat of fire and destruction if the duke did not submit. But neither the duke nor his wife would come back. Then King Uther sent the duke plain words, telling him to make ready for a siege, for the king intended to prise him out of even his strongest castle within forty days. The duke took this warning to heart, for he knew the spirit and the temper of the king. So he prepared two strong castles, one called Tintagel and the other Terrabil. Igraine, his wife, took charge of Tintagel and he commanded Terrabil. He secured all the gates and entrances and passageways, where a man might be surprised and die in a small space. With a heavy heart he paced the battlements, awaiting the enemy.

King Uther was as good as his word. In a short time his army marched out of the woods and meadows and surrounded the castle with countless pavilions of many colours. Looking down from the heights of the castle, the duke felt that he was cast adrift in a bright but angry sea. Then battle began, and many were slain.

When the fighting was going on, with no advantage to either side, King Uther fell sick. This was a great worry for his knights.

'How shall we overcome this castle without our king?' said Sir Ulfius. 'Sir, what is the cause of your pain?'

'Truly,' replied the king, 'I can tell you this: I am sick for anger and for love of Igraine. Without her, I shall never be a whole man.'

'Well, my lord,' said Ulfius, 'you may be at ease. There is a man hereabouts called Merlin, who is a great wizard. I will seek him out, for he has the means to cure you and make you whole.'

Then Sir Ulfius rode away, asking in villages and lanes and byways where Merlin might be found. But none knew, for Merlin was a most mysterious man. As he roamed the countryside, Ulfius came across a beggar most miserably dressed, whom the knight would have struck from the path. But the beggar held up his hand and the knight stopped as if he could not help himself.

'Look no further,' said the beggar. 'I am Merlin. I know already what you seek. If King Uther will reward me with what I ask, I will give him everything he desires. Go on your way to the king, and I will not be long behind.'

When Sir Ulfius returned to the camp alone, the king searched anxiously for the wizard. Suddenly, a voice sounded from behind him. 'I know everything in your heart,' it said. 'I am Merlin. Swear to me as a true king that you will do as I ask, and you shall have your desire.'

At once, a cross was fetched and the king swore his vow on the four Evangelists, and Merlin was satisfied. 'You shall do this,' he told the king. 'You shall lie with Igraine and get her with child in the first night. When that child is born it shall be mine to keep and to raise as I think best. But do not be afraid. This child will be worthy of your name.'

6

'Anything,' cried Uther. 'You shall have whatever you ask. But be quick. My heart is wracked for love.'

'This night,' Merlin promised, 'disguised as her husband, you shall lie with Igraine in the castle of Tintagel. This I shall accomplish by my art. Say nothing when you enter her chamber but go quickly to bed and wrap her in your arms, answering no questions, and please her with full manly vigour. Rise early in the morning, when I shall come to fetch you, and step lightly and without noise from her bed.'

In the evening King Uther covered himself in a cloak and left the camp. But the Duke of Cornwall had spies out who noticed that the king had slipped away from the siege. In the dark, the duke opened the gates and made a sudden attack on the king's army. But the struggle went badly for the duke, and he was killed in the black night even before King Uther had reached Tintagel.

Three hours after the death of the duke, Uther lay with Igraine in much happiness, and that same night she conceived the child Arthur. Before the break of day Merlin came to the bedside and whispered to the king to make haste, for the sun was already peeping at the rim of the Eastern world. King Uther arose and gave the lady Igraine a single kiss, as soft as dew. She stirred and murmured, 'Ah, husband'. Then she went back to sleep.

In the first light of the day came the messenger from Terrabil with the news of the death of the duke, so far from her bed, and Igraine could only marvel: who had slept with her in the likeness of her lord? She did not know what to do, except to mourn and hold her peace.

Then all the barons of Uther Pendragon, celebrating the death of the duke and knowing the inclination of the king's heart, prayed him to look kindly on Igraine. 'Our king,' said bold Sir Ulfius, 'is a lusty knight and wifeless, and my lady Igraine is a person of great beauty. If it might please the king to make her his queen, it would give us all great joy.'

With goodwill Uther agreed, and so in haste they were married on a summer morning. Then Queen Igraine swelled with child so that within half a year the king questioned her. 'By the faith you owe me,' he said as he lay fondly by her side, 'whose child is that within your body?'

At this question she was sadly cast down and did not know what to say.

'Do not be dismayed,' said the king, his hand resting tenderly on her swelling womb, 'but tell me the truth, and by the faith of my body I shall love you the better.'

Taking courage, the queen told him the strange thing that had happened. 'That is the truth,' said the king, 'for I myself came to you in the likeness of the duke. You need not worry. I am the father of your child.'

When the queen heard that all this was done by the art of Merlin, she was satisfied. But the shadow of Merlin crossed the threshold once more, and he said to the king, 'Make ready, Sir. When the child is born, remember that it is mine.'

'So be it,' the king replied, with some heaviness. 'Tell me what must be done.'

'There is a lord in your land who is a true and faithful man. His name is Sir Ector. Send for him and order him, as he loves you, that he and his wife must take care of the child and raise it as their own. When the child is born, deliver it to me unchristened at the private gate.'

Sir Ector was sent for and promised faithfully to do as the king wished, and for this he was given great rewards. Then the queen's time came and she gave birth to a baby boy. She washed the baby and held it close for a moment, and wrapped it gently in cloth of gold. She handed it to two knights and two ladies who took the child and delivered it to the man in beggar's rags at the inner gate, who then galloped away, with the bundle tied to his pommel, to the home of Sir Ector. When Ector had received the baby from Merlin, a holy man christened the boy and named him Arthur. Afterwards, the wife of Sir Ector nourished the child at her own breast.

Now, within two years King Uther fell sick and his enemies pressed hard upon him. The king, too ill to fight, was none the less carried in a horse-litter into the midst of battle. In this way, he encouraged his men to a great victory. But the effort left Uther so spent that for three days and three nights he lay speechless.

Merlin was called to the king's chamber, but after he had seen Uther he withdrew. 'There is no remedy,' he said sadly. 'God will have his way. But, barons, attend King Uther in the morning, and God and I shall make him speak one more time.'

On the morn, when all were solemnly gathered, Merlin cried aloud to the king: 'Sir, say truly, shall your son Arthur be king after your days?'

The king groaned and spoke, so weakly that hardly a mouse might hear. 'I give Arthur,' he barely whispered, 'God's blessing and mine. I bid him pray for my soul, that he may rightly and with honour claim the crown.' Then he yielded up the ghost and was buried as befitted a king, to the infinite sorrow of the queen, fair Igraine, and all the barons.

The king was dead. Who knew the new king, this prince, this Arthur? The barons had sworn no oaths; they had no allegiance to a prince they had never seen. The realm stood in great danger for a long while: every mighty lord strove to be king, thinking that he might hack his way through bodies and blood to the throne. Good people wept, and plague and dearth took over the land. Then the archbishop, on the advice of Merlin, sent for all the lords and gentlemen–at–arms to come to London at Christmas. The archbishop promised them a miracle to bring them order and reveal the true king of the realm.

The summons from the man of religion made the barons pause. What will men do if there is no authority? The horse runs wild without the reins. In truth, many knights were glad to stop the killing and these lords made their lives clean, to be more acceptable to God, before coming to the greatest church in London. After matins and the first Mass were finished, a great four-square marble stone rose up against the high altar. In its midst was an anvil of steel a foot tall, and stuck by the point into this was a naked sword. Gold letters were written about the sword, and this is what they said:

Whosoever pulls out this sword from this anvil and this stone is rightly the king of all England.

At this sign, all men stared and were amazed. Then, little by little, they approached the stone, taking its measure. Where was the danger? And when they received no hurt and the vision did not go away but remained solid and challenging, certain bolder warriors thought: why not? Ambition is the virtue of those who would be great. First one lord, and then another and another, heaved at the sword. But none could move it. At the end of the day, after all the Masses were done, and compline and benediction too, the sword was still there, stuck fast in the stone.

Then the archbishop ordained that ten good knights should guard the sword. On New Year's Day the barons assembled again, with jousts and tournaments, to test their power against the sword in the stone. They rode into the field, and had great sport. And it chanced that Sir Ector rode to the jousts with Sir Kay, his son, and young Arthur, who had been raised as a brother to Kay.

This Sir Kay was a new knight, only dubbed at All Hallowmass, but as he rode proudly towards his first joust he saw that he had left his sword at home. Just the act of a callow youth! He blushed to admit his mistake and so called Arthur privately to his side, and begged the young squire to hurry home and fetch his sword. Arthur was willing and away he went as fast as his horse would carry him. But at Sir Ector's house all the servants and retainers were gone to applaud at the jousts and there was no-one to find him the sword. Arthur was angry and said to himself, 'Without a sword my brother Kay will be shamed. I will ride to the churchyard and take that sword that is sticking from the stone.'

At the church, Arthur tied his horse to the stile. He looked about warily, but the sword was unguarded, for the knights who watched it were cheering in the lists of the tournament. Arthur took the sword by the handle and lightly but surely pulled it from the stone. Then he rode happily on his way and gave the sword to Sir Kay. At once, Kay recognized the sword for what it was. 'Look here, Sir,' he said to Sir Ector, 'Surely this is the sword from the stone. Must I now,' he added hopefully, 'be king of all this land?'

But Sir Ector, when he went and saw that the stone was empty, cuffed his son about the ears and made him swear on the Holy Book how he had come by the sword. So word came out that young Arthur had provided it.

'Were there any knights guarding this sword?' asked Sir Ector.

'Nay, not one.'

'Now I see clearly,' said Sir Ector to Arthur, 'that you have the royal sign upon you, and that you must be king of this land.'

'Why me?' said Arthur. 'And for what cause?'

'Sir,' replied Ector sternly, 'because God will have it so. Only the rightful king has the power to pull this sword. Now replace it where it was and let me see you pull it again.'

The sword was replaced and first Sir Ector tried to pull it free, and then Sir Kay. Both failed. But Arthur plucked it as easily as a plum from a pudding. At once, Ector and Kay sank to their knees.

'Alas, my own dear father and brother' said Arthur. 'Why do you kneel to me?'

'Nay, nay, my lord Arthur,' Sir Ector replied. 'I was never your father nor of your blood.' And he told Arthur how things had fallen out by the art of Merlin. All this was strange and unquiet news to Arthur. A king must follow a lonely path, with few to trust and many to fear. He grieved the loss of the good knight Ector, who had been as a father to him.

'Sir,' said Ector, seeing how wistful Arthur was, 'will you be my good and gracious lord when you are king?'

'Else were I to blame,' replied Arthur, 'for I owe all the world to you and my good lady your wife. Whatever you desire of me I shall not fail you. God forbid that I should fail you.' And straightaway Arthur promised that Sir Kay should be steward of all his lands, as long as Arthur reigned and Kay lived.

Then on Twelfth Day, on the feast of the Epiphany of Our Lord, Arthur proved before all the barons that he alone could pull the sword from the stone. Many were angry and muttered that it was their great shame to be governed by a mere boy of low blood. And so the matter was put off till Candlemass, and again till Pentecost, when all manner of lords sweated mightily to pull the sword, but again only Arthur could do it.

At this, even the commons were angry at the delay and cried out against the knights. 'We will have Arthur for our king,' they shouted. 'Let there be no more dilly–dallying. It is God's will that Arthur should reign. To hold out against him is futile. Our swords say that Arthur shall be king.'

When they felt the hot breath of the crowd and saw the sharpness of the swords, the lords gave way. Rich and poor fell to their knees, and Arthur forgave them all, even the doubters and those with jealous hearts and too much pride. He took the sword in his hands and offered it upon the altar where the archbishop stood. And that holy man blessed Arthur and knighted him right there, in front of the altar.

Soon Arthur was crowned and swore to the lords and the commons to be a true king, to stand with justice throughout all England in all the days of his life.

There was so much to do. The affairs of England were in sad disarray. Arthur went about the land with his arm raised against over-mighty lords. By acts of chivalry, and with God's help, he brought peace where there had once been war. But after many days in the saddle and under arms he grew weary of fighting. At Pentecost he journeyed to Wales, and announced a great feast in the city of Caerleon for the relaxation and joy of his knights. King Lot of Lothian and Orkney came to the feast, and King Uriens of Gore, and King Nentres of Garlot, and the young king of Scotland, and with these kings were many hundred knights.

King Arthur welcomed them all, for he believed that they had come from love of him and to honour him. He was full of joy and sent out rich presents. But none was accepted and his messengers were rebuked, for the other kings were still proud and would accept no gifts from a lowborn, beardless boy. They sent word that they had come instead to give him gifts of another kind, with hard sword-strokes between the neck and the shoulder. When he heard this, Arthur shut himself up in a strong tower with five hundred good men, and once again awaited the call of war.

Now, Merlin was also in Caerleon at this time and all the other kings were glad to see him. One question, in particular, they asked him: 'Why is that boy, Arthur, crowned your king?'

'He is Uther Pendragon's son,' Merlin replied, 'gotten on Igraine, wife of the Duke of Cornwall.'

'Then he is a bastard.'

But Merlin told them how Arthur was begotten after the death of the duke, and how Uther was wedded with Igraine. Some of the kings marvelled at Merlin's words. Some, like King Lot, laughed him to scorn, and yet others called him a witch. Then Merlin went to Arthur and comforted him, telling him to stand against his enemies as their king and chieftain.

Hard words passed between King Arthur and the other kings. Each side stood unyielding against the other. They parted with many oaths, daring one another to do their worst. Arthur returned to his tower and put his men into a state of readiness.

'What will you do now?' said Merlin to the kings. 'Better stop at once. You will not win were you ten times as strong.'

'Bold words,' cried King Lot. 'Should we be advised by you, a day-dreamer?'

With that, Merlin turned from the kings with contempt and went to Arthur with the promise of victory, saying, 'Fight not with the sword from the stone, the miracle blade, until you see that things are at the worst. Then draw the sword and strike your best blows.'

The battle began and the knights on both sides set about each other fiercely. The earth shook with horse thunder, with the howl of triumph and the gasp of the dying. Feet slipped in rivers of blood, and encumbered knights, tangled in arms and armour, lay in a red mire, waiting for their squires to come and raise them. Many were slain. The common people of Caerleon, affronted by the attack on their king, rose up against Arthur's enemies. They dealt roughly with the knights, pulling them from their horses, battering them down with staves and clubs, and slitting the throats of the fallen. The kings who contended against Arthur gathered together those of their men left alive and fled the field.

King Arthur wiped his brow and rested, leaning on a long spear. Victory had won him time. He would withdraw to London, but he knew well that the enmity of the northern kings still raged against him. So he took counsel with Merlin.

'Your enemies,' said Merlin, 'are in retreat for the time being, but they are still as strong as any men alive. This is my advice. Send across the sea to France for the two brothers, King Ban of Benwick and King Bors of Gaul. These are both marvellous good men. Swear a pact with them, to help each other in your need.'

And so it was that messengers were sent to Ban and Bors, who came about All Hallowmass to be welcomed with joy and feasts and tourneys. With all ceremony, King Arthur met them ten miles from London in a place by the river, under the willow tree, where pavilions were built and dressed in cloth of gold. And all the noble ladies, and the townsmen too, quit the city, jostling eagerly on the road to see who would do best in the jousts and the trials of honour.

Listen, stragglers on the road, the herald's trumpet is already sounding. Hurry! The procession has come to the lists, under flags and flying bunting, with painted shields, and with horses hooded and cloaked in many colours. The minstrels are playing, pipes and drums and bagpipes squeak and rattle and moan. The bold sound of brass brays into the air. Jongleurs and clowns contort and tumble, inciting the low fellows under the stands with many ribald gestures. But wait! The horses are impatient. That one can hardly be curbed. It breaks into an *estai*, a little canter, pawing the ground. The lists are ready. A sudden hush. The combatants have dressed their shields and begin to lower their lances.

Griflet, a flower of France, was the first that met with an English knight, whose name was Ladinas. They dashed together so eagerly that all men wondered at the shock. A long time they fought, their lances broken and their shields falling to pieces. Then horses and men plunged to the ground. The battle cries had died in their throats; they staggered with weariness. Still the heralds encouraged them, imploring them loudly, in God's name, to fight like men.

'Fair ladies,' they cried, turning to the stands, 'shall these good knights stain the green grass red without your approval? Where are

your voices? Show them your ribbons, your sleeves, your handker-
chiefs. Wave them bravely.'

But the French knight and the English knight were at their wits' end.
They could do no more, and presently they lay down and lay like dead
men. Thus, by hard knocks, they proved themselves for war, and the
hearts of enemy soldiers, had they seen this contest, would have
quaked.

Thus it came about that Arthur and Ban and Bors made a pact among
themselves, readied their armies and made war against eleven kings.
Then battle raged hard on hills and plains.

When King Lot spied King Bors, he knew him well. 'O Jesus, defend
us from death and horrible wounds,' he cried, 'for I see a king who is a
bold man and the best of knights.'

And then, for his greater discomfort, King Ban came into the field as
fierce as a lion, all dressed in stripes of green and gold. 'Ha, woe is me,'
lamented Lot. 'Here is the other brother, and there are no two fighters
to equal these. We must avoid them or die.'

The strokes of the swords rebounded again from the woods and the
fields. King Lot wept for pity when he saw so many knights meet their
end. Arthur and his two kings slew left and right, as hungry as winter
wolves among the mountain deer. It was terrible to behold bodies so
hacked and bruised. But always the eleven kings, well practised in
chivalry, never turned their backs, but withdrew step by step to a little
wood across a stream. There they rested, for at night it was not wise to
be caught in the open field. The eleven kings and their knights all inched
together, like men afraid and out of comfort. But still no man could pass
them. King Arthur marvelled at their deeds, though he felt a bitter
anger.

'By my faith,' cried King Ban, 'they are the best fighting men that ever
I saw. If those eleven kings followed you, no king under heaven would
have such knights.'

'I may not love them,' replied Arthur. 'They would destroy me.'

Next day, battle was renewed. In the thick of the press Arthur, Ban
and Bors killed on both hands until their horses went in blood up to the
fetlocks. But always the eleven kings and their knights closed ranks and
faced Arthur, which was a great marvel given the amount of the
slaughter. At last Merlin, on a huge black horse, loomed from the
evening mist with a pale sun behind him and called out to Arthur;

'Have you not done enough, you sorrowful king? Of sixty thousand that lived this morning you have left but fifteen thousand. It is time to say "Halt!" God is angry with you, that you are not yet done. Therefore those eleven kings will not be overthrown this time. Rest now, and reward your good knights with gold and silver, for they have matched themselves this day with the best fighters in the world.'

'That is the truth,' added King Ban and King Bors.

'These eleven kings,' Merlin went on, 'are no danger any more. They have more on hand than they are aware of, for the infidel Saracens have landed in their territories, burning and slaying, and have laid siege at Castle Wandesborow. Give freely to these two, Ban and Bors, and go on your way.'

With gratitude, Arthur accompanied the two kings from France on their way, riding after six days into the country of King Leodegrance, who claimed the help of his fellow kings in subduing certain rebellious lords. And here, in the palace, Arthur suddenly saw a face and a figure that remained with him in memory or by his side for the rest of his days. He saw the delicate smile of a lady in the act of going behind the curtain, a graceful presence that was soon gone. It was Guenevere, the king's daughter, and he ever after loved her.

At this time he did not stop, for the affairs of his realm called him on to Caerleon, where the wife of King Lot had come as if on an embassy, but in truth to spy out the court of King Arthur. With her, she had brought her four sons: Gawain, Gaheris, Agravaine and Gareth.

Now this lady was fair and artful and richly dressed, and she was attended with great state by many knights and ladies. She spoke boldly to Arthur and looked him in the eye, drawing out his heart till all at once he turned his face away. She went, and he called her to him again, for he desired her greatly and wished to lie in her bed. In this they were agreed. Arthur went secretly to her room and she gave her body to him, and Arthur got her with a child who was later named Mordred. This lady, Morgause, was the king's half-sister by issue from his mother Igraine, though Arthur had no knowledge that she was his sister. Morgause rested a month in Arthur's court and then departed.

When she had gone, King Arthur had a strange dream that caused him much fear. He thought he saw griffins and serpents that burnt and slew all the people in the land. In this dream he fought with them and they hurt him almost to death. He was sorely wounded before he could kill them.

When the king awoke, heavy with foreboding, he tried to forget his thoughts and made ready to go hunting. In the forest, he soon gave chase after a fine, strong hart. He spurred his horse and rode so hard that his horse staggered for want of breath and fell down dead. Seeing his horse dead, Arthur sat by a fountain, lost in thought, while his servant went to fetch him a new mount.

And as he sat he heard the noise of hounds, perhaps as many as thirty. Running towards him was the strangest beast he ever saw or heard of. This beast rushed to the well to drink, with a noise in its belly like the questing and howling of many hounds. The noise ceased while the beast drank, and afterwards it ran away with a thrashing of hooves. Arthur wondered and pondered, and soon fell asleep.

A knight came by on foot and said to Arthur, 'Knight full of thought and so sleepy, tell me if you saw a strange beast pass this way. I have followed this quest for the past year and have killed my horse. Either I shall achieve my quest or shed my best blood.'

'The beast is already two miles hence,' Arthur replied. 'Leave your quest to me, for this mystery touches on my thoughts, and I will follow it for a further twelve months.'

'Nay, fool,' the knight told Arthur. 'This quest belongs to me only, or to my near kin.'

And he laid hold of the bridle of the horse that the king's servant had just brought up and flung himself into the saddle, saying, 'My thanks to you, now this horse is my own.'

'Wait,' called the king. 'You may steal my horse but I can prove who is better on horseback, you or I.'

'Whenever you will,' shouted the knight as he galloped away. 'When the time is right, you will find me by this well.'

'What boldness makes this rash knight do these things?' Arthur wondered, as his serving-man ran to fetch yet another horse. 'Is this his quest or mine, bred out of my dreams? God puts mysteries in our paths. It is hard enough, then, to find the right way.'

He was worrying these matters further in his head when Merlin came to him in the form of a child of fourteen. Upbraiding the king for his forlorn looks, this beardless youth seemed to have knowledge beyond his years. He told Arthur the story of his begetting, which the king did

16

not know, and how he was suckled and raised. The king was angry and lifted his fist to the youth. Who was this mere child that he should know these things? And Arthur did not believe him.

Merlin went away, but soon returned as an old man. 'Are you troubled?' asked the old man in a kindly way. 'There is some grief in your looks.'

'I am heavy with thought,' Arthur replied, 'because a child has told me many strange things. How shall a child know these things?'

'Is it the child or the truth that you do not want to hear? Yes, that boy spoke the truth, and had more to tell you but for your anger. God is displeased with you. You have lain with your sister, and on her you have gotten a child who shall destroy you and all the knights of your realm.'

'Who are you?' said the king.

'I am the child, I am the old man, I am he who sees things unknown. I am Merlin. Listen, but do not marvel, for it is God's will that your body shall be punished for your foul deed. Your fate is hard, but mine is worse. I shall be cast in the earth quick after a shameful death, but you shall die an honourable man.'

Sadly, drawn together in their fate, king and wizard rode into Caerleon, where the king took thought on what he had been told. He asked Ector and Ulfius how he had been begotten, and they replied that it was as Merlin had said. So Arthur sent for Igraine, his mother, that he might hear it from her own lips. In haste Igraine came with her daughter, the beautiful Morgan le Fay, and the king welcomed them.

That night, when they were feasting, Sir Ulfius was taken with drink and turned on the queen. 'You are the most false lady in the world,' he accused her, 'and a traitress to the king's person.'

'Softly,' Arthur warned. 'Beware what you are saying. Those words must be made good.'

'I am well aware,' Ulfius replied. 'I throw down my glove to any who says to the contrary. If this Queen Igraine had told of your birth during the life of King Uther, then there would have been no mortal wars. Your barons, knowing whose son you were, would have obeyed you.' Slowly, Igraine lowered her eyes. She hardly dared to look upon the king.

'I am a woman,' she said, 'I cannot fight. Rather than I should be dishonoured, let Merlin speak for me. Know that everything that happened to me was as if to a victim. First I loved my lord the duke, then I loved my lord King Uther. What I did was according to Merlin's art. He took my child from me so that I never saw it, nor ever knew the name it was given. Well I know that, in both joy and grief, I bore a child to King Uther Pendragon. But what became of that child I do not know.'

Then Sir Ector, who could not keep back the tears, bore witness to this tale, and Merlin took the king by the hand, saying, 'Sir, here is your mother'. They came together and Arthur took his mother, Igraine, in his arms and kissed her, and they wept on each other. And then the king made a feast that lasted eight days.

Soon there came news to the court that a strange knight had set up a pavilion in the forest, blocking the path. No man could pass by unless he jousted with the knight. So Arthur rode out at daybreak to the place, where he saw a well-armed knight lolling at ease in a chair before the pavilion.

'Sir knight,' said Arthur, 'why do you bar the way, forcing unlucky men to joust with you? I advise you to give up that custom.'

'Good or bad,' replied the knight, 'that is my custom, whether you like it or not. Try to change it if you will.'

'Yes, I will amend it,' said Arthur.

'Then I shall defend it,' answered the knight.

Arthur dressed his shield and took a spear, and he and the knight rode so hard against each other that their spears were shivered in pieces. Then Arthur was angry. He drew his sword and smote the knight with many great strokes. They hewed and hacked at each other until the emblems flew from their helms into the field and the ground was spattered with their blood. Thus they fought, and rested, and fought again, hurtling together like two rams. At last, with a fierce clash of swords, the king's weapon broke in two.

'Yield or die!' cried the knight in triumph.

'Death is welcome when it comes,' said Arthur, 'but to surrender is to die of shame.'

With that, he leapt forwards, grappling, till the knight tore the helm from the king and would have struck off his head had not Merlin appeared and stopped that murderous blow. Quickly, Merlin cast an enchantment on the knight, who fell at once to the earth in sleep, while Merlin tenderly took up the king and bore him away.

'Alas, Merlin, what have you done?' said Arthur. 'Have you slain this best of knights by your magic crafts? He fought so well I would give my land to have him alive.'

'Hush, do not fret,' Merlin replied. 'He is only asleep. He will awake in good time to do you service. His name is Pellinore, that same worthy whom you saw in pursuit of the Questing Beast. He shall be the father of Percival of Wales and Lamorak of Wales, two sons greater in prowess and nobility than all men but one. And Pellinore shall tell you the name of your own son, the one begotten of your sister, who shall be the cause of the destruction of all your realm.'

Arthur listened, but he could not put his mind to the words. He was sore and battered, wounded and losing blood. Merlin led him to the hut of a hermit in the woods, a wise man practised in the use of salves and herbs. And there the king rested and was healed. After a while they rode forth again, and the king suddenly recalled the fight against Pellinore.

'My sword is broken,' he said to Merlin. 'Shall I fight with no sword?'

'Be not dismayed,' replied Merlin. 'Near this place there is a sword worthy of a king.'

They came to a lake of broad water, and in the midst of it was an arm clothed in rich silk holding a sword that dazzled in the light.

'That is the very sword I spoke of,' said Merlin. 'See there, the Lady of the Lake. She comes from a kingdom of rock within the water, a place as strange and wonderful as any on earth. She will come to you in a moment. Speak to her softly and with respect, and she will give you that sword.'

'Most fair lady,' said Arthur, 'what sword is that, the one held above the water? It is a fine blade and ready to do work. I would it were mine, for I have no sword.'

'Sir Arthur, O king,' replied the lady, 'that sword is mine. You shall have it. But give gift for gift. What shall I have in return?'

'By my faith, you shall have whatever you ask.'

'So be it. Step into that boat and row yourself to the sword. Take it, and the scabbard also. I will demand my gift when the time is right.'

Arthur rowed into the lake, and the arm gave up the sword to him and slipped away under the water. On the shore, the king considered his prize. He smiled and tested the sword, and smiled again. Then he rode on to a fork in the path where a tent of gaudy colour commanded the way.

'That pavilion,' said Arthur pensively, 'what does it signify?'

'It is Sir Pellinore's,' replied Merlin, 'he with whom you fought. He is distant now, pursuing other contests. But we shall meet him soon on the highway.'

'Good. Now that I have a sword I shall avenge myself with hard blows against him.'

'Do not do so, sir, for this knight is weary and not fit for honourable combat. Let him pass. In a short time he and his sons shall be useful to you.'

Sadly, Arthur put up his new sword and rested it in the scabbard.

'Which is better,' Merlin now asked him, 'sword or scabbard?'

'The sword, of course.'

'No, you are wrong. The scabbard is worth ten swords. That scabbard shall save you whole from all wounds, and from all loss of blood. Keep it always by your side.'

Just then, Sir Pellinore rode into view, but Merlin threw an enchantment on him so that he rode by unseeing, with his head in the air.

'I marvel,' said Arthur, 'that the knight would not speak.'

'Sir, he saw nothing. But had he seen you, it would have led to blows.'

So King Arthur came peacefully to Caerleon. His knights welcomed him with joy, glad that he was alive and well after he had ventured his arm and his honour in a stern fight, even as other poor knights had to do. But Arthur was not content. He brooded on the dark things that Merlin had told him about his son, the one begotten on his sister in sin. And seeing the king in this heaviness and knowing the cause of this complaint, Merlin advised him to kill all children born of lords and ladies on May Day. 'That is the safest thing,' said Arthur, and agreed. On pain of death, he ordered the children to be sent to him. In fear, many lords sent their babies, among whom was Mordred, sent by the wife of King Lot. Then all were put into a ship and consigned to the grim sea, though some were only four weeks old.

Now it happened that the ship was driven onto the rocks below a castle and wrecked. All the children were killed except for Mordred, who was cast up on the beach. By luck he was discovered by a kindly man, a native of those parts, who took the babe home and kept him and nourished him as his own, until Mordred was of an age to seek his fortune in the world.

But many barons of the realm, seeing their children cast away, were frightened and angered by the deeds of the king. They whispered with discontent, but they put the greater blame on Merlin, for they were in dread of King Arthur. They knew the duty that they owed to him as their lord, and so they held their peace.

✠ Balin le Savage ✠

There was a king called Rience, lord of north Wales and all Ireland and many other isles besides, who was a proud and mighty king and a good warrior. He had overcome eleven other kings. He had flayed the beards from their chins and worked them into the border of his cloak, and he intended to do the same for King Arthur. He sent a messenger to tell Arthur so. 'Say to the king: there's one space left in the border of my cloak where your beard will fit neatly.'

'O, most shameful!' Arthur replied. 'I see that your king has never yet met a man of honour, but I will have his head unless he does homage to me.'

Then Arthur summoned his barons and knights and went to Camelot to make his defence. When they were all gathered, a maiden came from the lady Lile of Avelion. She was richly dressed in a mantle trimmed with fur, but there was sorrow in her face. As she made her greetings to the king, her mantle fell open and Arthur saw a sword at her side.

'Lady,' he said, 'why that sword? Is it proper for a maiden? It befits you not.'

'That sword,' she replied, 'is a sad burden to me. Only a knight with clean hands and clean deeds may deliver me from it, a knight without villainy or treason. But where can I find such a man? I heard that there were noble knights at the court of King Rience. What did I find? All tried to draw this sword from the sheath, and all failed.'

This was a great wonder to Arthur. He offered to try the sword himself. It was not in his mind that he was the best knight, but he did it to encourage his barons. He put one hand on the sword and the other on the girdle of the lady, and tugged so mightily that she was pulled clear off her feet.

'Sir,' she said hastily, 'pull not half so hard. A small tug will draw the sword, if you be of gentle birth. But beware you be not defiled by shame or treachery.'

Then most of the barons tried, one by one, but none could do it.

'Alas,' the maiden cried, 'I thought this court had the best knights in the world.'

'By my faith,' said Arthur, 'there are good knights here, as good as any, but I see they cannot help you. That is a great sadness to me.'

Now, there was a poor knight in Arthur's court whose name was Balin. He had killed the king's cousin in an affray and was in prison for half a year. But he was a well-born knight from Northumberland of good and worthy name, so by intervention of certain high barons he was released. In the court, poor and ill dressed, he watched at the edge of the crowd, for he would not push forwards among so many noble men. He saw many knights try but fail to draw the sword. In his heart he knew he could do as well as any, had he but the chance. So when the maiden covered herself again in her mantle and turned from the court, Balin followed behind and called softly from the path.

'Lady, of your courtesy, let me try. Though I am poor and poorly clothed, my heart is pure.'

The maiden looked at the poor knight. He was a fine fellow, but how could one so tattered be without stain?

'Sir,' she said, 'I have suffered enough pain and trouble. What warrant is there that you might succeed where noble men have failed?'

'Ah, fair lady, look beyond clothes and raiment for worthiness. Manhood and honour are hidden within. Many a good knight rides unknown.'

'By God, you speak the truth,' she replied. 'And so, good sir, try your best.'

Balin grasped the sword by the handle and swiftly pulled it free. The blade was hard and fine and full of danger, and it pleased him much.

Then the king and all the court marvelled that Balin, so poor a knight, had done this thing, and many barons were jealous.

"'Tis true,' said the maiden. 'This is a worthy knight, the best that ever I have found. He shall do many marvels. Now, gentle sir, give me back the sword again.'

Balin jumped back dismayed. 'Nay, only force shall make me quit this sword.'

'O unwise man!' she warned. 'With that sword you will slay him you love most in the world. It shall destroy you.'

'I shall take whatever fortune God sends me,' Balin replied. 'But this sword you shall not have, except from my dead body.'

Then the maiden looked on him with sorrow. 'Soon, you shall repent. I grieve for you, and would have the sword for your sake, not mine.' She looked at him again: so noble a young knight, and with such a spirit and high heart. She shook her head and departed.

Soon Balin sent for horse and armour and went to take leave of King Arthur.

'Stay,' said the king. 'Do not leave our noble fellowship so lightly. You are displeased with me? Forgive me. I was misinformed against you. Rest here, and I shall advance you as your prowess demands.'

'God thank your lordship,' Balin replied, 'but adventure draws me onwards.'

'Well, do not tarry long away. You are right welcome here.'

But many knights of the court looked aside and muttered that Balin pulled the sword not by virtue, but by witchcraft.

As Balin made ready to depart, the Lady of the Lake came riding to the court and without more ado demanded of King Arthur the gift he had promised her when she gave him her sword, from out of the lake. This was the sword called Excalibur, which is to say Cut-steel.

'Give me the head of the knight that won the sword from the maiden,' said the lady, 'or else the head of the maiden herself. Indeed, I would take both heads, for he slew my brother and she was the cause of my father's death.'

'Nay, truly,' replied Arthur, 'on my honour I cannot grant you their heads. Ask for something else.'

'Nothing. I will ask no other thing.'

Just then Balin came by, with his sword girt by his side and his horse stepping eagerly on the road. He saw the Lady of the Lake and knew her to be the lady he had been seeking for three years, the one who had been the cause of his mother's death. He went boldly to her, saying, 'Evil woman, you would have my head, and therefore you shall lose yours.'

With a swift stroke of his sword, he smote off her head in front of King Arthur.

'For shame, what have you done?' cried the king. 'I owed this lady a gift and she comes here under safe conduct. You dishonour me, sir, and I shall never forgive you.'

'That I regret,' replied Balin. 'But this same lady, by enchantment and sorcery, has been the destroyer of many good knights. By her falsehood she caused my mother to be burnt.'

'Whatever your grievance,' said Arthur, 'her death has done me wrong. Therefore leave my court in all haste.'

So Balin took the head of the lady, all bloody as it was, and gave it to his squire to take to Northumberland, as an evidence that his foe was no more.

'But what shall you do now?' asked his squire.

'I shall seek King Rience, to destroy him or to die. And if perchance I capture him, then King Arthur will still be my good and gracious lord.'

As Balin left the court, a certain Lanceor, a knight of Ireland who was jealous of the prowess of Balin, offered to ride after him and avenge the wrong done to the king.

On a mountain they met, and Lanceor called out his challenge. With regret, Balin turned. He wished no harm to any in Arthur's court. But fight they must, for the challenge was given and taken. The shields were lowered, the long spears shook in their hands, the horses stamped the ground. Then they drove forwards. The blow from the Irish knight rang on the shield, but Balin's spear pierced through coat of mail and body and the horse's croup, leaving Lanceor as a corpse on the ground.

As Balin looked up from the body, he saw a lady on a white palfrey riding towards him as fast as she could whip the pony. When she saw the knight on the ground, the blood flew from her face and she burst into sorrow without measure. 'O Balin,' she cried, 'two hearts you have slain in that one body, and two souls you have lost.'

First she fell down in a swoon, then she rose up weeping. Snatching the sword from her dead love, she held it so fast that Balin could not take it from her. Then, of a sudden, she set the pommel on the ground and threw herself onto the blade. Unfriendly hand, thought Balin, to turn against yourself.

'O most cruel stroke,' he sighed. 'I repent me the death of this knight, surly and proud though he was, for I see there was much true love betwixt these two.'

So, heavily, he turned his horse and looked towards the vast and gloomy forest. As the shadows folded over him, he saw a knight riding at ease upon the path. Then his heart lifted, for he knew this knight by his device and his arms. It was his brother Balan. Joyfully, they saluted and came together, raising their helmets so that they might kiss each other in gladness.

Then Balan said, 'I heard in the Castle of Four Stones that you were delivered from prison and were seen in the court of King Arthur. At once, I came to find you. Well met, brother.'

Shortly he learnt all that had happened at the court of Arthur and how his brother had fallen out with the king, and how it saddened Balin, for Arthur was the best knight that reigned now on earth.

As they were talking, there came to them a dwarf together with a knight called Mark, who was king of Cornwall. When they saw the dead lady, the dwarf tore his hair for grief. But King Mark caused a fine tomb to be made, and he put in it the two bodies of Lanceor and his fair lady Colombe. As this was a-doing along came Merlin, who started back at the sight of these bodies. He looked angrily on Balin, saying, 'You have done yourself great harm because you did not save this lady.'

'By my faith,' Balin protested, 'I could not save her, for she slew herself so suddenly.'

'Because of the death of that lady,' Merlin told him, 'you shall strike a stroke more dolorous than ever man struck, except the one against Our Lord. For you shall hurt the truest knight living with a wound nigh incurable, and three kingdoms shall be brought to twelve years of poverty, misery and wretchedness.'

Then Merlin took his leave and King Mark, with frowning face, looked carefully at Balin. It was best to mark well a man of such a doleful future. 'Tell me your name,' said Mark.

But Balan, his brother, answered, 'See, he bears two swords. You may call him the Knight with the Two Swords.'

So King Mark departed to Camelot and the court of Arthur, while the brothers went towards King Rience. They had spoken with Merlin concerning this king and his great prowess. They had need of the wizard's counsel. For the sake of his lord Arthur, Merlin had promised to help them.

Deep in the woods, Merlin arranged an ambush for Rience. He advised Balin and Balan to take their horses aside and let them graze. Then, at a bend in the path where the way was crooked and trees were like a tent against the sky, the brothers lay down to rest, hidden in leaves and bushes. At midnight, they heard a noise.

'What is that?' they whispered.

'It is hooves on hard ground.'

'Is it King Rience?'

'It is the vanguard, jingling many harnesses.'

'Why, and where to?'

'They go to tell my lady de Vance that King Rience would lie with her tonight.'

'And what is that, coming apace?'

'The king is riding at ease, amid the low sounds of laughter.'

'Now' said Balin; 'Quick' said Balan. And they leapt suddenly into the way with swords naked, hacking to the right hand and to the left, till the escort fled in fear of these devils from the woods and King Rience was left alone. Balin would have killed him had not the king yielded at once.

'Good knights, slay me not,' he cried. 'My death shall win you nothing, but by my life you may profit.'

'There's truth in that,' said the brothers gladly. So they bound him and laid him on a horse-litter and dragged him away. In the dawn they came to Camelot and delivered King Rience to the guards of the court, and went on their way to sleep. After a time, when King Arthur had broken his fast, he summoned the prisoner.

'Sir king,' he said, 'take this welcome, such as it is. By what adventure came you here?'

'By a hard adventure indeed.'

'Who won you?'

'The Knight with the Two Swords and his brother, two knights of great prowess.'

Arthur knew not these names but Merlin, who was standing by, said, 'It was Balin and his brother Balan, both good men. There lives not a better knight than Balin. Yet how sad it is for him, because he shall not endure.'

And all marvelled that this knight was a man of such misfortune. At every step he had tried to do service to Arthur, his good and gracious lord. Yet every step was his undoing.

'Now I owe him much,' said Arthur, 'and I have served him ill for his kindness. But where are these brothers?'

'Balan you shall see no more,' replied Merlin. 'As for Balin, he will not be long from you. He is the one that shall give the Dolorous Stroke, from which shall fall great vengeance.'

'I would to God he would abide with me,' said Arthur, 'for the sake of his life.'

Within a day or two after, King Arthur fell somewhat sick. He pitched his pavilion in a meadow and lay down to sleep. The day was comfortable and the air soft, but he got no rest. For very soon there came the clatter of a horse and a knight rode by making a great wail.

'Why this sorrow?' said Arthur, rising from his bed.

'You can give me no help,' replied the knight, and abruptly passed by.

Now, the king was displeased by this uncivil fellow and called Balin to him, saying, 'Fetch that knight again, either by goodwill or force, for I would know why he mourns so greatly.'

But the knight would not return until Balin offered to take him by force. At this, the knight gave way and went along under Balin's safe conduct. Hardly had they reached King Arthur's pavilion when there came one invisible and thrust a spear right through the body of the sorrowing knight.

'Alas, I am slain under your safe conduct,' he cried to Balin. 'It was Garlon that struck me. Take my horse, which is faster than yours, and ride to the forest, where you shall find a maiden. Follow my quest, as she shall lead you, and avenge my death.'

Thus was treachery done to the knight Sir Herlews by a certain Garlon, for which wrong Balin felt himself at fault. As he was a knight of chivalry, he swore revenge. He took the shaft of the spear to be a memorial for the knight's lady, and rode with her on her quest. They had not ridden far when they met a knight out hunting who, after he had heard the sorrowful tale of the lady, offered to help them. They rode on together till they came to a hermitage by a churchyard. In this place of dread and strangeness there came all at once another invisible blow from Garlon that killed the knight who was called Perin.

Balin searched the empty air on all sides. 'What is this traitor knight that rides invisible?' he wondered. 'Now he has wronged me twice.'

Around the hermitage lay only woods, and the sigh of the wind, and the distant song of birds. Balin buried the knight Perin and rode on with the maiden. Three or four days later they came to the house of a rich man who made them at ease. As they sat at supper, with many good things to eat and a great fire burning in the hall, Balin heard a grievous moan coming from a chair nearby.

'What noise is that?' said Balin, starting back.

'Be not afraid,' replied the host. 'Lately I jousted with the brother of King Pellam and twice smote him down. But he took revenge on my son, who cried with pain, as you have just heard. He laments because he cannot be healed till he has some blood from the body of the knight that struck him. Alas, the knight rode away invisible and I do not know his name.'

'Surely, I know that base fellow,' said Balin. 'He is Garlon, the same who has slain two knights that went with me. I would rather meet him now than have all the gold in the realm.'

It happened that King Pellam had ordered a great feast to be held within twenty days, that any knight could attend if he brought his wife or paramour.

'Let us go,' said the host, 'for our enemy shall be there.'

'Then I promise you,' said Balin, 'part of his blood to heal your son.'

They journeyed for fifteen days through a land that did not welcome them. The way was dark and rough. With relief they came to the castle, even though it was King Pellam's castle. The feast was about to begin. The guards on the gate admitted Balin and the maiden, but the host must stay outside, for he had no lady. After Balin was bathed and dressed in clean clothes of the finest cloth, the steward of the castle would have removed his sword. But Balin stopped him, saying, 'It is my custom to have my sword always by my side.' So the steward let him be, and he went into the hall of the castle and sat among the worthy knights with his lady before him. And soon, after he had looked into every space and even into every crooked corner, Balin spoke in a low voice to one nearby, saying, 'Is there not a knight here, whose name is Garlon?'

'Yonder he goes, he with the black face. Is he not a marvel? For he may go invisible, and thus destroys many good men.'

Then Balin put his eye steadily on Garlon till Garlon noticed him. He came and smote Balin across the face with the back of his hand, saying, 'Knight, why do you stare at me so? For shame, eat your meat and be gone.'

Balin rose up fiercely with his sword and cut Garlon's head open to the shoulders. Then he took from his lady the shaft of the spear that she carried always in memory of her dead lover, and he drove it through the body of Garlon. 'With that shaft,' he cried, 'you killed a good knight, and now it sticks from your own gut.' Therewith Balin called outside to his host, saying, 'Here is blood enough to heal your son.'

At once, there was a riot in the hall. Men sprang up from the table and would have fallen on Balin had not King Pellam himself intervened. 'For the love of my brother,' the king shouted, 'no hand but mine shall touch him. Knight, make ready, for you shall die.'

Then Pellam took in his hand a grim weapon and struck at Balin. The force of this blow shattered Balin's sword and Balin turned and ran from chamber to chamber seeking a weapon, and always Pellam was close behind. At last, he came to a dim chamber ornamented with the richest cloths and coverings that ever man did see. There was a bed arrayed with cloth of gold, and a silent figure was shrouded within the bed. A table of gold stood on silver legs beside the bed. Upon the table was a spear, strong and sharp, all chased with wondrous work.

Balin snatched up the spear, then turned and let King Pellam run onto the weapon. The blood burst forth like a spring freshet, and the king swooned to the floor. The roof and walls crumbled and fell, and stones tumbled upon Balin so that he could not move hand or foot. The castle became nothing but a hill of stones, brought down by the Dolorous Stroke, and lay upon Pellam and Balin for three days.

After three days Merlin found Balin and took him from the ruins. He got him a good horse, for his was dead, and bade him ride out of that country.

'Where is my maiden?' said Balin. But Merlin answered him, saying, 'Lo, see where she lies dead.'

Then Balin departed from Merlin with these words: 'In this world we shall never meet more.' So he rode through fair countries and towns, and found people dead, slain on every side. Those left alive cried in

LEWIS EGERTON SMITH MEMORIAL LIBRARY

their pain, 'O Balin, what damage you have caused! The Dolorous Stroke that you gave to King Pellam destroyed three countries. Do not doubt that vengeance will fall on you at last.'

Balin was glad to be past those lands. He rode eight days before he saw a tower in a forest, and beside it was a great warhorse tied to a tree. Nearby a knight sat on the ground, mourning. Loath to disturb him, Balin turned aside to admire the horse. But still he heard the knight's lament. 'Ah, lady,' he groaned, 'you promised to meet me here at noon. I curse the day that ever you gave me this sword, for with it I shall kill myself.' At this, Balin ran forwards and held him fast.

'Let go my hand,' cried the knight, 'or else I slay you.'

'There is no need. I promise my help to find you your lady.'

'What is your name?'

'It is Balin le Savage.'

'Ah, sir, I know you well enough. You are the Knight with the Two Swords. I am Garnish of the Mount, a poor man's son, but by my hardiness Duke Hermel has made me a knight and given me lands. It is his daughter that I love, and she me, as I think.'

Then the two knights went together to her castle and searched for her from chamber to chamber. After a while Balin was weary of this and went outside to take the air. He went into a fair little garden and saw the lady under a laurel tree, lying on a quilt of green silk with a knight in her arms, in a fast embrace and kissing each other, with grass and herb under their heads. He was a foul knight, and she a fair lady. And when Garnish came and saw them, he went mad for sorrow and his mouth and nose burst with blood. Of a sudden he drew his sword and struck off both their heads. Then he turned on Balin, saying, 'O Balin, you have brought me much sorrow, showing me this sight that I would have passed by.'

Balin protested. 'I did it so that you should see and know her falsehood. God knows, I would have you do the same for me.'

But Garnish could not endure it. With no further word, he pulled his sword and thrust himself onto the blade up to the hilt.

'Men suffer,' cried Balin, 'while I stand by.' And with heart cast down he hurried away, lest folk should think he had slain all three. Where could he run to? Death was not so much. A good knight faced it willingly. But to keep it with you, like baggage in your train. So he went where his horse's feet took him, and after three days he came to a cross set in the road, stamped with letters of gold that said: 'No knight may ride alone towards this castle.'

He saw an aged man walking on the path, who stopped Balin with a thin hand. 'Balin le Savage,' he said, 'turn back. You pass your bounds if you come this way.'

At this the man vanished. Then Balin heard a faint horn blow, as it would sound for the death of a beast. 'That blast,' he said, 'is blown for me, for I am the prize and yet I am not dead.'

Then a crowd of ladies and many knights came with light steps to welcome him into the castle, where there was dancing and minstrelsy and all manner of joy. In the small hours the lady of the castle came to him and took him by the hand. 'Knight with the Two Swords' she said, smiling, 'you must joust with the keeper of the island nearby. No man may pass here without a joust.'

'This is an unhappy custom,' replied Balin. 'Travelling men are oft weary and their horses too. But though my horse be tired, my heart is ready. I am content that my death be here.'

'Take my shield,' said a knight beside Balin. 'Yours is not good. I pray you, take this one that is bigger.'

He took the unknown shield and rode out to the shore of the lake.

The day was just breaking and the sun sat fair on the still water. The mountains lifted their heads into the sky, and the forest was as green as my lady's silk gown. Balin put himself and his horse in a large boat for the island. When he came to the other side, a maiden saw him and cried, 'O knight Balin, is that you I see? Why have you left your own shield? Your device was known, that men might see whom they fought. But now?'

'I repent,' Balin replied, 'that ever I came to this country. But, for shame, I may not retreat. It is an honourable matter to take what adventure may come to me, be it life or death.'

Then he looked over his armour with great care, and he saw that he was well armed. He made the sign of the cross and mounted, and was ready.

He saw a knight riding towards him dressed all in red, and he himself was in the same colour. At a short distance, the red knight of the island stopped. He thought that this stranger might be his brother Balin, because of his two swords, but he knew not the device on the shield. Any knight might wear two swords. No matter: there was nothing to be done but to fight.

31

First one horse, and then the other, stirred into a gallop. The first clash was so fierce it sent both knights swooning to the ground. Balin rose slowly. He was weary of travel and bruised. At once Balan was upon him, and smote him again and again till Balin, reeling, made a hard reply with that unhappy sword. And so they fought till they staggered and their breaths failed. Then they sat apart a little and rested.

While he was panting for breath, Balin looked up to a tower nearby and saw that it was full of ladies. They waved their hands, making their long sleeves flutter, and flew ribbons, red and green, into the wind, and shouted good cheer unto the hurt men below.

'Is it for them we fight?' Balin wondered. 'I do not know.'

They set to again and wounded each other sorely, and the earth about was all flecked with red. Their hauberks of mail were undone and gaping, and the naked flesh beneath gashed with seven wounds, to the least, and each wound was enough to kill the greatest giant.

At last, the younger brother, Balan, withdrew a little and sank onto the ground. Scarce able to kneel, his brother looked on him and marvelled. 'What knight are you? Never before did I find a man that matched me.'

'I am Balan, brother to the good knight Balin.'

Balin's face blanched beneath the spent blood. 'Alas,' he cried, 'that ever I should see this day.' And he fell forwards to the grass as if he were dead.

Crawling on hands and feet, Balan went to his brother and pulled off the helm, but he hardly knew that face, so hacked and hewn and bleeding. 'O Balin, my brother,' he cried, 'we have slain each other, and all the wide world will grieve for us. Alas, I knew you not. I saw the two swords, but you bore another's shield.'

When she saw that the knights were near to death, the lady of the tower brought helpers to bear them away. 'We came both from one womb,' said the brothers to her, 'that is to say our mother's belly. Let us lie at last both in one pit.' And the lady, weeping, granted them their wish.

Balan soon died, but Balin lasted till the midnight hour. In the black night, with no noise, he gave up the ghost. And so they were buried both, and in the morn Merlin came and wrote on the tomb in golden letters:

Here lies Balin le Savage, the Knight with the Two Swords, he that gave the Dolorous Stroke.

✣ The Fellowship of the ✣ Round Table

In the beginning of Arthur, after he was chosen king by fortune and by grace, many of the barons did not believe that he was Uther Pendragon's son, and for this cause kings and lords made war against him.

'Alas, I have had no rest,' said Arthur, 'not even for one month, since I was crowned king of this land. And I shall never rest until I have met all my enemies in a fair field. This I shall do in good time. For I swear that my true liege people shall not be destroyed through my default. Who shall help me? Go with me those of you that will, and abide with me to the end.'

The knights of his court and many others from the far parts of the land spoke to one another, saying, 'You know well that Sir Arthur has the flower of the chivalry of the world with him. He is so courageous of himself that he comes to the field with few people, and still he triumphs, as he proved in the great battle with the eleven kings. Therefore let us hurry to join him, riding night and day.'

So many worthy knights came to his court.

Now, King Arthur for most of his days was ruled by the counsel of Merlin, and by this means he overcame many. He would not move, in war or peace, but by the advice of Merlin. So it happened one time that Arthur said to Merlin, 'Though the barons give me no rest, it would ease my heart if I took a wife. Then I should have comfort. What say you?'

'A man of your bounty and noblesse,' Merlin replied, 'should not be without a wife. Is there any that you love more than another?'

'Indeed, I love Guenevere, daughter of King Leodegrance, who holds in his house the Round Table that belonged to my father Uther.'

'As to her beauty,' replied Merlin, 'she is one of the fairest alive. But I fear your choice. Were your heart not so set, I could find you a maiden equal to her. But when the heart points forwards, a man is loath to go back.'

Merlin warned the king that Guenevere would do him no good, for she would love another. But Arthur would not give way. So Merlin went with a doubtful heart to King Leodegrance of Camelerd, and told him that King Arthur desired to have Guenevere for his wife. This news was good tiding to Leodegrance, for Arthur was a noble king. Gladly he gave his daughter, and with her he sent King Uther's Round Table, and a hundred knights besides, to be her marriage portion.

After King Arthur, in all haste, had ordained for the marriage and coronation, he said to Merlin, 'Find me in all the land the fifty knights with the most prowess and the most honour.'

Merlin searched far and wide, but only eight-and-forty knights could he find. These, after prayer and solemn music, took their seats, and the Bishop of Canterbury blessed them in their places. Then they arose and went to do homage to King Arthur, so that he would maintain them in his court. When this was done and the knights had departed, Merlin found the name of each written in gilt letters on his seat. But two of the seats were still unfilled.

Not long after, young Gawain came to the court and begged a gift of the king.

'Ask,' said Arthur.

'Sir, make me a knight that same day you shall wed Guenevere.'

'Willingly I grant it, for you are my sister's son.'

Then another came to the court, a poor man, and with him was a fair youth of eighteen riding a lean mare. When he saw the men of the court, the eyes of the poor man were dazzled.

'Who is King Arthur?' he asked.

'Yonder he is,' replied the knights with contempt. 'Can you not see?'

'O king,' the man cried, 'flower of all knights, Jesu save you. I have heard tell that, in the time of your marriage, you will grant a gift to any that asks.'

'True,' said the king, 'so long as it harms not my realm or estate.'

'Sir, I am Aries the cowherd, and here is my son. I beseech you, make him a knight.'

'This is a great thing you ask,' said the king, smiling. 'Tell me, does it come from you or your son?'

'O sir, from my son. I have twelve other sons, and they will labour as I tell them, and right glad to do it. But this child will not work for me. He is always shooting arrows, or casting darts. He is ever looking for knights and battles, gaping on courteous folk with his mouth open. Night and day he desires of me to be made a knight.'

The king beheld the youth, whose name was Tor, and he saw that he was well made and had a bold face. 'Fetch me your other sons,' said Arthur to the cowherd. And when this was done, the king saw that they were all of a lump, rustic folk very like Aries himself. But Tor was much more than any of them.

'Take your sword from the sheath,' said the king to Tor, 'and require me to make you a knight.'

Tor alighted from his horse and knelt, giving King Arthur a sorry, rusted sword. The king smote him on the neck with the sword, saying, 'I pray God you may be a good knight, and if you are worthy and show prowess you shall be a knight of the Round Table. Now Merlin,' Arthur went on, 'say whether this Tor shall be a good knight or not.'

'Yea indeed,' replied Merlin, 'he should be good, for he is of a king's blood.'

'How so?'

'This poor man, Aries the cowherd, is not his father. King Pellinore is his father.'

This was grievous news to the cowherd. But his wife was fetched, and she answered full openly that a stern knight had her maidenhead half by force, while she was out milking.

'He begat my son Tor,' said the wife, 'and took my greyhound, to keep as a token of my love.'

The cowherd looked on her sadly. 'I knew not this,' he said, 'but I well believe it, for he has no qualities of mine.'

But Tor turned to Merlin with some heat: 'Sir, dishonour not my mother.'

'Good youth, it is more for your honour than hurt,' Merlin replied. 'Your father is a good man and a king. He may advance both you and your mother, for you were begotten before she was wedded.'

'Tis true,' said the wife. And the cowherd took from that what comfort he could.

So King Pellinore was called to the court, and when he beheld Tor he was much pleased. Then there was music and feasting, and Tor was the first to be made knight at the feast, and Gawain after him. King Arthur was content and looked over the company with much joy till he saw the two empty seats and demanded of Merlin why this was so.

'None but the best,' replied Merlin, 'shall sit in those places. And in one of them, the Seat Perilous, he who is hardy enough to sit there, though he shall have no equal, shall be destroyed.'

At once Merlin took King Pellinore by the hand and placed him in one of those seats, which caused young Sir Gawain great envy. With black brow he turned to Gaheris, his brother, saying, 'It grieves me sore that yonder knight is honoured, for he slew our father King Lot. Now I shall kill him.'

'Not yet,' Gaheris cautioned him, 'for I am only a squire, and when I am made knight I will help our revenge. So, brother, bide your time. It would be a sorry thing to trouble this high feast.'

Then the time of merriment continued, and the king was wedded to the Lady Guenevere at Camelot, in the church of St Stephen. Afterwards, at the high feast, as every man sat according to his degree at the Round Table, a white hart leapt into the hall and close on its quarters was a white brachet, which is to say a female hound, with a pack of black running dogs bawling and baying behind. As the deer clattered hooves by the Round Table, the brachet tore a piece from its buttock, so that the wounded animal jumped into the face of a knight and knocked him over. In anger, the knight took fast hold of the brachet, ran from the hall and rode away with the hound.

'What tumult is this?' cried Arthur. 'It shames our feast.'

Soon there followed a lady on a white palfrey, lamenting, 'That brachet was mine. The knight has stolen it.' But hardly had she cried out when a grim knight on a black horse snatched her up and bore her away, still wailing and crying for the loss of her hound. King Arthur was right glad to be rid of her noise. But what was the cause of the mystery of these events?

'Sir knights,' he called out to the Round Table, 'now comes your test. Let us shape these things to our understanding. Sir Gawain, fetch me again that white hart. And Sir Tor, you must bring back the brachet and the knight, or slay him for his discourtesy. And King Pellinore also, fetch back the wailing lady and the grim knight, or again slay him.'

The king need say no more. Each knight, eager for adventure, made ready for his quest: the art of knighthood was to put wrongs aright and keep God's law. First Sir Gawain rode out, with his brother Gaheris as his squire; full gladly they went, for they were young.

They followed the hart by the cry of the hounds and came to a great river. As the white hart plunged and swam, Gawain was stopped on the bank by a loud voice saying, 'Sir knight, do not pursue that deer unless you would joust with me.'

'I cannot do other than follow my quest,' replied Gawain. So he spurred his horse into the water and met the knight on the other side, exchanging hard blows till Gawain's weapon burst the brains from the helm of the knight.

'That was a mighty stroke,' said Gaheris to his brother, 'for a young knight.'

Then the two of them let slip their greyhounds, which chased the hart towards a castle and into it, and even to the innermost chamber, where the hounds killed it. As Gawain and Gaheris followed, a knight came in anger with drawn sword, and striking dead two of the greyhounds he drove the others yapping from the castle. He looked about fiercely and saw Sir Gawain.

'Why have you slain my hounds?' said Gawain. 'They did but follow their nature. Avenge your anger on me, not on my dumb beasts.'

'That, too, I will do,' said the knight. 'My sovereign lady gave me that white hart. As I live, its death shall be avenged.'

After they had fought for a while, foot to foot, the knight was stunned and fell hard to the earth. He yielded to Gawain and cried mercy for his life. But Sir Gawain had no mercy. 'Die,' he replied, 'for slaying my hounds.' He unlaced the man's helm and would have struck off his head had not a lady, with arms outspread, rushed from the castle. She came so suddenly upon them that she stepped between the raised sword and the fallen knight. So, by misadventure, Gawain struck the head from the lady and not the knight.

'O shameful deed,' cried Gaheris in alarm. 'Should not you give mercy to them that ask? A knight without mercy is without honour.'

Astonished at the death of the lady, Gawain told the knight to rise. But he cared not for mercy, nor for living, now that his true love was dead.

'Sorely I repent it,' said Gawain, 'for I thought to strike at you. Oftentimes, a bad act makes a worse befall. Go you now to King Arthur, and tell him of your adventure, in this quest for the white hart.'

Then, for dread of something worse, the knight rode towards Camelot, with one slain greyhound behind the saddle and the other across the neck of his horse.

Gawain went into the castle and wearily unarmed. He was ready to sleep. But Gaheris put out his hand, saying, 'Are you mad? Will you unarm here, among your enemies?' He had no sooner said these words when four well-armed knights thrust open the door and challenged Gawain.

'You new-made knight,' they taunted him, 'you have shamed your knighthood. A knight without mercy is dishonoured. Also, the death of that fair lady cries "Foul" to the world's end. You shall beg mercy from us before you depart.'

Now Gawain and Gaheris were in jeopardy for their lives. One of the knights, an archer, shot an arrow through Gawain's arm. He and his brother would have been slain had not certain ladies, hearing the din of battle, come and begged grace for these young knights, who were so fresh and comely. At the fair words of the ladies, the other knights gave way. But they bound Gawain and Gaheris and took them prisoner.

Next morning, as Gawain was wailing piteously of his wound, one of the ladies heard him.

'Sir knight,' she said, 'what cheer?'

'Not good.'

'It is your own fault, for the slaying of that lady was a foul deed. But are you not King Arthur's kin?'

'Yes, truly. I am Gawain, son of King Lot of Orkney, and my mother is King Arthur's sister.'

Then, for Arthur's sake, the four knights forgave Gawain his deed and sent him back to Camelot with the white hart's head, so that his quest might be accomplished. But for penance and the error of his conduct, he was made to ride out with the dead lady's head hung about his neck and with her body stretched before him on the horse's mane. Thus he rode into Camelot, and the king and the queen were greatly displeased by the slaying of that poor lady.

So Queen Guenevere set a court of high ladies to judge Gawain. When they had deliberated, they ordained that ever after Sir Gawain should be the champion of all ladies and gentlewomen, to be always courteous, to fight their quarrels and never to refuse mercy. And Gawain swore on the four Evangelists to this end.

Next it was the turn of Sir Tor to go out on his quest and seek the knight with the white brachet. He mounted and rode out with the gladness of a young heart, but soon he came to a narrow place where a dwarf barred his way. The dwarf, who had been hiding in the woods, stopped him, saying, 'A gift, I pray you'.

'Well?' said Tor.

'Suffer me to do you service, I know you ride after the knight with the white brachet, and I can bring you to him.'

'Take a horse,' said Sir Tor, 'and ride on with me.'

They rode for a long while through the forest till they came to two pavilions. On one was hung a red shield, and on the other a white. Sir Tor dismounted and drew his sword. With quiet steps he went to the pavilions and saw, in the first one, three maidens asleep in the same bed, and in the other a lady also asleep, with the white brachet lying at her feet. Then the hound bayed. At once the ladies awoke and ran from the pavilions. But Tor caught the brachet and held it fast, so that the lady saw it and called out, 'Knight, you shall not go far with that hound.'

'I shall take whatever adventure God should send me,' Tor replied, and he turned his horse towards Camelot.

But the road was longer than he thought and the eye of the moon was winking in the heavens, so he and the dwarf stopped for lodgings at a hermitage. There was some grass and oats for the horses, but scant food for the men. They supped on hard fare and rested themselves on the bare ground. In the morn, Sir Tor devoutly heard a Mass and took his leave as the sun rose, begging the hermit to pray for him. Then, with sore body and empty belly, he went on till he heard a roaring behind and a knight all out of breath galloped to them, saying, 'You there, halt. Give me my brachet that you took from my lady.'

The knights addressed each other, rearing back on their coursers. Both were well armed and well horsed, and they traded mighty blows.

After a time, when he saw the other knight grow faint, Tor doubled his strokes, drove the knight to the ground and ordered him to yield.

'That I will not,' said the other, whose name was Abelleus, 'while life and breath last, unless you give me the brachet.'

'Nay,' replied Tor. 'It is my quest to fetch the brachet, or you, or both.' And he got ready to make a prisoner of Abelleus.

At once a maiden came riding fast, calling out, 'I beseech you, gentle knight, for love of King Arthur, grant me the head of this false Abelleus, for he is a most outrageous murderer.'

'That I am loath to do,' Tor relied. 'Let him make amends for the wrong he has done you.'

'How can that be?' the lady lamented. 'He slew my brother before my very eyes. I knelt half an hour in the mud to beg for the life of my brother. He was a good knight whose only harm was to try with this villain an adventure of arms. Despite my anguish, he cut off my brother's head. Therefore, give me his in return.'

Now when Abelleus heard this he was afraid, and began to beg for mercy.

'Tis too late,' Sir Tor told him. 'Before, you spurned my mercy unless you had your brachet. Now you shall suffer.'

Abelleus tried to flee, but Tor thrust him down, put his foot on his chest and struck off his head.

The lady was satisfied to be avenged, and in thanks to Sir Tor she took him to her lodgings, where she and her husband gave him good cheer and good ease. In the morn, as he went on his road, the people of the house waved to him, saying, 'Fair knight, if you travel this way again, our house is always at your command.'

On the third day, at noon, Tor came to Camelot. The king and the queen and all the court were happy at his coming, for he had departed but a new-made knight on his first quest. He had only an old battle-horse, borrowed armour with many a dent, and a borrowed sword. He had no other help but himself alone. Now right boldly he told his adventures, and the king and queen heard them with great joy.

But Merlin said, 'Nay, these are but japes to what he shall do. For he shall prove a noble knight, as good as any living. Mark well, for you shall see it.'

Two quests were done, and now King Pellinore rode out from Camelot to seek his adventure. Passing into a wild part of the land, he saw a maiden with a wounded knight in her arms, and she called out to him, saying, 'Help me, for Christ's sake, King Pellinore.' Had she cried out a hundred times more, Pellinore would not have paused, so hot was he after his quest. As he pressed his horse forwards, she cursed him: 'I pray to God that, before you die, you shall have as much need of help as I do now.' Soon the knight in her arms gave up his last breath. Then she took her lover's sword and slew herself in grief.

What was it to King Pellinore? He knew not and cared not for that knight. Urgently he rode into the valley beyond, questioning all he met. After some time he heard from a poor labourer that the knight and the lady he sought were not far away. They waited in a meadow where a kinsman of the lady had overtaken them and challenged the knight. One would have her by force, and the other would rule her by right of kin. But the lady was crying with all her heart, for she knew some blood was like to flow.

In haste, Pellinore rode between the knights and parted them, and heard their claims.

'She is mine,' said one. 'I won her by prowess of arms at King Arthur's court.'

'Untrue,' said Pellinore, 'for I know you well enough. You came suddenly, bursting in upon the high feast, before any was ready to resist. You snatched this lady. It is my quest to return with both you and the lady, or die for it. Sir, come with me.'

'Nay,' replied both the knights who had been fighting. 'This affray is ours alone.' And they both assailed King Pellinore with all their power. Pellinore's horse was slain under him. In a rage, he struck at that knight and chopped through his helm to the chin. Then the other, the lady's kin, would fight no more, but knelt and said, 'Take my cousin the lady, and as you be a true knight put her to no shame or villainy.'

Now, since Pellinore lacked a horse, the defeated knight promised to provide one, and he took Pellinore to lodge the night with him and the lady. He was Sir Meliot of Logris and she was called Nimue, and that night they gave Pellinore good wine and good entertainment. In the morn, at the gate, stood a fine bay courser with Pellinore's saddle upon it. The lady was also mounted and ready to go with him to Camelot, so they rode some time in silence till the path led into a steep valley full of stones, which caused the lady's horse to stumble and throw her. She fell hard and near fainted with pain.

'Alas sir,' she cried, 'I cannot go on, for my arm is out of joint.'

So they rested there for the night. King Pellinore made a cover of bushes and pulled off his armour, and lay down with the lady beside him. They were near unto sleep when, a little before midnight, they heard the trotting of horses. 'Listen,' whispered Pellinore, with his finger to the lips of the lady. Quietly he put his hand to his sword and waited.

Out of the dark came two knights riding from north and south. Without seeing Pellinore and the lady, they drew together and saluted.

'What tidings at Camelot?' asked one.

'By my head, I have been to the court of King Arthur and have seen there such a fellowship as may never be broken. Well-nigh all the world is gathered with Arthur, and with him is the flower of chivalry. I ride north to warn our chieftains of this fellowship.'

'As for me,' said the other, 'I have the remedy. There is one of us at Camelot who has made himself right close to Arthur, and I am taking him a deadly potion to poison the king. Our chieftains may lie easy. It shall be done.'

'But beware of Merlin,' warned the other, 'for he knows all things by the devil's craft.' And so they parted, each on his way, well satisfied.

When the morning came and the lady was somewhat eased of her pain, Pellinore rode on whistling, content that he knew the plot against King Arthur. But this contented mood did not last long. In a while he came to the place where he had left the lady with her wounded knight. About him he saw the remains of bodies, mauled and eaten by lions or wild beasts, so that only the head of the lady was to be seen whole. Then King Pellinore wept, because he had abandoned those unlucky folk in the heat of his quest. He gave the remains of the knight worthy burial, and charged a hermit to pray for the man's soul. Then, to show his own fault, he tenderly took up the head of the lady and rode on towards Camelot, casting his eye often to the long yellow hair and the fair dead face of the lady.

When King Pellinore approached the court of Arthur, the king and the queen were right glad to see him coming. But when they saw the head of the lady and heard of his adventure, they gave him stern and sorrowful looks. And Merlin set on him fiercely, saying, 'Truly, you have reason to repent. That dead lady is your own daughter, begotten on the Lady of the Rule, and her name was Elaine. Since you would not stay and help her, you shall see your best friend fail you in your time of greatest distress. That God has ordained for you.'

'So be it,' said King Pellinore in all sadness, 'but God may yet forestall my destiny.'

Then King Arthur called to him the knights of his Round Table, and among them were Gawain and Tor and King Pellinore.

'Sir knights,' he said, 'by your quests you have learnt the lesson of our fellowship, and thus stand worthy to be one of us.' And to those that were not rich, he established them, and gave them lands.

And then, by holy oath, King Arthur charged them never to do outrageous wrong nor murder, and always to flee treason; also, to be not cruel, but to give mercy to all that asked, upon pain of banishment from Arthur's court; and always to help all maidens and gentlewomen, upon pain of death. Also, no knight may fight for greed or for a wrongful cause.

And this was the oath that all knights of the Round Table swore every year at the high feast of Pentecost.

King Pellinore had brought to Arthur's court the lady called Nimue, who was one of the maidens of the lake, and she stole the heart of Merlin. He was besotted with her. Because of her, he fell into a dotage and would let her have no rest. And she was kind to him and was always by his side, till she had learnt from him everything that she desired.

At this time Merlin spoke much with King Arthur. 'My task is done,' he told the king. 'I have strengthened your arm and made your foot sure. Now, for all my craft, I shall not last long, but shall be put in the earth quick.' Then he warned the king of many things that would befall. In particular, Arthur must guard well his sword and scabbard, for a woman he trusted was likely to steal them from him.

'See how you shall miss me,' Merlin said to the king. 'When I am gone, you would give all your lands to have me with you again.'

'Since you know your future,' replied the king, 'prepare for it. By your craft, turn aside this misadventure.'

'Nay, it cannot be,' said Merlin. And so he left the king.

Within a short while, Nimue, the Maiden of the Lake, departed from Arthur's court, and Merlin went with her wheresoever she travelled. Often, he spirited her away privily by his subtle craft. But she was afraid and made him swear that he would put no enchantment on her, or he would never have his will of her. So he swore, and they went together over the sea to the land of Benwick, and saw many strange wonders, and returned again into Cornwall. Always, Merlin was plotting to have her maidenhead. She grew weary of him and would gladly have abandoned him, but she feared him as a devil's son, and she could not be rid of him by any means.

After they came to Cornwall, Merlin showed Nimue an enchanted cavern that lay under a great stone. Nimue tempted Merlin to go under that stone, so that he might explain the marvel of it to her. Then she made the stone to fall when he was still inside, and he could never come out for all his craft. So she departed and left Merlin.

When Merlin was gone from him, King Arthur still had no other task but to make his realm peaceful and his people safe. It was weary work, with hard riding, much travel and sore pain. His enemies drew him into many jousts and battles, and ofttimes the earth was red with the blood of good knights. When these deeds were done, and his body was bruised with heavy strokes, Arthur was glad to rest and to take his ease with feasting and hunting.

Once, when the din of battle was somewhat past, Arthur was hunting with King Uriens, who was his sister's husband, and with Sir Accolon of Gaul. They chased a great stag, driving it to the water, where the hounds grappled with it and tore at its throat. Then Arthur put an end to that stag, and blew on his horn that the hunt was done.

At the edge of the water, as the king was looking about the world, he saw a little glittering ship come to the sands, and its sails were all of silk. Arthur peered into the ship, but he saw no earthly creatures within. So he called to the two knights and they all went aboard. By then it was dark. Suddenly a hundred bright torches lit the ship, showing twelve maidens of great beauty who welcomed King Arthur on their knees. These maidens led the three knights to a chamber with many delights. The men marvelled that they had never seen such a supper and such entertainment in their lives. After supper, each one was led to a rich bed, and so they were laid easily in sheets of softest silk. 'Do we dream?' they wondered, and fell asleep.

On the morrow, when he awoke, King Uriens was in Camelot, abed in the arms of his wife, Morgan Le Fay. But King Arthur awoke in a dark prison, hearing about him the complaints of many woeful knights.

'Who are you that make such a noise?' said Arthur.

'We, alas, are twenty knights, all prisoners. Some of us have lain here these seven years, and many men, formerly of our number, have died in this same prison.'

'For what cause?'

'We will tell you. The lord of this castle, Sir Damas, contends with his brother Sir Ontzlake for this estate. Ontzlake is well beloved, but Damas is evil, for he is without mercy and a coward. Sir Ontzlake would fight for this livelihood and land, body to body, as a true knight should. But Damas will not do it, unless he can find a knight to fight for him. But none will fight for Damas. So he waylays good knights, and imprisons them, till one should fight his cause. But none of us can fight and die for one so false and full of treason. So we are like to die here in prison, haggard with hunger and scarce able to stand.'

'God deliver you,' said Arthur. 'It is hard, yet had I rather fight than die in prison. I will do battle, that I may be delivered and all these prisoners also.'

Thus was it agreed with Sir Damas. And when Arthur was prepared, well horsed and with arms keen and ready, a maiden came to lead him to the lists.

'Lady,' said Arthur, 'have I not seen you in the court of Arthur?'

'Nay, sir,' she replied, 'I was never there.' Yet she was false, for she was one of the maidens of Morgan le Fay.

Now, while King Arthur was making ready in prison, Sir Accolon awoke from deep sleep. He found that he was balanced on the very edge of a dark well from which water spouted in a silver pipe into a marble trough. Accolon was afraid. He feared the blackness of the hole before him, which seemed to pull him forwards. Quickly he made the sign of the cross, thinking himself betrayed by the maidens in the ship, who were surely devils, not women. Then a little ugly man, with a great mouth and flat nose, came to tell him that Queen Morgan le Fay, whom Accolon loved, would have him fight with a certain unknown knight at the hour of prime. And as a token of her care for Accolon, she sent him the sword Excalibur and its scabbard, which Arthur had given his sister Morgan to guard. With the sword, the little man gave this message from the queen: 'Do battle to the uttermost, without mercy, as you have promised to the queen, in the privacy of your love.'

'Recommend me to my lady queen,' replied Accolon. 'It shall be done as I have promised, or else I shall die. But tell me, has she prepared an enchantment for this battle?'

'You may well believe it,' said the little man.

Thereupon Accolon set out, attended by six squires whom Queen Morgan had sent to lead him to the house of Sir Ontzlake. It was devised that Accolon should be the champion of his host against Sir Damas, for Ontzlake was wounded in both thighs and unable to fight. Thus both Damas and Ontzlake had their champions ready. In the morning, after Mass, at about the prime hour, the two champions rode out in proud array to do battle. As Arthur was riding to the field from one side, a maiden came from Morgan le Fay to hand him a sword that looked like Excalibur, and its scabbard also, saying, 'Your sister sends you your sword, for the great love she holds you.'

And King Arthur gave thanks in his heart, for he knew not that the sword was counterfeit and brittle.

Then the two knights went eagerly to fight, and gave each other many great blows. But Arthur's sword did not bite like Accolon's, which hurt Arthur sorely on every stroke. His blood ran from him fast, and he began to dread death. It was a marvel he stood on his feet, but he was so full of knighthood that nobly he endured his wounds. All the people were sorry for him. He wished for some pause and rest, but Sir Accolon called him always to battle, saying, 'Fight, as a champion should'. Then, in sudden rage, Arthur smote Accolon so mightily on the helm that the blade of his sword snapped.

'Knight,' cried Accolon in triumph, 'now you are overcome. You are weaponless and have lost much blood. Yield, for I am loath to slay you.'

'I may not,' replied Arthur, 'for I have promised to do battle to the uttermost. It is better to die in honour than live in shame. Yet you shall be shamed if you slay me weaponless.'

'Now keep you from me,' cried Accolon, 'for you are but a dead man.'

In the field, close by where the knights fought, there was a maiden of the lake who had come there for love of Arthur. She knew how Morgan le Fay had tricked the king of his sword and how the queen wished for his death. As Accolon raised the sword to give the fatal stroke, the maiden, by enchantment, caused Excalibur to fall from his hand. Arthur snatched up the sword and knew at once that it was his Excalibur, saying to it with reproach, 'You have been from me all too long, and much damage have you done me.'

Then, with his last strength, he rushed on his opponent and struck him to the earth. He pulled off the helm and gave Accolon such a blow that the blood started from his ears and mouth.

'Tell me,' cried Arthur, 'who you are, or I shall slay you.'

'Sir knight, I am of the court of Arthur. I am Accolon of Gaul.'

At this reply, Arthur remembered him and was dismayed. 'Who gave you this sword?' he asked.

After a long silence, Accolon spoke. 'Woe comes from this sword, for by it I have gotten my death.' And he told Arthur how Morgan le Fay, King Uriens' wife, had given it to him.

'O Accolon,' replied the king, 'know now that I am King Arthur.'

'Fair sweet lord, have mercy on me, for I knew you not.'

'You shall have mercy. Though you are a traitor, I blame you the less. My sister Morgan le Fay, by her craft, made you consent to her false lusts. Against her, doubt not that I shall be avenged.'

Then Sir Accolon cried aloud to all the knights gathered there, saying, 'O lords, this noble knight whom I have fought with is the most worshipful man in the world. It is himself, King Arthur, our liege lord, that by a misadventure I might have slain.'

When they heard this, all the people fell on their knees and cried for mercy. And Arthur granted them mercy. But he did not forgive Sir Damas, who had been the cause whereby a king and his own knight errant had done great damage to each other. He took from Damas his lands, and gave them to his brother Ontzlake. And he bade Damas to ride only on a palfrey, for a battle courser did not become a man of such meagre spirit. Then both Arthur and Accolon were weary with pain and loss of blood, so they went haltingly to the quiet of an abbey. The good nuns of that place bound their wounds and fetched leeches to cure them. King Arthur came slowly to better health, but Sir Accolon had bled too much and died within four days.

Meanwhile, Morgan le Fay thought that her brother Arthur was dead. This was the chance she had wished for, when she might kill her husband Uriens. And she would have done it, taking a naked sword to his chamber as he slept, had not her son, Sir Uwain, come suddenly and caught her by the arm.

'What act is this, mother?' said Uwain. 'Yet I can hardly call you mother, but it seems an earthly devil gave me birth.'

Then Queen Morgan was ashamed, and promised never more to do the devil's work. On this covenant, her son forgave her. As she passed from the chamber with a face of shame, she met a messenger who told her of Arthur's safety and Accolon's death. Her heart swelled with sorrow till it well-nigh burst at the death of her lover. But she kept grief from her countenance and suffered in secret. She called for her fastest horse and fled from the court, and rode to the abbey where Arthur lay.

'Hush,' she said to the nuns, 'do not wake him. A man so badly hurt must needs rest.' So when the nuns went away, she looked to steal Excalibur again from Arthur. But he kept it, even in sleep, in his right hand. She dared not wake him, but took the scabbard only and departed.

When King Arthur awoke, he was angry at the loss of his scabbard. He bade Sir Ontzlake saddle horses, and the two of them together rode after Morgan le Fay. Soon they had a sight of her, but she heard them following. Putting spurs to her horse, she galloped to a lake and threw the scabbard far into the water, saying, 'Whatever may become of me, my brother shall not have this'. The queen watched the scabbard sink, weighed down with gold and jewels, and then rode on to a valley of rocks where, by the touch of enchantment, she turned herself and all her guards into great marble stones. Thus Arthur passed them by, and Morgan and her knights took again their own forms.

Unable to find Morgan le Fay, Arthur returned to Camelot. Then was King Arthur wonderfully angry and said to King Uriens, 'My sister, your wife, betrays me, and your family must be of her counsel. You I will hold excused, for Sir Accolon confessed to me that he was the lover of your wife, and that she would have destroyed you too. But your son, Sir Uwain, I hold suspect. Let him go from my court.'

At this, Sir Gawain rose up in heat, saying, 'If you banish my cousin-german, you banish me also.' And so the two departed.

After the two knights had been together for many a day, they went their different ways. Sir Uwain rode to the west and Sir Gawain to the north. As he travelled at ease into the forest of adventure, taking whatever fortune might come to him, Gawain entered a large glade. As he came from shade into soft light, he heard the sound of weeping and the clash of arms. He saw at a distance, beside a cross set in the ground, a most comely knight, armed only with a spear, making battle against ten men. This knight was crying with a great wailing, but he smote down his ten enemies one by one, both man and horse. Yet when the ten were on foot and rushed at him, the knight stood stone still and suffered them to pull him off his horse. They bound him hand and foot and tied him under the horse's belly, and so led him away.

'O Jesu, this is a doleful sight,' said Gawain to one who stood and watched. 'What knight is this that suffers such indignities?'

Then Gawain learnt that the name of the knight was Sir Pelleas. He was a most worthy man who had proved himself at a great joust to be the best knight for prowess, and had won thereby a fine sword and a circlet of gold. This circlet he gave to the fairest, who was Ettard, a great lady in that country. But she was so haughty and proud that she scorned him. She would never love him, she said, though he should die for her. So he wandered after her, wherever she would go. And thus he came to this land and lodged at a priory, where every week she sent knights to fight him. He fought, but always suffered himself to be bound and taken away, so that he might see his love. But Ettard used him most shamefully, sometimes making her knights bind him under the horse's belly and other times tying him to the horse's tail.

It was a great sorrow to Gawain that knighthood should be so abused and a worthy man made to suffer. On the morrow, he went to speak with Sir Pelleas, for he was minded to help. 'Do as I shall devise,' he told Pelleas. 'Change horses and armour with me. Then I shall go to the castle of your love and tell her I have slain you, offering your armour as proof. Thus I shall gain her thanks, and work her heart towards you. Ofttimes remembrance makes affection where there was none before.'

Sir Gawain promised true faith to Pelleas, then changed harness and horses and rode to the pavilion of the lady, set in the summer field before the castle gate. But when Ettard saw at a distance the armour of the rider, she fled to the castle battlements.

"Tis not Pelleas,' Gawain called up to her. 'It is another. Rejoice, I have slain Sir Pelleas.'

'Pull off your helm,' said the lady doubtfully, 'that I may see your face.'

When this was done and the lady saw a knight so young and fresh, she was glad and made Gawain welcome.

'I hated that knight Pelleas,' said Ettard, 'for I could never be quit of him. As you have slain him and saved me from him, I shall be your woman.'

They went within the castle and had good cheer. After supper they were alone and talked long with one another, and each looked on the other's face with much happiness.

'Madam,' Gawain sighed at last, 'I love a lady, but by no means does she love me.'

'She is to blame,' Ettard replied. 'You are so well-born a man, there is no lady in the world too good for you.'

'Ah, will you do all that you may, by the faith of your body, to get me the love of my lady?'

'Yes, truly, by the faith of my body.'

Then Sir Gawain said, 'It is yourself I love so well. Now, hold you to your promise.'

The lady Ettard looked at him a long moment, and said slowly, 'I may not choose, unless I be forsworn.' And so she granted Gawain all his desire.

In the month of May she and Gawain went out to the pavilion, where the new flowers grew, and embraced each other to their hearts' joy. Then they made a bed and lay there together for two days and two nights. On the third day Sir Pelleas armed himself right early and set out for the castle. He had not slept, for he awaited Gawain, who had promised to return before the night was done. Therefore, in the first light of the third day, Pelleas came to the pavilion in the field. He found Sir Gawain lying asleep in bed with Lady Ettard, with their arms twined fast about each other. Then the heart of Sir Pelleas well-nigh burst for grief, and he fled from that place because he could not abide the sight.

In half a mile, he turned and came back. He thought he would slay them both. He saw them again, still asleep, and near fell from his horse in sorrow. But his sword dropped from his hand. 'Though this knight be never so false,' he said to himself, 'yet I cannot slay him sleeping, for I will never destroy the high order of knighthood by such a base deed.' And he went away.

But in a little while he turned again, minded once more to kill them. In blind rage he tied his horse to a tree and went into the pavilion with his sword naked in his hand. There they still lay, innocent in sleep. And again he could not do it. So he laid his naked sword across their throats and rode away.

Sir Pelleas went home forlorn and told his squires and knights, 'For your faithful service, take all my goods. I will go to my bed and never arise again. When I am dead, take the heart out of my body and bear it to my Lady Ettard on two silver dishes. Tell her how I saw her play false with Sir Gawain.' Then he unarmed himself and went moaning to his bed.

In the sun's heat, Gawain and Ettard awoke within the pavilion with the touch of the naked steel against their throats. Ettard looked and knew well that it was Pelleas' sword.

'Alas,' she cried to Gawain, 'false knight, you have betrayed me and Pelleas both.'

Without reply, Sir Gawain rose hastily and dressed himself, and fled into the forest.

Now it happened that Nimue, the Maiden of the Lake, was riding through that country, and she learnt from a knight of Pelleas what had come to pass.

'This is great shame and nonsense,' said Nimue. 'I warrant this Pelleas shall not die of love. And this proud lady, she shall soon be in as evil a plight as Pelleas is now. Those who have no mercy on a valiant knight shall find no further joy.'

Within two hours she brought Lady Ettard to Pelleas' bed, where he lay insensible, as if dead. Then Nimue threw an enchantment on Ettard, saying to her, 'For shame, to murder such a knight.' And at once Ettard loved Pelleas sorely.

'O Lord Jesu,' she cried. 'How is it befallen that I love him whom I most hated before?'

'It is God's righteous judgement,' replied the Maiden of the Lake.

Soon Sir Pelleas awoke. He saw Ettard, and then he hated her more than any woman alive. He turned his face from her, saying, 'Away, traitress. Come never again in my sight.' So she went mournfully away.

'Sir Pelleas,' said Nimue, 'now arise from your bed. Take your horse and come with me out of this country. You shall love a lady that loves you.'

'That I will,' replied Pelleas, 'for this Ettard has done me despite and shame. But now I am free of her, thanks be to Jesus.'

'Nay,' said the maiden, 'thank me.'

So they went away together, wherever the maiden might lead. Lady Ettard died of sorrow, but Nimue rejoiced Sir Pelleas and they loved each other all the days of their lives.

✚ The Knight of the Kitchen ✚

t was the custom with King Arthur, when the fellowship of the Round Table met for the feast of Pentecost by the wild sands of Wales, that he would not go to eat until he had heard or seen some great marvel.

One year, a little before noon on the day of Pentecost, Sir Gawain looked from the window and saw three men come riding, with a dwarf behind on foot. When the horsemen alighted and handed their horses to the dwarf, Gawain saw that one of the men was taller than the other two by a foot and a half. Then Gawain said to the king, 'Sir, go now to your meat, for here comes some strange adventure.'

Soon there came into the hall two stalwart fellows with the third, as large and fair a man as ever was seen, leaning on their shoulders. As they approached the high table, the tall young man stretched up easily.

'God bless you,' he said to the king. 'I come to ask three gifts, which you may grant without dishonour, hurt or loss. One I ask now, the other two I shall ask in twelve months' time.'

'Ask,' said Arthur.

'Give me meat and drink sufficient for this twelvemonth, and then I shall ask again.'

'My fair son,' the king replied, 'ask better. This is but a simple asking, hardly worthy for a man of honour.'

'Nay,' said the youth. 'I ask that and no more.'

'So be it. You shall have meat and drink enough. But what is your name?'

'That I cannot tell,' said he.

Then the king marvelled that such a goodly young man should not know his own name. But he ordered Sir Kay, the steward, to provide the best of food and drink, and to keep and lodge him in a manner fit for a lord's son.

But Sir Kay muttered to himself, 'No need for that, for I dare say he is a villain born. A man of good blood would have asked for horse and armour. Since he is nameless, I shall call him Beaumains, that is to say Fair-hands, for his hands are indeed large and fine. Into the kitchen he shall go, and there he shall have greasy broth every day. In a twelve-month he shall be as fat as a pork hog.'

At this, Sir Gawain and Sir Lancelot were angry. But Kay sat the young man down with the boys of the scullery and there he ate. After he had supped, both Gawain and Lancelot came to him privily and offered him good cheer. But Beaumains would do only what the steward commanded. Thus he was put in the kitchen and lay nightly on a pallet amid the lads in the back rooms, under thin covering. So he endured all that year and never displeased man or child, but was always meek and mild. Only, when there was jousting or sport, none could tear him away. And when the great stone was cast, none came within two yards of his throw. Then the steward would say, 'Now, how do you like my kitchen boy?'

Thus the year went round again, and once more the Round Table met most royally at Caerleon. This time, as King Arthur prepared to eat, a maiden came suddenly to the high feast, saluted the king and asked for his help.

'For whom?' said Arthur. 'What is the adventure?'

But the maiden would say no more than that she came for a lady of great renown who was besieged by a tyrant called the Red Knight of the Red Glade. This was a most dangerous knight, with the strength of seven men, and he was destroying the lady's lands.

'Fair maid,' said Arthur, 'here be many good knights well able to rescue your lady. But no knight of mine shall venture for a lady who is nameless.'

At once Beaumains spoke up, saying, 'Sir king, God thank you for my twelvemonth in your kitchen. Now I ask my other two gifts.'

'Speak, upon my peril,' said the king.

'Sir, first grant me this adventure of the unknown lady, for it belongs to me. Then bid Lancelot du Lake to ride after me and make me knight when I shall require him, for I will have none make me knight but him.'

All this was granted, as Arthur had promised. But the maiden was angry, saying boldly, 'Fie on you, sir king, shall I have none but your kitchen page?' In a rage, she took her horse and departed.

Though he had neither shield nor spear, Beaumains mounted a horse with trappings of cloth of gold, and looked fierce enough for men to marvel at. Then he rode after the maiden and Sir Kay followed him, to test his boy from the kitchen.

'Beaumains,' the steward called out. 'What, sir, do you not know me?'

'Yea indeed,' said Beaumains, turning his horse, 'I know you for an ungentle knight, and therefore beware of me.'

So they rushed at one another and Beaumains with his sword beat the steward from his horse, leaving him almost dead. Then he took the shield and spear from the steward and rode away. All this was seen by the maiden and Sir Lancelot. The defeat of Sir Kay was a surprise to Lancelot. He thought that he would also try the prowess of this kitchen boy. So they hallooed at each other and came together like boars in rut, slashing and thrusting for nigh on an hour. Lancelot marvelled at the strength and skill of this man, whose fighting was so full of peril and more like that of a giant than a knight. Sir Lancelot had much ado to keep himself from being shamed. At last he called out, 'Beaumains, fight not so sore. Our quarrel is not so great but we may leave off.'

'True,' said Beaumains, letting out breath, 'but it does me good to feel your might. Yet, my lord, I was not at my limit.'

'In God's name,' Lancelot admitted, 'I could do no more.'

'Am I thus approved for knighthood? In this, how do I stand?'

Then Beaumains begged that he might be made a knight. And Sir Lancelot agreed, on condition that he should know the new knight's true name.

'Sir, I shall tell you, so long as you do not reveal me. I am Gareth, brother to Sir Gawain, by the same father and mother.'

'Ah, I am more glad of you than ever. For I always thought you would be of good blood, and that you came to court for more things than food and drink.'

Then Sir Lancelot dubbed him and gave him the order of knighthood. After this, Lancelot went back to Arthur's court, recovering on the way the bruised body and sore feeling of poor Sir Kay. But Sir Gareth was once again Beaumains, the page of the scullery, as he returned to his quest in the cause of the maiden and her lady.

He rode hard and overtook the maiden, but she turned her face away, saying, 'What, are you here again? You stink of the kitchen. Your clothes are foul with grease and tallow. Go back, you bawdy kitchen page. I know you well. Your name is Beaumains, an idle lout, a table-wiper and dish-washer.'

'Good maiden,' said Beaumains mildly, 'say what you will. I shall see this adventure to the end, or else I shall die.'

'Fie on you, knave. Soon you will trade all the kitchen broth you ever supped to be elsewhere.'

And thus they rode on in stiff silence into the gloom of the woods. As they entered, there came a man fleeing as fast as he could, crying out, 'Help me! Six thieves have taken and bound my lord, and I fear they will slay him.'

At once Beaumains galloped to those thieves, pursued them and harried them until they were all slain. He untied the knight, who thanked him gravely and offered him reward. But Beaumains would have none except what God gave him, for he must follow the maiden, though she still berated him with the stink of the kitchen. But as it was growing dark, the maiden gladly went to the safety of the knight's castle, and Beaumains rode after. The knight gave them comfort and set them both at table. But the maiden cried again, 'Fie, fie, sir knight, you are discourteous, to set a kitchen page before me. You might as well stick a swine before a maiden of my high lineage.'

These words made the knight ashamed of her, and he took himself to eat with Beaumains at a sideboard. They had good cheer, and after went softly to rest.

On the morn, when they departed, Beaumains and the maiden came to a ford over a river which was defended by two knights.

'What do you say,' the maiden taunted him, 'will you match yonder knights or turn aside?'

'I would not turn,' he replied, 'were there six or more.'

Thereupon he splashed into the shallows and forced a passage. He stunned one knight so that he fell and drowned, and he cleaved the head of the other right through the helm. Then he beckoned the maiden and bade her courteously to ride through.

'Alas,' she lamented, 'that a kitchen knave should destroy two such doughty knights. Do you think you did nobly? Nay, I saw the first knight stumble, fall and drown. The other, you crept behind him and slew him by mishap. Do not make yourself proud.'

'Fair maiden, give me good words,' he replied, 'and then my care is past. For I fear no knight, whomsoever he might be.'

'Follow me further and you shall be slain. I see that all you do is by misadventure, and not by the prowess of your hands.'

'Well, madam, say what you will. But wherever you go, I shall follow.'

So they rode again till the time of evensong, and always she chided him and would not let him rest. At dusk they came to a dark place where the Knight of the Black Glade hung his banner and black shield on a hawthorn tree. Nearby his great spear stuck in the ground and his black horse munched the grass. When he saw them, the Black Knight shouted a challenge, saying, 'Maiden, have you brought this knight of King Arthur to be your champion?'

'Nay, fair knight,' she replied. 'This is but a scullery knave that was fed in Arthur's kitchen.'

'Then what is this bold array? 'Tis a shame that he keeps you company.'

'Sir, I cannot get rid of him. Would to God that you might slay him. He is an unhappy knave that by luck and misadventure has already undone several good men.'

'It is a wonder,' said the Black Knight, 'that any worthy knight will have ado with him.'

'They do not know him. Because he rides with me, they take him for a well-bred knight.'

'Well, I grant you that he is a likely and strong-looking person,' said the Black Knight. 'I will win from him his horse and harness, for it would shame me to do him any further harm.'

Then Beaumains replied undaunted, 'In spite of you, I shall pass through this glade. As for my horse and harness, get them if you can.'

'Do you say that, boy?' the Black Knight laughed. 'Now let your lady go, for it does not become a kitchen knave to ride with such a lady.'

'You lie,' cried Beaumains hotly. 'I am a gentleman born and of better birth than you, and I will prove it on your body.'

In great anger, they fought. And Beaumains, so large and strong, knocked the Black Knight on one side and on the other until he lay all bloody on the earth and died. Then Beaumains took his black horse and handsome black armour and rode after the maiden once more. But she reviled him again till he chided her, saying, 'I warn you, fair maiden, that I will not leave you until I have been beaten or slain. Therefore do not spend all day rebuking me, for I shall see the end of this journey, come what may.'

So Beaumains rode on after the maiden, who never ceased to assault his ear with insult and rebuke. In a little time they came to a new-mown meadow that lay in front of a fair city. In the field were many bright pavilions and much preparation for joust and tourney. Five hundred knights were getting ready their arms. Shields of many colours and the fine clothes of fair ladies all shone in the sun.

'Look there at yonder pavilion the colour of Inde,' said the maiden. 'In there is Sir Persant of Inde, the most lordly knight that ever you saw.'

'Be he never so brave,' replied Beaumains, 'here I shall stay till I see him under cover of his shield. Let him come, and do his worst.'

Now, seeing the boldness of his arm and the courtesy and mildness of his tongue, the maiden began to repent her hard words. 'Sir,' she said, 'now I wonder who and what you are. You speak well, and boldly you have fought. That I have seen. Therefore, I pray you, save yourself. You and your horse have done hard trials, and I fear we stay overlong from my lady's siege, which is but seven miles hence. I dread lest you catch some hurt from this strong knight. Yet Sir Persant is nothing to him that lays siege to my lady.'

'It is shameful for me to withdraw now,' aid Beaumains. 'Have no doubt but that I shall deal with this knight within two hours, and then we shall come to the place of your siege by daylight.'

'O Jesu, what manner of man are you? Surely you must come of noble blood. For never did woman rule a knight so foully and shamefully as I have done you. Yet always you suffered me meekly.'

'Madam,' he replied, 'a knight must suffer whatever a maiden pleases. The more you rebuked me, the more I was inwardly angered, and the more I wreaked my wrath on those who came against me. Your words furthered me in my battle, and caused me to prove myself. Though I had meat in Arthur's kitchen, yet I might have had food enough in other places. But I did it to test my friends. Gentleman or not, I have done you gentle service, and perhaps I will yet do you better service before I leave you.'

'Fair Beaumains,' she cried, 'forgive me all I have said or done against you.'

'With all my heart,' he replied, 'and since you now speak kindly to me, it gladdens my heart. Now there is no knight living that I cannot match.'

By this time Sir Persant had come into the field well armed. He thought that Beaumains looked a worthy knight, by his clear face and his large and heavy limbs. So the two knights fought, as men of honour will do. The fight was long and hard, with many grievous blows given and taken. But after two hours Beaumains prevailed over Sir Persant and made him yield, and at the plea of the maiden granted him mercy. When he had recovered somewhat, Persant thanked Beaumains for his courtesy, and he took him and the maiden to the pavilion in the meadow, where they drank wine and ate spices, and rested awhile. Then, in the evening, they supped again and went cheerfully to bed.

Now, when Beaumains was abed, Sir Persant called his daughter of eighteen years, a mere girl and a beauty, and charged her upon his blessing to go to the knight's bed. 'Lie down with him,' said her father, 'take him in your arms and kiss him, and make the night sweet for him.'

The girl did what her father said. Quietly she undressed and laid herself down by Beaumains' side. This made him awake with a start. He drew back suddenly, catching the covering, and demanded to know who she was.

'I am Sir Persant's daughter,' she said, 'come here by my father's wish.'

'Are you maid or wife?' said he.

'Sir, I am a clean maid.'

'God forbid that I should defile you. Fair maid, arise at once from this bed, or I will.' Then he kissed her but a single time, gently, and so she departed to her father.

'Truly, whoever he be,' said Sir Persant, 'doubtless he comes from noble blood.'

On the morn, as Beaumains and the maiden made ready to leave, Sir Persant asked where they were going.

Arthur pulls out the sword from the stone

Above: Merlin, King Arthur's magician

Left: King Arthur, depicted on a medieval tapestry

Sir Lancelot in combat

'This knight with me,' replied the maiden, 'goes to the siege that keeps my sister pent up in the Castle Dangerous.'

'Ha,' said Persant. 'That is the work of the Red Knight of the Red Glade, a most perilous fighter and a man without mercy. God save you from that knight, for he has the strength of seven men. But he does great wrong to the lady. But are you not Lynet, her sister?'

'Indeed, sir, I am Lynet, sister to Dame Lyonesse.'

Then Sir Persant told them of the dangers that lay ahead, and sent them riding from his gate with warnings and a blessing. Fearful for the fate of her sister, Lynet ordered a misshapen little man to hurry before them to carry the news of their coming to the castle. When Lyonesse heard what sort of doughty knight was coming to help her, she was right glad and had prepared for him good food and drink. Then the little dwarf took to a certain hermitage two gallons of wine in silver flagons, two large loaves of bread, with fat baked venison and dainty fowls beside, all so that Beaumains might refresh himself and grow strong, for Lyonesse knew well that the knight he must meet cared for nothing but murder.

The dwarf led Beaumains and the maiden to the hermitage, and then departed. As he went back to the castle, a stern knight in red armour on a tall courser stopped him. He knew at once that this was the Knight of the Red Glade, a most perilous man.

'Sir,' the little man replied to the knight's questioning, 'my lady's sister, Lynet, has been at the court of King Arthur and has brought a champion with her.'

The Red Knight laughed. 'Her trouble is for nothing,' he boasted. 'Had she brought Sir Lancelot, Sir Tristram, Sir Lamorak or Sir Gawain, I would think myself good enough for them all. But who is this worthy? Is he one of the four I have mentioned?'

'No, none of those, but still a king's son.'

'His name, then?'

'I will not tell you. But Sir Kay, the steward, scorned him with the name of Beaumains.'

'Well, I care not,' said the Red Knight with contempt. 'Whoever he is, I shall soon deliver him to a shameful death.'

That night Beaumains lay at the hermitage, praying in God's name for right action and good conscience. Upon the morn, he and Lynet heard Mass and broke their fast. Then they took horse and rode not far to a plain before a large castle. In the distance they saw much smoke and heard a great noise of siege. As they came near, they saw upon the trees armed knights hanged by the neck, with swords in their scabbards and gilt spurs upon their heels.

'What means this?' said Beaumains.

'Fair sir,' replied Lynet, 'do not lose your courage at this sight. All these poor knights came hither to rescue my sister Lyonesse. But the Red Knight of the Red Glade killed them in this shameful manner, without mercy. And he will do so to you, unless you better him.'

'Now Jesu defend me,' said Beaumains, 'from such a villainous death. I would rather be slain in a manly way, in plain battle.'

'Then trust him not,' she warned, 'for in him is no courtesy.'

They rode towards the castle and saw that it was double-ditched, with full warlike walls. On the far side the sea beat upon the battlements. In a field before the castle the Red Knight had hung the horn of challenge, a huge horn of elephant bone hung in a sycamore tree.

'I pray you,' Lynet said, 'blow not that horn till high noon, when his strength will decline. It is now about prime, and his strength is increasing to the equal of seven men.'

'For shame, fair maiden,' Beaumains chided her, 'were he the strongest knight that ever was, I would not avoid him at his most mighty. I will win honourably, or die like a knight in the field.'

Then he spurred his horse straight to the sycamore and blew such a blast on the horn that all the siege army and all the castle rang with the sound. Knights leapt distraught from tents and pavilions, and the embrasures of the castle walls were suddenly filled with eyes. But the Red Knight of the Red Glade listened and went calmly to arms. Two barons set his spurs upon his heels, and all was blood red, his armour, spear and shield. An earl buckled his helm and brought him to his red steed. So he rode to a little valley under the castle walls where all might behold the battle. And among the onlookers was Dame Lyonesse. As Beaumains cast his eyes towards the skies, he saw her in the window. She made curtsey to him below, and held out her hands.

With that, the Red Knight called to Beaumains, 'Sir knight, leave your looking and behold me. I warn you well, she is my lady. For her, I have done many strong battles. Have you not reason to beware of yonder knights that hang upon the trees? Now it shall be your turn, so make ready.'

Then they put their spears in their rests and came together like roaring lions. They hit each other so hard that the breastplates of the horses split and the surcingles burst. The riders tumbled down with reins and bridles tangled in their hands. Then the two knights sprang to their feet with sword and shield, and fought past noon and did not stint till both stood wagging and tottering, panting, blowing and bleeding. Once more they set to, and grappled and grovelled on the earth with little advantage either way till evensong, when they agreed to rest. So they sat down on two molehills in that valley, and each unlaced his helm and let the cool wind play about his weary head.

When his helm was off, Beaumains looked again to the window and there he saw the Lady Lyonesse making him such a glad and welcoming face that his heart rose high. Sternly he turned to the Red Knight, saying, 'Now sir, let us cease sporting. Let us do battle to the uttermost.'

'Yea, you have said it,' replied the other. So again they hurled their sore bodies at each other. This time Beaumains fought with such fury that soon he had the Red Knight on the ground, with a foot on his neck and his helm torn off. Then the Red Knight yielded and begged for mercy. But Beaumains thought on the knights in the trees, with their poor necks stretched, and he was not minded to be merciful. There was then a great wail from the field, and many earls and barons prayed on their knees for the Red Knight's life, that he might amend himself for his misdeeds, which were in the past and yet could not be undone.

Mercy, our Saviour knows, is above all a quality of knighthood. So Beaumains granted life to the Red Knight, on condition that he go to the court of King Arthur and yield himself up, and do homage and fealty for his lands. Also, he must make his peace with Sir Lancelot, with whom he had an old quarrel about a woman.

Then the maiden Lynet tenderly unarmed Beaumains. She staunched his wounds and bathed the gashes of his flesh. For ten days he rested in a little tent, hardly stirring for soreness. After this time he was well, and ready to go to the castle.

After Beaumains was rested and made whole again, he dressed himself in fine clothes and rode to the castle. But he found the gate closed against him. He saw the unfriendly faces of many armed men, pulling up the drawbridge and letting down the portcullis. Marvelling at this, he looked towards the high window. Then he heard the voice of Dame Lyonesse saying, 'Go on your way, Sir Beaumains, for as yet you shall not have wholly my love. Therefore go and labour in worthiness this twelvemonth, and then you shall hear new tidings.'

'Ah, fair lady,' he said in great surprise, 'what is this? I am sure I have bought your love with a part of the best blood in my body.'

'Courteous knight,' she replied, 'do not be displeased. Your great trials and your good love shall not be lost. Therefore go and be of good comfort. A twelvemonth will soon be done. And trust me, I shall be true to you and never betray you.'

She went from the window. In sorrow Beaumains rode away from the castle, wandering he knew not whither, until it was dark night. At last he came to a broad water with a lodge nearby. He dismounted and gave his horse to the dwarf that waited on him. Then he laid his head on his shield and slept.

As soon as he was gone from the castle, Lyonesse summoned her brother Sir Gringamore. 'Ride in haste after Sir Beaumains,' she said, 'and catch him while he sleeps. Then privily snatch up his dwarf and carry him away. The dwarf knows the right name and kindred of this knight called Beaumains, and till I also have that knowledge I shall never be merry in my heart.'

Sir Gringamore rode with whip and spur, and came upon the sleeping Beaumains in the middle of the night. He tied his horse to a thorn at some distance and very quietly he stalked up behind the dwarf, who was dozing as he watched. Then he tucked the little man under his arm and dashed away. But all the while the dwarf bawled lustily, waking Beaumains, who dressed with all speed and gave chase. He rode through marsh and field and dales. He looked for the shortest way in the dark, and many a time he and his horse plunged into mire and bog, head over heels, till a countryman going to market in the dawn pointed out the road to Gringamore's castle.

Already Sir Gringamore and his sisters had met there, and the dwarf was in the chamber with them. Right easily he answered Dame Lyonesse, telling her that his master was in truth Sir Gareth, brother of Gawain and son of Orkney's king.

As they sat talking thus, Sir Gareth, he who was also Beaumains, came roaring at the gate with his sword drawn, demanding the delivery of his dwarf, or else he would do great harm to all within. Proud Sir Gringamore would have withstood him. But Dame Lyonesse laid her hand on her brother's sleeve, saying, 'Let go his dwarf, for I would not have him angry. I owe him my service for what he has done for me, and I love him before all others. I would not have him know me as I was, but now beginning again as someone new.'

So Gringamore let go the dwarf who went at once, as became him, to take the reins of his master's horse in the courtyard below.

'Well, my little fellow,' said Gareth, 'what an adventure we have had for your sake.' He put his hand on the rough, crooked head, and together they went in.

Then Dame Lyonesse came forth, dressed like a princess and as fair as the summer morn, and many tender looks passed between her and Gareth. That evening in the castle there was much mirth, with dancing and singing, and sweet music from the minstrel. The time fled away, and the more Sir Gareth beheld the lady, the more he loved her, so that he burnt beyond reason. When they went to supper, he could not eat for love.

Sir Gringamore was well pleased at the looks that passed between the lovers, for Gareth was of noble blood. 'Stay with us as long as you like,' he said. And Gareth agreed with a glad heart, for he most wished to be with this lady. He kissed her many times, and she promised to love him and to have none other all the days of her life. Then they plighted their troth, to love each other and never to fail while breath lasted. Now they burnt so hot they could not be content with seeing and talking, but were minded to satisfy their lusts in secret. So Lyonesse took Gareth aside in a corner and told him to sleep in the hall, and there she would come to his bed around midnight.

This secret was not so easily kept. They were both young and ardent, and not used to such trickery. When she knew what would happen, Lynet was a little displeased that her sister would not wait for the time of her marriage. For the honour of the lovers, she thought to cool their hot lusts. By enchantment, she ordained that they should not have their delight until they married.

After supper, when all were yawning and going to their beds, Gareth said plainly that he would go no further than the hall. Of all places, he said, that was most convenient for a knight errant to rest in. So a great couch was fetched and a feather bed put upon it, and Gareth lay down. At midnight Dame Lyonesse came to him, naked under a mantle tipped with ermine. She lay beside him and forthwith he folded her in his arms and began to kiss her for his very life.

Then there came into the hall an armed knight, in a shining halo of lights, who rushed at Gareth with a battle-ax in his hands. Gareth leapt from bed, caught up his sword and fended off the blow from the ax, which nonetheless slipped from the guard and opened a great wound in the thick of his thigh, cutting through veins and sinews. At once Gareth answered with a fierce swing of his sword and smote the head from the shoulders of the knight. But Sir Gareth was bleeding so fast that he fell to the bed and swooned.

All the people of the household came running at the noise and were much amazed at the sight. Sir Gringamore was sore angry at this dishonour to his guest. And Lyonesse made a great wail and tried to staunch the bleeding as best she might. But Lynet took up the severed head, anointed with a salve both it and the shoulders from which it came, and stuck them fast together. Then the knight rose up lightly and went on his way. Sir Gareth, recovered somewhat from his swoon, saw this and sadly said to Lynet, 'Maiden, we rode together through the perilous passages. I never thought this would be part of your doing.'

'My lord,' she replied, 'I will stand by all I have done. It was done for your honour, and for the honour of our house.'

The wound healed and after a time Gareth was near mended whole, and sang, gamed and had good cheer again. Then he and Lyonesse once more burnt hot in lust, and she covenanted that she would come to his bed as before. But again an armed knight came, with lights about him as if from twenty torches. Gareth was more ready this time, and fought the knight all about the hall with great anger and malice. He struck down the impertinent knight and lopped off his head, and hewed it into a hundred pieces, which he hurled from the window into the ditches of the castle. But this great effort burst open his old wound, so once more he fell faint from loss of blood.

The sorrow of Dame Lyonesse at this second blow was a grief to see, and she wept as if she would die. But Lynet came again and fetched all the gobbets of the head from the ditch outside. Then she anointed them and stuck them all fast as before, and the knight went on his way.

'Well, Dame Lynet,' said Gareth, bleeding upon the bed, 'do I deserve this from you?'

'Indeed, sir, and thus I save your honour, and the honour of us all.'

Now, while this happened in the castle of Gringamore, none at the court of King Arthur knew where the kitchen boy Beaumains had gone and how he fared. So when the knights defeated by Beaumains in his travels came to the court to do homage to Arthur, as Beaumains had commanded them, the king questioned them closely. But none could give him news.

'Sir king,' said the Red Knight of the Red Glade, 'I tell you nothing, for it is full hard to find him. Such young knights errant as he, when they are about their adventures, stay in no place.'

Then the king sent a messenger to Dame Lyonesse, who was still with Sir Gareth. But Gareth was not yet ready to be discovered. He let it be devised that a great tourney be commanded for the Assumption of Our Lady between the knights of Dame Lyonesse and the knights of the Round Table. He that proved himself the best for prowess would win the Lady Lyonesse and all her land.

Upon the appointed feast, King Arthur and his knights went to the castle of Lyonesse. And there in great state and majesty a tourney was held between the best knights in the world. Here Sir Gareth fought, still under disguise, and he was so large and young and big with power that he did wondrous and worthy acts of battle. All men marvelled at his force until Arthur in amazement sent a herald to spy upon this unknown knight under the yellow shield. When the herald drew close, edging up to Gareth from his blind side, he saw golden letters appear about the helm, saying: 'This is Gareth of Orkney'.

Then Sir Gareth was discovered. His brother Sir Gawain rode to him, and then they embraced and wept a good while before they would speak. While they sat thus upon the ground, Dame Lynet spurred her mule and came quickly to King Arthur, who was but two miles hence, and told him the adventure that had come to pass. Right there, King Arthur ordained the setting of a camp, so that his beloved nephews might rest and recover. And nothing was wanting in that camp that house or country could provide, or gold and silver get.

'How now, Lynet,' said Arthur, 'why stay you? Gallop apace to Dame Lyonesse, and bring her to her knight Sir Gareth.'

Thus summoned, she came. She was arrayed in robes of cloth of gold, and in that company of kings and queens at Arthur's court she was not the least fair.

'Look on this lady,' said the king to his nephew Gareth. 'Will you take her as paramour, or to have as your wife?'

'My lord,' he replied, 'know well that I love her above all ladies living.'

'What,' said Arthur, 'is the wind in that door? You cannot love so well but that I shall increase it. I would rather lose my crown than hurt your hearts. And now, fair Lady Lyonesse, what say you?'

'Most noble king,' replied the lady, 'I would rather have Sir Gareth as husband than any prince or king ever christened. If I may not have him, I promise you I shall have none. He is my first love, and he shall be the last.'

'In truth,' Gareth then said to her, 'if I do not have you as my wife, no lady nor gentlewoman shall ever rejoice me again.'

Then provision was made for the marriage, at Michaelmas, by the sea sands of Kinkenadon in that beauteous country. Word went out throughout the land, and all the lords and ladies came gladly to that day. And, Lord, what joy and good cheer they had.

✠ Sir Lancelot du Lake ✠

A mong the knights of the Round Table there were some who increased so much in arms and in worth that they passed all their fellows in prowess and noble deeds. In especial, this was the case with Sir Lancelot du Lake. In all tournaments and jousts, both for life and for death, at no time was he ever overcome, except by treason or enchantment. Therefore Queen Guenevere held him in great favour above all other knights, and it is certain he loved the queen also, above all other ladies of his life.

After Sir Lancelot had resorted at the court of King Arthur for some long time, and had rested and disported himself with play and games of jousting and the like, he thought he would prove himself in strange adventures. He sent to Sir Lionel, saying, 'Nephew, make ready, for we two will go and seek adventures.'

So, armed at all points, they rode from a forest onto a deep plain. The sun was high, and about noon Sir Lancelot had a great desire to sleep. Nearby Lionel saw a wide-spreading apple tree, and said, 'Brother, yonder is a fair shade. Let us rest there.'

Then Sir Lancelot stretched under the apple tree, with his helm under his head, and slept while Sir Lionel watched.

Soon after, three knights galloped by, fleeing for their lives, and behind them followed a fourth knight, as large and grim and boldly armed as any seen. The strong knight overtook the first, and smote him to the cold earth. Then he tumbled the second, man and horse, to the ground, and rounded on the third, striking a mighty blow of his spear on the horse's arse. The big knight jumped to the ground and bound his three prisoners with the reins of their own bridles.

'This is a heavy man, a worthy man,' Lionel marvelled. 'It is meet that I try him myself.'

So Sir Lionel stole away privily, without waking Lancelot, and rode in haste after the big knight, calling loudly for him to turn. Then they fought. But the knight was too strong for Lionel, who was thrown up in the air and out of the saddle so that he landed in a lump without wind. The knight bound him also, and laid him across his own horse. He gathered the reins of all the horses, and went to his castle with the four unfortunate men lying like bundles of rags across their horses' backs.

When the knight came to the castle, he stripped his prisoners all naked and beat them with thorns, and threw them in a deep dungeon where many more knights were making a piteous noise.

Now, when Sir Ector heard that his brother Lancelot was gone from Arthur's court to seek adventures, he was angry with himself that he was left behind. He went after him, to search out whatever might happen. Soon he met a forester on the road and said to him, 'Good fellow, what adventures are nigh at hand in this country?'

'Within a mile,' the man replied, 'is a strong manor behind a deep dyke, with a ford on the left hand. Over the ford stands a wizened tree hung with many shields of fair knights. By a hole in the tree, there hangs a copper basin. Strike it thrice with the butt of your spear and you will soon hear strange tidings, enough to please the greatest lust for adventures.'

When Sir Ector came to the tree he saw hanging there the shield of his kinsman Sir Lionel, and many more besides that belonged to his fellows of the Round Table. This grieved his heart and he promised in his mind to avenge his brother knights. As his horse drank peacefully at the ford, Ector beat on the basin like a madman. At once the large knight appeared, saying with a grim smile, 'Come, sir, out of the water, and make ready to suffer on land'.

Then Sir Ector set his spear, and the feet of his horse threshed the waters of the ford to foam, and Ector gave the knight such a great buffet that his horse turned about twice.

'That was boldly done,' cried the knight. 'It was a knightly blow.'

Thereupon he drove his horse at Sir Ector, barging him, seizing him under the arms and lifting him clean from the saddle. Then he carried Sir Ector to his own hall like a swaddling child, and dumped him in the middle of the floor, saying, 'Know and fear me, for I am Sir Turquin, and you have done this day more unto me than any knight did these twelve years.' Then he stripped Sir Ector and whipped him with thorns, and cast him into the deep dungeon where he could make sorrow with his fellows.

'Alas, brother,' said Ector to Lionel, 'are you here too? But where is Sir Lancelot?'

'I left him asleep under an apple tree. What is become of him I cannot tell. Alas, unless Sir Lancelot help us, we may never be delivered, for I know no other knight to match this Turquin.'

While these things happened betwixt Turquin and his prisoners, Sir Lancelot awoke in the cool of the day, and rode away into thick woods where he could find no highway. At last, in a little clear vale, he saw a pavilion of red cloth with a bed inside that called him to sleep. He unarmed wearily, and fell asleep.

In the dark, when the knight of the pavilion returned home, he saw a body within the bed that he took to be his paramour. He entered under the covers beside Sir Lancelot and began to kiss him right heartily. When Lancelot felt a rough beard kissing him, he leapt from one side of the bed, and the knight leapt from the other, and they both reached for their swords. Then they ran all unclothed from the pavilion, slashing at each other in the blackness, till by luck Lancelot cut the knight with a sore wound. At once the knight cried mercy, and told Sir Lancelot the cause of their mistake.

'I repent that I hurt you,' replied Lancelot, 'but I dreaded some treason.' He carried the knight back to the pavilion. As he staunched the wound, the knight's lady came and made a great moan over her lord.

'Peace, my lady and my love,' said the knight, who was named Belleus. 'This is a good man and a knight adventurous. He has wounded me by misfortune, and now he staunches my blood.'

On the morn, Sir Lancelot commended the knight and his lady to God and went on his way in search of Sir Lionel. By many paths he came again to the apple tree where Lionel had left him. He saw there a maiden sitting on a white pony, as if waiting for him. She greeted him by name, and at his questioning told him all that had befallen Sir Lionel at the hands of Sir Turquin. 'Now, good Lancelot,' she urged him, 'hurry to help him.' So she brought him to the ford and the tree where the basin hung.

Sir Lancelot let his horse drink while he beat on the basin so hard that the bottom fell out. But no man came. Then Lancelot rode to the manor, prowling the gates and the walls for nigh on half an hour before he saw a big knight coming, leading a horse with a bound man athwart its back. As they came nearer, Lancelot thought he should know the bound knight. Then he saw that it was Sir Gaheris, Gawain's brother.

So he cried aloud, 'Bold knight, now put down that wounded man, and let us two prove our strengths. I am told that you have done despite and shame to many knights of the Round Table. So now defend yourself.'

'Are you too of the Round Table?' Turquin mocked him. 'So much for you and all your fellowship. I despise you all.'

'That is one word too many,' said Lancelot.

Without more prattle, they came together as fast as their horses might run. Their meeting was like the crashing of winter seas. For two hours or more they fought, but neither could find the bare or undefended place that means woe or death. At last, both breathless, they stood leaning on their swords.

'Now fellow,' gasped Sir Turquin, 'hold your hand a while and tell me what I ask.'

'Say on.'

'You are the biggest man that ever I met, strong-armed and well-breathed. Indeed, you are very like the one knight I hate above all others. If you are not that man, tell me your name and we shall make accord. I will deliver my prisoners, to the number of three score and four. Then you and I shall be fellows together, and never fail.'

'Well,' replied Lancelot, 'what man is he whom you hate?'

'Sir Lancelot is his name. He slew my brother Carados at the Dolorous Tower. If ever I meet him, I vow one of us shall find his end. In search of him I have slain a hundred good knights, and as many more I have maimed utterly, while still others have died in my prison. Now, say not that you are Sir Lancelot.'

'I see well,' said Lancelot, 'if I were that man, there should be mortal war betwixt us. Then know, sir knight, that I am truly Lancelot du Lake, son of King Ban of Benwick, a very knight of the Round Table. Now do your best.'

'Ah, Lancelot,' cried Turquin, 'you are now as dear to me as any man. Welcome to death!'

Again they took up arms and bespeckled the ground with their best blood. At last Sir Turquin began to wax faint, and his shield dropped somewhat for weariness. Seeing this, Lancelot leapt within Turquin's guard, got him by the beaver of his helmet and plucked him down on his knees. Then he tore off his helm and smote his neck in sunder.

Sir Lancelot unbound Gaheris and went with him towards the manor of Turquin. At the gate, he looked on the old gnarled tree and saw the many sad shields hanging there.

'What a sight is this,' he said to Gaheris. 'There is Kay's shield, and many more belonging to knights of the Round Table. And there, alas, are those of my brothers Sir Ector and Sir Lionel. I pray you, good Gaheris, release them and greet them all from me. Bid them sack the manor of such stuff as they please and go to Arthur's court to await me. For I must go on now to meet my adventures, as I have promised this maiden on the white pony.'

Then Gaheris released all the knights and told them that their freedom was Lancelot's doing, who killed Turquin with his own hands. Happily, the knights sought arms, armour and horses. When they were dressed and armed, they called to the forester to bring four mules laden with fat venison. That night they ate right well on venison roasted, baked and boiled, and after a full supper they lay at ease in feather beds.

Meanwhile, Sir Lancelot took the highway again, saying gently to the maiden, 'Will you need any more service of me?'

'Nay, sir, not at this time,' she replied. 'But Jesu preserve you, for you are the most courteous and meekest knight that now lives. One thing only you seem to lack. You are without wife, and I hear say that you will take none, which is the greater pity. It is noised that you love Queen Guenevere, and that she has enchanted you to love no other. No maid nor lady rejoices you, wherefor many in this land, of high and low estate, make great sorrow.'

'Fair maid,' he said, 'people may speak of me as they please. But to be a wedded man, I think not. For then I must couch with my wife, and leave arms and tourneys, battles and adventures. And as for taking my pleasure with paramours, that I refuse for dread of God. Lecherous knights will never be fortunate in war. Either they are undone by simple folk, or by mishap and their cursedness they slay better men than themselves. All things about a lecher are unhappy.'

So she left him, and Sir Lancelot rode on for two days. On the third, as he was passing over a long bridge, a foul churl came suddenly and smote his horse on the nose, and rudely demanded why Lancelot crossed that bridge without a licence.

'Why should I not choose this way?' said Lancelot.

'You may not choose,' said the churl, lashing at him with a huge iron-bound club. Lancelot answered him back with a stroke of the sword that divided the churl from his hair to his paps. But the village folk at the end of the bridge all cried to Sir Lancelot, 'A worse deed you never did. Beware, for you have slain the chief porter of our castle. He will be avenged.'

Straightways Lancelot went to the castle and tied his horse to a ring on the wall of a pretty green court. It seemed a good place to fight in, so he prepared himself for battle. When he was ready, he called out to the many faces that peered from the windows, 'Knight, whoever you are, come forth, for you are unhappy'.

Very soon two giants came upon him, well armed all save their heads, with horrible clubs in their hands. Sir Lancelot ran at the first one, thrusting the point of his sword through the unguarded neck. The second, seeing what passed with his brother, fled like a madman, but Lancelot tripped him and slew him. Then he went into the hall of the castle and delivered up three score maids and ladies, gentlewomen all, who had laboured at the silk-works of the giants for seven years.

Then Lancelot departed, commending them to God. As he rode along with ambling steps, without hurry or aim, except to see what adventures might come to him, suddenly his path was crossed by a black hound, sniffing as if on the track of a wounded deer. He followed the hound and saw on the earth a track of blood. With its nose in the dirt, the hound led Lancelot a long way, over an old, feeble bridge to an old house. Lancelot pushed the door of the house and entered a dim hall hung with many cobwebs. In the middle of the floor lay a dead knight. The hound whimpered and went to lick the wounds of the dead man.

A lady came forth from the dimness into the hall, weeping and wringing her hands. She saw Sir Lancelot and said, 'O sir, here is too much sorrow. My husband is slain, and he who did this deed is himself sore wounded and never likely to recover, for which I have no regret.'

'Who was your husband?' said Lancelot.

'His name was Sir Gilbert the Bastard, one of the best of men. But I know not the name of he who slew him.'

'Now God send you better comfort,' said Sir Lancelot.

Going from that gloomy place into the woods again, he met a maiden who knew him well. She greeted him. 'Well found, my lord. On your oath of knighthood, give me your help. My brother is sore ill, and cannot stop bleeding from the wound he got from Sir Gilbert the Bastard when he fought and slew him in plain battle. A sorceress, who dwells here besides, this day told me that my brother would never be whole till I find a knight to go into the Chapel Perilous. There he will find a sword and a bloody cloth that the knight was lapped in. Only that sword and that piece of cloth will heal my brother's wounds.'

'This is a marvellous thing,' said Lancelot. 'But what is your brother's name?'

'He is Sir Meleot de Logris, your fellow of the Round Table. But hurry along this highway, and it will bring you to the Chapel Perilous. I shall abide here, till God speed you to me again.'

In haste Sir Lancelot rode to the chapel and saw by the door many rich shields turned upside down. And about the door he saw thirty knights, taller by a yard than most men, blocking his way with evil grins. The look of them made Lancelot's heart quake. But he drew his sword and raised his shield, ready to do battle with those men in black armour with black shields. Yet in a sudden moment they scattered on every side, and he went through boldly into the chapel. Inside there was nothing but ghostly light and a corpse covered with a silk cloth.

Lancelot stooped and cut away a piece of that cloth, and as he did so the earth shook a little. In fear he snatched up the sword of the dead knight and ran from the chapel. In the yard beyond he heard the grim voices of the tall knights, saying, 'Sir Lancelot, lay that sword aside, or you will die'.

'Live or die,' he shouted back, 'I keep hold of it. Fight for it, if you want it.'

He rushed through the knights, who stopped him not, to the gate of the chapel yard. There a maiden stood who said to him, 'Sir Lancelot, leave that sword, or you will die for it.'

'I will not leave it,' he said, 'under no entreaties.'

'Well said,' she replied, 'for had you left the sword, you would never again see Queen Guenevere. Now gentle knight, I require you to kiss me but once.'

'Nay, God forbid.'

'Ah, sir, had you kissed me all the days of your life would be over. But now, alas, I have lost all my labour. I ordained this chapel for thy sake. I have loved you this seven years, though I knew you loved none but Queen Guenevere. Since I may not rejoice you and have your body alive, I had no other joy in this world but to have your body dead. I would have embalmed it and kept it all my days, and daily I would have embraced you and kissed you, in despite of Queen Guenevere.'

'Jesu preserve me,' said Lancelot with blanched face, 'from your subtle crafts.'

At once he took his horse and rode away with all speed, leaving her forlorn and in such sorrow that she died within a fortnight. And her name was Hellawes, the sorceress.

With hard riding, Lancelot soon returned to the sister of Sir Meleot, who clapped her hands when she saw him and wept for joy. Together they went to the castle where Meleot lay, as pale as water for loss of blood. Then Sir Lancelot touched his wounds with Sir Gilbert's sword and wiped away the blood with the piece of cloth, and presently Sir Meleot was as whole a man as he had ever been.

When this task was done, Sir Lancelot took his leave. He still had strange countries to see and many fortunes to meet. He journeyed as the path took him, in valleys, plains and mountains, till in a certain place he heard two bells ringing. He saw a falcon tangled in the branches of a high elm, caught by the long leashes that streamed from its feet. As it threshed in the branches its little bells rang, and Lancelot felt sorry for the bird.

While he was looking upwards, a lady called to him, 'O Lancelot, flower of all knights, help me get my falcon. If I lose it, my husband Sir Phelot will slay me.'

'Lady,' he replied, 'since you know my name, I will do what I may. Yet God knows I am an ill climber, and the tree is very high, with few boughs to help me.' But he unarmed and put off his clothes down to his shirt and breeches, and with might and force climbed up to the falcon. He untangled the leashes and threw the bird down to the lady below.

As soon as she had her falcon in her hand, her husband Sir Phelot stepped suddenly from a grove, with naked sword in his hand, and said, 'You, knight Lancelot, now I have you as I want you'. And he stood at the bole of the tree, ready to kill him.

'Lady,' said Lancelot with reproach, 'why have you betrayed me?'

'She did it,' said Phelot, 'as I commanded her. But there is no help for you. The hour is come when you must die.'

'Shame on you,' said Lancelot, 'an armed knight to kill an undressed man by treason.'

'You get no further grace from me.'

'Truly, that shall be to your shame. But take my harness and hang my sword on a bough, that I may reach it if I can. Then do your best to slay me.'

'Nay, I know you better than that. You get no weapon from me.'

'Alas,' cried Lancelot, 'that ever a knight should die weaponless.'

He reached around him in the tree until he found a heavy spike of a branch, which he broke away with his body. Then he climbed lower. When he was just above his waiting horse he leapt to the other side, to get the horse betwixt him and the knight. Sir Phelot ran after him, lashing with his sword, but Lancelot put away the stroke with the heavy bough. Then he returned a crushing blow to the head of the knight, so that he fell in a swoon. He picked up the knight's sword and struck his head from his body.

When she saw this, the lady cried out weeping. But Sir Lancelot turned on her, saying with anger, 'You are the causer of this death. With falsehood you would have slain me, and now it is fallen on you both.'

Without more words Lancelot dressed and armed himself as fast as he might, lest the knight's people come to find him. Then he took horse and departed, with thanks to God that he had escaped this adventure.

Now Sir Lancelot was somewhat weary for travel. He wished to see again the face and person of Queen Guenevere. So, two days before the feast of Pentecost, he came home to the court of Arthur, all stained and bespattered from the road. The king and all his knights, and the queen also, were most glad of his coming. And there were in the court at that time many whom Sir Lancelot had helped and comforted in his adventures. With loud voices they spoke the praise of this knight.

Then Sir Lancelot had the greatest name of any knight in the world, and he was the most honoured by both high and low.

One time, upon Whit Sunday, a hermit came to King Arthur as the knights sat at the Round Table. And when the hermit saw the Seat Perilous left empty at the table, he asked the king why that seat was void.

'One only shall sit there,' said Arthur, 'and he shall be destroyed.'

'Know you who that man is?'

'Nay, I know not.'

'But I know,' said the hermit, 'though he that shall sit there is as yet unborn and ungotten. But his time comes, for this same year he shall be gotten. Then he shall sit in the Seat Perilous, and he shall win the Holy Grail.' The hermit said his words, and went on his way.

Now, after the feast of Pentecost Sir Lancelot set out on adventures once more, as is the manner of knighthood. He rode through country strange to him, seeking new fortune. In a wild part, as he passed over the Bridge of Corbin, he saw a tall tower in a town full of people who cried out to him, 'Welcome, Sir Lancelot, you are of such renown we know you by your device. O flower of knighthood, help us in our danger. Within this tower is a dolorous lady, suffering pains these many winters, for she boils in scalding water. Sir Gawain was here and could not help her, so he left her in pain.'

'I am as likely as Gawain,' said Lancelot, 'to leave her in pain.'

'Nay, we trust that you shall deliver her.'

'Well,' he replied doubtfully, 'then show me what I shall do.'

They brought Sir Lancelot into the tower and unlocked the doors of iron into the scalding chamber. Inside it was as hot as any stew, and in the hot mist Lancelot saw a lady as naked as a needle. Five years before Queen Morgan le Fay had by enchantment put the lady into the pains of that heat, because the queen was jealous of her beauty; nor might the lady be delivered until the best knight in the world came to rescue her.

When the heat had rushed from the door, Sir Lancelot led her from the scalding chamber and the people brought her clothes. She arrayed herself, and Lancelot thought that she looked a fair lady, a most fair lady, just one jot less beautiful than Queen Guenevere herself. Then she and Lancelot went to the chapel of the tower to thank God for her deliverance. And all the people, rich and poor, as they gave thanks also, thought on one more request to ask this good knight. 'My lord,' they said, 'since you have delivered this lady, save us also from a serpent that lives here in a tomb.'

They brought him to the place, and Sir Lancelot could not deny them. He came near the tomb and saw these letters writ in gold:

Here shall come a leopard of kings' blood, and he shall slay this serpent. And the leopard shall engender a lion in this foreign country, and this lion shall surpass all other knights.

Sir Lancelot lifted the tomb and out came a fiendish dragon, spitting fire from its mouth. He drew his sword on the dragon, skipping nimbly to avoid the horrible flames. They fought long but at last, by a lucky stroke, Lancelot cut through the dragon's neck. While they were fighting many had come to watch, and among them was King Pelles, the good and noble knight.

When the dragon was dead, Pelles saluted Sir Lancelot. 'I am King Pelles,' he said, 'king of the foreign country, and near kinsman of Joseph of Arimathea. What, sir, is your name?'

'Know you well, sir, my name is Sir Lancelot du Lake.'

Then they made much of each other, and so went into the hall to take their repast. As they ate, a dove entered at the window with a little censer of gold in its mouth. Suddenly there was such a savour, as if the chamber were flooded with all the spices of the world. And there appeared on the table every manner of meat and drink that they could think on. Next a maiden came in, holding a golden vessel betwixt her hands. Then the king and all about him knelt devoutly and offered their prayers to God.

'O Jesu,' said Lancelot softly, 'what may this mean?'

The king replied with reverence, 'This is the richest thing in the world of men. This is the Holy Grail. When this thing goes about, the Round Table shall be broken.'

When this sight was gone, leaving all in amazement, King Pelles still made much of Lancelot, for he schemed to this intent: he wished Sir Lancelot to lie with his daughter Elaine and get a child upon her. Such a child would be named Galahad, and he would grow into the good knight by whom all the foreign country would be brought out of danger. By Galahad also the Holy Grail would be won.

Thus Pelles schemed, but it was not easily done. For the enchantress Dame Brisen told him that Lancelot loved none but Guenevere. Therefore, it must be the work of enchantment to make him lie with Elaine. So Brisen sent a false messenger to Lancelot, bearing as a token a ring such as Guenevere was wont to wear.

'Where is my lady the queen?' said Lancelot with most eager joy.

'At the Castle of Case, but five miles hence.'

Lancelot rode there in all haste, and was received right worthily by such servants as a queen would have about her. The queen, they told him, was abed. Dame Brisen led him to a bedchamber and gave him a cup of enchanted wine. He drank and soon became so besotted and mad that he would brook no delay. He leapt from his clothes and into the bed, thinking that maid Elaine was Queen Guenevere. He was glad indeed; and so was Elaine, that she had Sir Lancelot in her arms. For she knew that that same night Galahad would be gotten on her, he who would prove the best knight of the world. All long night they twined together in joy and gladness, and the windows were covered so that no chink of light might disturb them.

Well after dawn, when the sun was high, Sir Lancelot awoke and went to the window. As he drew the covers and opened the window, the light flowed in and the enchantment was gone. Then he knew himself for what he was, and knew also that he had done amiss.

'Alas,' he cried, 'that I have lived so long, for I am surely shamed.'

He went to the bed and took his sword in hand, saying, 'Traitress, who are you with whom I have lain this night? Prepare to die.'

But Elaine sprang from the bed all naked and knelt before him shivering. 'Good courteous knight,' she implored him, 'descended from kings' blood, have mercy on me. I am Elaine, daughter of King Pelles. Slay me not, for you have planted in my womb he who shall be the most noble knight of the world.'

Sir Lancelot thought on this and considered it well, and then he forgave her. For the fault was not hers. She was a fair lady, and lusty and young, and as wise as any maid living. So he took her in his arms and kissed her, and wiped away a tear. Then he dressed and armed himself and made ready to depart, at which she said to him with a voice mild and sad, 'My lord, I beseech you see me again as soon as you may, for I have only obeyed my father's prophecy. By his command I have given you the greatest riches and the fairest flower, which is the maidenhead that I shall never have again. Therefore, gentle knight, owe me your goodwill.'

So Sir Lancelot took sweet leave of young lady Elaine and rode away to the Castle of Corbin. And when her time came she was delivered of a fine child, and this baby was christened Galahad.

About this time King Arthur came back in triumph from his wars in France and ordained a celebration, a great feast for all the lords and ladies of England. King Pelles spared no cost to send his daughter Elaine to the feast. She was finely arrayed in the richest robes, and a hundred lords and ladies were of her party on the highway. When she came to Camelot, she dazzled the eyes of the court, even the eyes of the king and queen. But Queen Guenevere gave her good greetings with her face only, not with her heart. And when Sir Lancelot saw her, he was so ashamed he would neither salute her nor speak to her, and yet he thought her as fair a woman as he had ever seen. This coldness made Dame Elaine so heavy she felt her heart would burst, for she loved him out of measure.

'This unkindness,' she wept to her woman Brisen, 'near kills me.'

'Peace, madam,' said Dame Brisen. 'Tonight I undertake he shall lie with you.'

In the evening, the queen commanded that Elaine should sleep in a chamber near unto hers, under the same roof. Then Guenevere sent for Lancelot and told him to come to her chamber in the night, saying, 'Or else I am sure you will go to that woman's bed, by whom you had Galahad.' And Lancelot promised her faithfully. But Brisen, by her crafts, knew this promise.

When all folks were abed, Brisen came to Lancelot's side and whispered, 'Sir Lancelot, do you sleep? My lady Guenevere lies waiting for you.' Lancelot threw on a long gown and grasped his sword. Then Brisen led him by a finger to Elaine's bed, though he knew it not. As they welcomed each to the other's arms, and began to kiss and fumble, the queen sent her own woman to fetch Sir Lancelot to her. But the woman found the bed cold and the knight away.

Then the queen was nigh out of her wits, writhing like a mad woman, so that she slept not four or five hours. In the chamber close by, Sir Lancelot embraced his lady and then fell asleep. Soon he began to talk in his sleep, calling often the name of his love Queen Guenevere. He chattered like a jay, and so loud that the queen, all restless in her chamber, heard him say her name. Then she was more mad than before, and began to choke and cough very loud in her confusion. At this, Lancelot awoke. He heard the hemming and hawing in the next chamber and suddenly saw where he was. Then he knew well that he lay not with the queen. As he leapt wildly from the bed in his shirt, he met Guenevere coming in at the door. She rebuked him fiercely, saying, 'False traitor knight, avoid my sight, avoid my chamber, and never more abide in my court.'

'Alas,' cried Lancelot in despair, and in his shame he ran to the bay window and threw himself into the garden, plunging through thorns that scratched his face and body all over. Half-naked still, he rushed from the garden, as wild and mad as ever man was. And so he wandered for two years, so strange that none might know him.

When Dame Elaine saw her love leap from the window, she turned to the queen and rebuked her.

'Madam,' she said, 'you are greatly to blame, for now you have lost him. Alas, you do great sin and dishonour to yourself, for you have a lord of your own. There is no queen in the world that has such a king as you have. And, but for you, I might have the love of Sir Lancelot. I have true cause to love him, because he has my maidenhead and I have gotten his son Galahad, who in his time shall be the best knight in the world.'

'Dame Elaine,' replied Guenevere, 'when it is daylight I charge you to avoid my court. And for the love you owe Sir Lancelot, keep all this to your own counsel, or else it will be his death.'

'As for that, madam, I dare say he is marred for ever. That is your doing. Neither you nor I are like to rejoice him again.'

'Alas,' sighed Queen Guenevere and 'Alas,' sighed Elaine, 'for now I know we have lost him for ever.'

On the morn, Elaine departed in sadness from the court. And when King Arthur and his knights heard what had befallen, and how good Sir Lancelot was gone mad, they made great moan. For, as Sir Bors said, 'All kings, Christian or heathen, may not find such another knight, of such nobleness and courtesy, such beauty and gentleness. Alas, what shall we do, those of us who are of his blood?'

Then Queen Guenevere took fright at this complaint. She knelt before Sir Bors, Sir Ector and Sir Lionel, those who were of Lancelot's blood, and begged them to seek him, saying, 'Spare neither cost nor goods. Find him by all means, for I know that he is out of his mind.'

Swiftly they went away, taking from the queen's treasure enough for their expense. They rode from country to country, through wastes and wilderness, asking all manner of travellers if they had seen a naked man, in his shirt, with a sword in his hand. Thus they rode for nigh quarter of a year, along and about in many places, and ofttimes they were most poorly lodged for Lancelot's sake. But never a word did they hear of him. So they returned home for the time being, with hands and hearts empty.

Meanwhile Sir Lancelot suffered and endured, running wild and mad from place to place, under snows and rains and hot sun. He lived on fruit and what else he could win from tree, hedge and field. He drank cold water from stream or ditch for two years. He had but little clothing, except his shirt and breeches.

One time in his wandering he came to a pavilion in a meadow and saw a white shield hung in a tree, with two swords and two spears standing near. Some remembrance of deeds of arms touched him, even in his madness. He leapt to one of the swords and began to beat about the shield with a noise of ten men fighting.

At once a little man came forth and tried to take the sword from Sir Lancelot. But Lancelot caught the little man and near broke his neck upon the ground, so that the cries brought from the pavilion a knight dressed in scarlet trimmed with fur. As soon as this knight saw Lancelot he deemed him to be out of his wits, and therefore soothed him with fair speech.

'Good fellow,' he said, 'lay down that sword. It seems to me that you have more need of sleep and warm clothes than a sword.'

'Nay,' shouted Lancelot, 'come not so near, or I will slay you.'

Then Lancelot flew at him, and hit him such a buffet upon the helm that the stroke troubled his brains. He fell to the earth with blood bursting from his mouth, nose and ears. After this blow, Lancelot ran into the pavilion and dashed into the warm bed, and the lady who was already there abed tumbled from the other side in her smock. When she saw her lord lying stunned upon the ground, she wept so loud that her noise roused him. Weakly he shook his head and said, 'What madman is this? Such a blow I never had before from any man's hand.'

'Do not hurt him,' said the little man to his master. ''Tis not honourable to harm a man out of his wits. Yet doubtless he was once of some nobility, fallen mad from heartache. It seems to me he much resembles Sir Lancelot, whom I saw once at the great tournament of Lonazep.'

'Jesu defend,' replied the master, whose name was Bliant, 'that ever noble Sir Lancelot should be in such a plight. Go to the castle and bring me a horse-litter, that we might bear this poor man home.'

They took up Sir Lancelot, still lying in the feather bed, and carried him in the horse-litter to the Castle Blank. Then they tied him hand and foot for his own safekeeping, and gave him good meat and drink to bring him back to his bodily strength. But his wits they could not recover. Thus Sir Lancelot lived for more than a year and a half.

Yet he was still not whole in his wit. For another half-year he languished. Then Sir Lancelot heard the noise of a great boar hunt going about the castle, with shouting and hallooing, and horns a-blowing. One of the huntsmen was taking breath under a tree, with his horse waiting and his sword and spear leaning against the saddle. When Lancelot saw this, he leapt on the horse, took the weapons and followed the hunt. After a long chase, Lancelot cornered the boar and dashed at it. But the beast turned nimbly, tore out the lungs and the heart of the horse, and slashed Sir Lancelot through the brawn of his thigh even to the bone. In a rage, he drew his sword and struck the head from the boar with one blow.

All this was seen by a hermit of the woods who went to help Sir Lancelot, asking him how he was hurt.

'Fellow,' said Lancelot in churlish anger, 'this boar has given me a sore bite.'

'Come with me,' replied the hermit, 'and I shall heal you.'

But Lancelot chased the hermit away. The hermit did not go far. He soon found a party of horsemen going through the woods, and together they fetched a cart to carry Sir Lancelot, who did not resist because he was now feeble from loss of blood. They took him to the hermitage, where his wound healed slowly. But the hermit was a poor man and could not find good sustenance for Lancelot, so he waxed feeble both in body and wits. He was as mad as before.

After a time Lancelot ran into the forest, looking like a scarecrow. By fortune his steps took him to the city of Corbin, where Dame Elaine was living. As he ran through the market, boys and young men ran after him, jeering at his madness, throwing turves and offal at him, tripping and striking him. Those Lancelot could lay hands on, he broke their bones, so that they wished they had been elsewhere. But the naked madman was a marvel to behold, and the noise and riot of his passage brought forth the gentlefolk from the castle to see him. They saw that he seemed to be a goodly man, though sore troubled and annoyed. There was some nobility about him, even in madness. They were sorry for him and put him in a little house, with clothes for his body and some straw to lie on. Every day they threw him some meat and set drink by his door, but few dared touch him or hand him food.

At Candlemas it so befell at Corbin that the nephew of King Pelles was made knight. After the ceremony he gave presents of gowns and robes to many about the court. Among these was Sir Lancelot, the fool without wits, who was awarded a scarlet robe. When he put this on and walked with lords and ladies, he seemed the handsomest and best-made man in the court.

Thus dressed, Sir Lancelot entered a little garden and lay down by a well to sleep in the heat of the day. Soon Dame Elaine and her maid came to play in the garden, and they saw this sleeping, goodly man.

'Peace,' said Elaine softly, 'say no word.'

Then she looked closer and knew him truly for Sir Lancelot, and she fell so much to weeping that she was sick. She ran to King Pelles, crying, 'O father, help me now if ever. Sir Lancelot lies sleeping by our garden well, and he is distracted out of his wits. He has on a scarlet robe and nought else besides.'

'I may hardly believe it,' said the king, 'but hold you still, and let me deal.' He called to him his most trusted people, and they carried him asleep to the chamber in the tower where the vessel of the Holy Grail stood. Then Lancelot was laid down and the priest uncovered the holy vessel, and it shone around the chamber. And so by miracle and virtue of the Holy Grail, Sir Lancelot was made whole and recovered his wits. In a little time, he awoke and groaned and sighed, saying, 'Good folk, I am so sore'. He looked about him suddenly, and marvelled that King Pelles and Dame Elaine were there. He regarded himself, and felt shame at his condition.

'Lord Jesu, how came I here?' he said in wonder. 'For God's sake, my lord, tell me.'

Then all that had come to pass was told to him, and again he hung his head and said, 'For the love of Christ, keep your counsel that I was mad, for I am sore ashamed that I have been thus miscarried. Now I am banished from Logris forever, that is to say banished out of the land of England.'

For a fortnight he lay without stirring, till all his hurts were better. Then he sent for Dame Elaine.

'Lady,' he said, 'you know how for your sake I have had much travel, care and anguish. I know well that I did you wrong when I drew my sword upon the morn I lay with you. Will you now, for my love, beg from your father some little place where I may live? For I may never come again to the court of King Arthur.'

'Sir,' she replied, 'I will live and die with you, or for your sake. Where you will be, my lord Lancelot, doubt not that I will be with you, to do you all the service that I may.'

So Sir Lancelot departed with Dame Elaine to the Castle of Bliant, a place upon an island removed from men, which they called the Joyous Isle. And here he hid under the name of Le Chevaler Mal Fet, that is to say 'the knight who has trespassed'. He dressed in sable, and his shield was sable. On this isle he made a statue of a queen all in silver and another statue of an armed knight kneeling before her. Once every day he would look towards the realm of Logris, towards the court of King Arthur and Queen Guenevere, and his heart would nigh burst.

Now, even on this isle Sir Lancelot still had remembrance of past days and the adventures that had befallen him. And when he heard that there was jousting not three leagues from his castle, his heart yearned for that noble exercise of arms. So he announced a great tourney at the Joyous Isle, which was attended by five hundred knights. For three days together Lancelot did mighty deeds of arms and overcame all who stood against him. This contented him well, and at the end of the tourney he made a great feast.

While they feasted with banners and music and dancing, and all manner of good cheer, Sir Percival and Sir Ector rode through that country and would have gone to the castle. But they could find no bridge over the water to the Joyous Isle. As they were searching, they saw a lady with a sparrowhawk on the far bank. They called to her, to know who was in the castle.

'Fair knights,' she replied, 'in this castle is Elaine, the most beautiful lady of the land. And with her is a knight, as mighty a man as ever lived, who is called Le Chevaler Mal Fet.' Then she told them how the knight had come mad to this place, and how he had been cured. 'Ride a way round the shore,' she added, 'and you shall find a boat for yourselves and your horses.'

When they found the boat, Percival dismounted and halted Ector, saying, 'Abide here awhile, until I know what manner of knight he is. It would be shame for both at once to do battle with him.'

So Percival went over the water, and right gladly the knight of the isle fought with him. They were both strong men in prowess and worthiness. From noon to eve they fought, then they rested all breathless. 'You fight boldly,' said Lancelot. 'My name is Le Chevaler Mal Fet. Now tell me, gentle knight, what is your name?'

'Truly, it is Sir Percival de Gales, brother to the good knight Sir Lamorak, and King Pellinore was our father.'

'What have I done to fight with you?' cried Lancelot. 'You are a knight of the Round Table, and once I was your fellow.'

He threw aside his sword and shield and fell on his knees, so that Sir Percival marvelled what he meant. 'Knight, whosoever you may be,' he said, 'by the high order of knighthood, tell me your true name.'

'So help me God, I am Sir Lancelot du Lake, son of King Ban of Benwick.'

'But how is this?' said Percival. 'I was sent by Queen Guenevere to seek you two years ago. Yonder, on the other side of the water, is your brother Sir Ector. Now, for God's sake, forgive me whatever offence I have done to you.'

'It is soon forgiven,' replied Sir Lancelot.

Sir Ector was sent for, and all night long they spoke, and many other nights besides, to tell each other the tales of their adventures. Thus they passed the time in joy and mirth. But when Percival and Ector were ready to depart, they asked Sir Lancelot what he would do now, whether or not he would go with them to King Arthur.

'Nay, that may not be,' said Lancelot. 'I am too shamed to go there ever more.'

'Sir, I am your brother,' replied Sir Ector, 'and you are the man in the world I love the most. I would never counsel you to do anything dishonourable. But King Arthur and all his court, and in especial Queen Guenevere, made such a grief at your absence that it was a marvel to hear. It has cost my lady the queen twenty thousand pound to seek you out. Will you disappoint her? And remember, my lord, your great renown, for there is none living that bears such a name. Therefore, brother, make ready to ride to the court with us, and I dare say never a knight will have a better welcome than you.'

Sir Lancelot thought well and long. Then he said, 'Well brother Ector, ride on, and I will be with you'.

So he departed the Joyous Isle, and Dame Elaine watched him go in great sorrow. She could not prevent him, for his life must be lived amid great matters. Within five days Lancelot came to Camelot, that in English is called Winchester. The king, the queen and all the knights welcomed him with the greatest joy, and when they heard the whole of his adventure the queen wept as if she would have died.

'O Jesu,' said King Arthur, 'I marvel for what cause you went out of your mind. I and many others deem it was for love of fair Elaine, by whom you are noised to have gotten the child Galahad.'

'My lord,' he replied, 'if I did any folly I have paid my price.'

The king spoke no more. But all Sir Lancelot's kin knew the lady of his love and the cause of his madness.

✠ Sir Tristram and ✠ La Beale Isoud

In the country of Liones there was a man called Meliodas, a most likely knight and a king also, but one that held his land under obeisance to King Arthur. By fortune, he wedded Elizabeth, sister of King Mark of Cornwall. Within a while Elizabeth waxed great with child. She was a meek lady and well she loved her lord, and he loved her, so there was great joy betwixt them.

But another lady had long loved Meliodas. When she saw she could not have him, and knowing he was a great huntsman, she removed him from the hunting field by enchantment and made him prisoner in an old castle. Elizabeth missed her lord and became nigh out of her wits. Even though she was great with child, she summoned a gentlewoman and ran into the forest to seek Meliodas.

Deep in the forest she could go no further, for she began to labour of her child. There, in trees and dark bushes, she had many grim throes. Her gentlewoman helped her all she might, and so by miracle of Our Lady of Heaven she was delivered with great pains. But she had suffered so much weakness and cold that deep draughts of death took her. Needs she must die and depart from this world, there was no help for it.

'When you see my lord Meliodas,' she whispered dying to her woman, 'tell him what pains I endure here for his love. I die for his sake, and I am full sorry to depart from him out of this world. Therefore pray him to be friend to my soul. Now let me see my baby, for whom I have had all this sorrow.'

Then she looked sweetly on her child and said, 'Ah, little son, you have murdered your mother. I suppose that you, who are a murderer so young, will grow into a manly man. Good gentlewoman, because I die of this birth, I charge you that this child shall be christened Tristram. Pray tell this to my lord Meliodas, for Tristram names a child of sorrowful birth.'

Therewith the queen gave up the ghost and died. Her woman laid her in the shade of a great tree, and lapped the baby as best she could against the cold. And there she waited till the barons that were looking for Elizabeth came by and they saw the queen was dead.

In the meantime Meliodas had escaped his prison. But when he heard of his queen's death, his sorrow was such no tongue might tell it. He buried her most richly and christened the baby as she had commanded, calling him Tristram, the sorrowful-born child.

Seven years Meliodas endured without a queen, and all this time Tristram was nourished well. Then the king wedded again, and his wife had children. But young Tristram alone rejoiced the land of Liones, and the queen was jealous for her own children. She ordained a poison for Tristram. A poison was put in a silver cup for him to drink. But the queen's own child, being thirsty and finding the cup by fortune, drank freely of it and suddenly died. The king understood nothing of this treason. But when the queen again tried poison, the king himself found the cup and would have drunk, had not the queen run crying and pulled the cup from him.

Then the king, remembering how her first-born was poisoned, drew his sword and with a great oath demanded what manner of drink this was. She said the truth. 'Well,' replied Meliodas grimly, 'therefore you shall taste of the law.'

By the assent of the barons she was damned to be burnt. A great fire was made, but just as she was led to execution young Tristram knelt before the king his father and besought a boon. 'Well?' said the king.

'Sir, grant me the life of the queen my stepmother.'

'It is unrightfully asked,' replied the king, 'for you ought to hate her, she who would have poisoned you. It is for your sake that I have cause to condemn her.'

'I beseech you, sir, forgive her. God will forgive her, and I do. Grant me my boon, for the love of God.'

Meliodas turned away, saying, 'I grant you the gift of her life. Go to the fire and take her, and do with her what you will.'

After this, the king would never have more ado with her, at bed or at board. Nor would he suffer young Tristram to abide at his court any longer.

So it was ordained that a well-learned gentleman, whose name was Gouvernail, should take young Tristram into France, to learn languages, and nurture, and deeds of arms.

'Sir,' said Gouvernail to Tristram, 'it is meet that a young squire learns many things. It is best to begin with God. Put your entire trust in Him. He will never desert you. For those things you lack, ask Heaven. Then be ever humble, and banish pride from your heart. Be generous, give freely to the knight without portion, to the landless man, to the poor labourer, to the widow and the orphan. Share among them your wealth, your gold and silver, your rich furs, both the thick *gris* and the light *vair*. The more you give away, the more honour you will have, and thus the richer you will be.'

For seven years in France Gouvernail taught Tristram many things. He loved God. He was envious of no man and destroyed the good name of none. He learnt to serve his lady, and to this end he was joyous day and night. He was gentle, sweet and pleasant. He was not silent in counsel, but spoke according to season and gravely. He was neat in dress, slandered none, gave with generous heart. By long practice, he knew well how to sing and dance, and he was fierce in jousts and deeds of arms. In time of peace, it needs must be that he get his lady's consent and go about to seek adventures.

'After God's name,' said Gouvernail, 'in especial remember two things: spare no pain, peril or labour to win love. And be worthy of your fathers, for the old saying truly says, "The son of a cat ought to catch mice".'

In seven years Tristram had learnt all that he might and came home again to his father King Meliodas. He was a worthy young man. He had applied himself on harping and on instruments of music, and he was a harper passing all others. As he grew in might and strength he laboured ever in hunting and hawking, no gentleman more, and he knew all manner of beasts of the chase. Thus all gentlemen that bore arms honoured Tristram for the goodly knowledge that noble men should have and use, and shall do so to the day of doom. In this way men of worship may distinguish a gentleman from a yeoman, and a yeoman from a villain. He with gentle qualities draws all men unto him, to follow noble customs.

It befell at this time that King Agwisance of Ireland sent unto King Mark of Cornwall for the tribute that Cornwall had paid for many winters. King Mark was seven years behind with payment. He was unwilling to pay and sent a message to Agwisance saying, 'If you will have your tribute, send me a trusty knight that will fight for your right.'

At this the King of Ireland was wonderfully angry. He called to Sir Marhaus, the good knight and the brother of the queen.

'Brother Marhaus,' he said, 'I pray you go to Cornwall for my sake, and do battle for our tribute.' And Sir Marhaus consented, for he wished to have ado with right worthy knights, and advance by deeds of arms.

There was sorrow in Cornwall when Sir Marhaus arrived. He was one of the most famous knights of the world, and there was none in Cornwall that dared have ado with him. Thus Sir Marhaus abode in his ship at anchor, and every day sent to King Mark for his tribute, or else to fight. High and low, the king looked for a champion. Some counselled him to send to King Arthur for one of his knights. But Sir Marhaus was a knight of the Round Table, and any of that fellowship would be loath to battle with him.

Soon word came to the court of Meliodas how Sir Marhaus abode fast by Tintagel and none dared fight him. When young Tristram heard this he was ashamed for the men of Cornwall.

'It is to our dishonour,' he told his father, 'that Sir Marhaus should depart to Ireland without battle. If I were made knight, I should match him. I pray you, father, let King Mark make me knight. Then I shall meet this champion of Ireland.'

'Let it be so,' replied King Meliodas, 'as your courage shall rule you.'

Then Tristram rode to his uncle Mark, saying, 'Sir, if you will give me the order of knighthood, I will do battle with Sir Marhaus.'

When the king knew his name, and saw that he was well made and big, though but young in age, he made him knight and sent him forth unto Sir Marhaus. And when the king and barons of Cornwall beheld how Sir Tristram departed to fight for their land with such high courage, both men and women wept to see so young a knight put himself in jeopardy for their cause.

King Arthur in bed with Queen Morgause, his half-sister

Above: Knights jousting

Right: Lancelot relating his feats to King Arthur and
Queen Guenevere

King Arthur depicted as a great ruler. The crowns represent
his kingdoms

Sir Tristram went to the island, where six ships lay at anchor. Under the shadow of the ships hoved Marhaus of Ireland. Tristram mounted and dressed his shield and harness, saying to his man Gouvernail, 'Where is this knight with whom I must have ado?'

'Do you not see him, sir? He is ahorse under the shadow of the ships, with spear in hand and shield at the ready.'

'Ha,' cried Tristram, 'now I see him well enough. Now commend me to my uncle Mark. Let him know that I will never yield for cowardice. If I am slain, let him inter me in Christian burial. And now, upon your life, come not near this island until the battle is done. I shall win, or I shall be overcome.'

Gouvernail departed weeping and Tristram advanced into the sight of Sir Marhaus, who looked on him kindly.

'Young knight Tristram,' he said, 'why are you here? Repent of your courage, for I have been tried and matched with the best knights of the world. Go back, I counsel you.'

'Fair and well-proven knight,' Tristram replied, 'know that I am a king's son born, and I shall fight with you to the uttermost to deliver Cornwall from your tribute. Know also that your noise and fame, as one of the most renowned knights of the world, gives me courage to have ado with you. I trust to God that I shall be worthy of this trial.'

Then they fought for more than half a day and both were sore hurt, so that their fresh blood flowed from gaping flesh. But Sir Tristram was younger and better-winded than Sir Marhaus, and on a sudden with a mighty stroke he smote Marhaus through the helm and into his brainpan. Thrice he pulled to free the sword. When that was done, Sir Marhaus rose grovelling, threw his weapons aside, tottered to his ships and fled away.

'Sir knight of the Round Table,' Tristram shouted after him, 'why do you flee? You do yourself and your kin great shame. I would rather be hewed in an hundred pieces than withdraw.' But Sir Marhaus fled and answered no word.

He sailed to Ireland hurt unto death. When the surgeon searched his wound they found in his head a broken piece of Tristram's sword. But they could not save him, and so he died. His sister, the queen, kept that piece of sword, and ever as she looked on it she thought always of revenge against Tristram.

But Sir Tristram also was sore wounded, for the spear that had struck him was envenomed. None in Cornwall might help him. Needs he must go to Ireland, where that poison was known. They put his bed in a fair ship, and he took his harp with him. And when they bore him unto the shore of Ireland, he sat in bed and played so sweetly and merrily on his harp that the king and queen had heard no harper like him in all the land. He said his name was Tramtrist, a knight wounded for love. Then the king found in his heart great favour for this Tramtrist. He put Tramtrist in the keeping of his daughter, the fairest maid of the land, and wise about the working of poison. She bound his wound and cured him.

So Tramtrist cast his love to La Beale Isoud, the king's daughter. He sang and played to her and taught her to harp, and her dreams began to rest upon him.

Now Sir Palomides, the Saracen, was also at the court of Ireland, and every day he gave La Beale Isoud gifts, for he loved her well. He was a mighty man, and ready to be christened for her sake. Thus there grew great envy betwixt Tramtrist and Palomides.

About this time the king gave word of a great joust, and Tramtrist was in uncertain mind whether to partake.

'Why will you not have ado at this tournament?' asked La Beale Isoud. 'Sir Palomides will be there, to do what he may. Therefore, Tramtrist, I pray you be there, or else Sir Palomides is like to win the degree.'

'As you will, so be it,' said Tramtrist humbly. 'I will be at your command.'

On the day of the jousts Sir Palomides came unto the lists with a black shield and overthrew so many knights that people marvelled at him. Many were adread to fight him. Then Isoud arrayed Tramtrist in harness and a white horse and let him out at a privy gate, so that he came into the field like a bright angel. Anon he smote Palomides to the earth amid a great shout of the people. The Saracen was ashamed at his fall and went lightly to withdraw. But Tramtrist overtook him and bade him yield or die. Palomides looked into his face. He feared more buffets, so he yielded.

'Well said,' cried Tramtrist. 'Now I charge you first, upon pain of your life, that you forsake my lady La Beale Isoud and draw not to her. Next, this twelvemonth and a day you shall bear no armour nor harness of war. Promise or die.'

'Alas,' Sir Palomides lamented, 'forever I am ashamed.' Then in anger and despite he cut off his harness and threw it away, and Tramtrist rode smiling back to the privy gate and La Beale Isoud.

Thus Tramtrist was long cherished in the court of Ireland. And upon a day the queen and Isoud made a bath for Tramtrist. As he lay in the bath, and they roamed up and down his chamber, the queen saw his sword upon the bed. She drew the sword. She beheld it a long while and saw there was a great piece broken out of the edge. Then she remembered the piece of sword lodged in the brainpan of the good knight Marhaus, her brother.

'Alas, daughter,' she said to Isoud, 'this is the traitor knight that slew my brother, your uncle.'

When Isoud heard this she was sore abashed, for well she loved Tramtrist, and full well she knew the cruelness of her mother.

The queen ran to her own chamber and fitted the piece she kept into Tramtrist's sword. Then she gripped that sword fiercely, rushed straight to the bath and would have riven Tramtrist through his naked body had not a squire got her in his arms and pulled the sword from her. Then the queen told the king of the traitor in their midst, and the king demanded of Tramtrist who and what he was. The tale came out, he could no longer hide it, how Tramtrist was truly Sir Tristram, who had honourably overthrown Sir Marhaus in battle. Then the king was sad. For though he might cherish Sir Tristram for his qualities, yet he must banish him as the slayer of the queen's brother.

'My lord king,' replied Sir Tristram, 'I thank you for the great goodness you and my lady your daughter have showed to me. I promise, as I am a true knight, I shall be your daughter's servant in right and in wrong. I shall never fail to do as much as a knight may do.'

Then he went sadly to take leave of La Beale Isoud. He told her who and what he was, and promised to be her knight all the days of his life.

'O gentle Tristram,' she said, 'your departing makes me full of woe, for I never saw a man who had so much of my goodwill. And therefore I promise you that I shall not be married this seven years without your assent.' And then she wept with all her heart.

So Sir Tristram went to the sea, and with good wind came back to King Mark in Cornwall. King Mark was more than glad to see him. But then there arose a jealousy betwixt them, for they both lusted after the same lady. This lady favoured Sir Tristram and welcomed him to her bed, despite her husband. And ever after King Mark cast in his heart how he might destroy Tristram. He thought to send him into Ireland for La Beale Isoud. King Mark said he would wed her, for Tristram had so praised her beauty and her goodness. Yet all this was done in despite, with the intent to slay Sir Tristram.

Tristram departed, for he owed obeisance to the king his uncle. Sailing on the sea road to Ireland, he met a broad tempest that drove him back to England, fast by Camelot. And full glad he was to find the land again. When he was ashore and had hung his shield upon his pavilion, it befell that two knights that were brethren summoned King Agwisance of Ireland to Arthur's court, to answer treason before his liege lord. Agwisance, said Sir Blamor, had slain Blamor's cousin in Ireland by treason.

Now, it was custom in those days that a man accused of treason or murder should fight his accuser body for body, or else find another knight to fight for him. King Agwisance was heavy in mind, for Sir Blamor was a knight of great prowess. As the king was casting about for some champion, Gouvernail, Tristram's man, went to his master and told him of the king's distress.

'These tidings, thanks to God,' rejoiced Tristram, 'are the best I heard these seven years. Now the King of Ireland has need of my help. To win his love, I will take this battle upon me, for the good he showed me in Ireland and for the sake of my lady his daughter.'

He went to King Agwisance and proffered his help, saying, 'Sir, I will take this battle upon two conditions. One, that you swear to me that you are right in this matter of treason. Second, if God give me grace to speed in this battle, then you will grant me whatsoever reasonable thing I ask.'

'You shall have,' said the king, 'whatsoever you ask.' And Tristram answered, 'It is well said.'

Then Sir Tristram and Sir Blamor fought before the judges, and after long battle Blamor was smote down upon his side on the earth. Then Sir Tristram stood long and beheld him.

At last Sir Blamor might speak, and gasped out, 'Sir Tristram de Liones, as you are a noble knight, slay me. I would rather die with honour than live with shame.'

But Tristram knew not what to do. He started aback and knelt before the kings that were the judges, and besought them to take this matter in their hands. Then the judges gave Sir Blamor mercy, for he had fought nobly, and though Sir Tristram had beaten his body, he had not beaten his heart.

When this justice was done King Agwisance and Sir Tristram together went into Ireland, and the noise of Tristram's battle for the king went before them, so that all the people made joy at this noblesse. But the gladness of La Beale Isoud no tongue might tell, for she loved Sir Tristram above all earthly men.

In Ireland, upon a day, Tristram said to the king, 'Now, sir, it is time to ask my boon. Give me La Beale Isoud, your daughter, not for myself but for my uncle King Mark. He would have her to wife, and I have promised him so upon my honour.'

'Better than all my land,' replied Agwisance, 'I would that you wed her yourself.'

'Nay, if I did then I were shamed forever in this world, and false to my promise.'

'Well, take her to do with her what you please. I would that you wed her yourself. But if you give her unto King Mark, that is in your choice.'

And thus it was. In short time La Beale Isoud was made ready to go with Sir Tristram, and with them were Dame Bragwaine, her chief gentlewoman, and Gouvernail, Tristram's man. As they departed, Isoud's mother gave unto Bragwaine and Gouvernail a drink to give King Mark on the day that he wed. 'And then,' said the queen, 'I undertake that either shall love the other all the days of their lives.'

It happened on the sea journey that Tristram and Isoud were thirsty as they sat within their cabin. They saw by them a little flask of gold, and it seemed by the colour and smell that it was noble wine. Tristram took it up, laughing to see such good cheer. He drank freely and then she drank also, and they thought that they had never tasted so sweet or good a wine. As soon as the drink was in their bodies, it fixed their love so that it might never leave them for better or worse. And this love did not depart them to the end of life.

So they came unto King Mark at Tintagel. And anon the king and La Beale Isoud were richly wedded. After the feast, when Dame Bragwaine was sent to fetch herbs in the forest, two ladies that hated and envied her caught her and bound her hand and foot to a tree. There she was held fast for three days till, by fortune, Sir Palomides found her. He cut her free and brought her to a nunnery.

When Queen Isoud missed her maiden she went to the forest to seek her. Full of heavy thoughts, Isoud rested by a well and sighed for her countrywoman. Suddenly Palomides came before her, saying, 'Madam Isoud, grant me my boon, and I shall bring you Dame Bragwaine safe and sound.' Because she loved her woman, Isoud was unadvised and granted all his asking.

Soon Sir Palomides brought Bragwaine from the nunnery to the court, and in the presence of Mark demanded his boon from Queen Isoud.

'What say you, my lady?' said the king.

'It is even so, as he says,' replied the queen, abashed.

'Well, madam, if you were hasty to grant a boon, it must be given. I ordain that you perform your promise.'

'Then know,' said Palomides, 'that I will have your queen, to lead her and govern her however I wish.'

The king stood still. What would he do? He bethought him that Sir Tristram would rescue her, so he hastily said, 'Take her with the adventures that shall befall of it. I suppose you will not enjoy her long.'

Then Sir Palomides took her softly by the hand, saying, 'Madam, grudge not to go with me, for I desire nothing but your own good.' He set Isoud behind his saddle and rode on his way.

At once King Mark sent for Sir Tristram. But he was a-hunting and nowhere to be found. Sir Palomides kept close by Isoud but after some adventure she slipped from him in the deep forest and ran to hide in a castle. From the window she saw him following hard, so she had the gates strongly shut. Then Palomides took off bridle and saddle and set his horse to pasture. In the meadow before the gate he sat like a man bereft, caring nothing for himself.

When Tristram returned from hunting and heard what had passed, he was angry beyond measure. He leapt to horse and galloped like a madman, seeking Isoud. At last, by fortune, he came to the castle and saw Sir Palomides asleep at the gate while his horse peacefully grazed.

'Now go,' said Tristram grimly to his man Gouvernail, 'and bring him this news. Bid him arise, for his mortal foe is come.'

Gouvernail went near and said aloud, 'Sir Palomides, arise and put on your harness.' But Palomides heard him not, for either he slept or he was mad.

Again Gouvernail came to him and stirred him with the butt of his spear, saying, 'Sir Palomides, make ready quick. Sir Tristram, your mortal foe, hoves yonder.'

Therewith Sir Palomides rose stiffly and took horse and harness like a man in a dream. They fought and Sir Tristram smote him down, while La Beale Isoud watched from the window with anxiety of heart.

'Alas, though I love him not,' she cried, 'it were pity to see Sir Palomides slain. Then he would die unchristened. I would be loath that he should die a Saracen.' She came down from the window, and begged Sir Tristram to fight no more.

'Ah, madam,' he protested, 'will you shame me?'

'Nay, I will nothing for your dishonour, but for my sake spare this unhappy Saracen.'

Then Sir Tristram gave way to her asking, and she turned to Palomides, saying, 'I charge you, go out of this country all the while that I am herein.'

'I will obey your command,' replied Palomides, 'though it is sore against my will.' And so he departed with great heaviness.

When Sir Tristram brought the queen again to King Mark there was great joy of her homecoming, and they lived content for a long while. But there was a knight in the court named Sir Andred, who was envious of Tristram though he was his nigh cousin. He lay in wait to see what was betwixt Tristram and La Beale Isoud, to discover them and slander them. Upon a day he saw them close talking in a window, and he told it to the king. Then Mark took a sword and came at Sir Tristram, who ran beneath his arm and pulled the sword from his hand.

'Where are my knights?' shouted the king. 'Slay this traitor.' But none dared make a move.

When Tristram saw this he shook the sword at the king, looking as if to kill him. King Mark fled and Tristram followed after, striking him five or six times with the flat of the sword, so that the king fell upon his nose. There Tristram left him, and called his men unto him. They armed themselves and rode away into the forest. At this departing, King Mark was angry beyond measure and asked his barons what best to do about Tristram. Sir Dinas, the steward, advised him to beware, for many good knights would hold with Sir Tristram.

'He is called peerless of any Christian knight, except perhaps Sir Lancelot,' said Dinas. 'If he go to King Arthur, he may get such friends as can defy your malice. I counsel you, sir, to take him again into your grace.'

The king assented, and sent for Sir Tristram under a safe conduct. So Tristram came back and was welcomed, and once again there were games and play.

So Sir Tristram went as before, going to La Beale Isoud whenever he might, day and night. And still his cousin Sir Andred watched to find them together, until upon a night he spied the hour of their meeting. At midnight he took twelve knights and set upon Sir Tristram suddenly, when he was naked abed with Isoud. Andred bound him fast, hand and foot, and brought him on the morn before the king. King Mark ordained that Sir Tristram be led to a chapel that stood upon the rocks of the sea, and there wait to be judged.

When that time came, Sir Tristram looked on the faces of his judges, thinking that he must die.

'Fair lords,' he said, 'remember what I have done for Cornwall, and in what jeopardy I have been for the good of you all. Therefore, as you are gentle knights, let me not thus shamefully die. For I daresay I was as good as any knight, or better.'

'Fie, false traitor,' replied Sir Andred. 'For all your boast you shall die this day.'

'O Andred, Andred, you who should be my kinsman are now my enemy. If I had you alone, you would not put me to death.'

'No?' said Andred in rage, and drew his sword to slay him.

With all his might Sir Tristram of a sudden wrenched his hands free from the two knights that held him. He leapt upon his cousin, Sir Andred, twisted the sword from his hand and struck him to the earth. Then he turned upon those that kept him, and he a naked man with a sword in his hand. After hard battle he killed ten knights, drove the others from the door and secured the chapel. Outside there was a great cry, and a hundred or more rushed to help Andred. Sir Tristram locked fast the chapel door, broke the bars of a window and jumped all naked onto the crags of the sea below, where none could reach him.

When Gouvernail and some other of Tristram's men had found their master and pulled him from the rocks with ropes, they took him to the leper-house where Andred had shut La Beale Isoud. Then Sir Tristram fetched her from that ungodly place and hid her at a manor in the forest. But King Mark searched her out, and when he found that Tristram was gone to disport himself, Mark carried her home. In the meantime Sir Tristram was waylaid in ambush and shot in the shoulder with an envenomed arrow. He came fast back to the manor as best he could and saw the tracks of many horses, and he knew that his lady was gone. Then King Mark took Isoud and guarded her strait so that by no means might she see Tristram, or he her. Sir Tristram endured for a long while, with great pain in his poisoned shoulder. At last there was no help for it but he must go into Brittany to be cured of his ill.

In Brittany there was a fair lady named also Isoud, called la Blanche Mains, she of the white hands. She was the daughter of King Howel, and was full wise in the healing of wounds. When she had cured him, Tristram was grateful and took up arms for the king her father. He smote the king's enemies and slew more than a hundred knights. Then King Howel embraced him, saying, 'Sir Tristram, all my kingdom I will resign to you.'

'God defend,' said Tristram, 'for I am beholden unto you for your daughter's sake.'

By the encouragement of King Howel and his son Kehydius a love grew betwixt Tristram and Isoud la Blanche Mains, for she was good and fair and of noble blood. And in the midst of this pleasure Sir Tristram had almost forgotten La Beale Isoud.

So upon a time Sir Tristram agreed to wed Isoud of Brittany. After they were wedded, they went joyfully to bed. Then Tristram remembered his first lady, La Beale Isoud. Suddenly he was all dismayed. He had embraced and kissed his wedded wife, but now he made none other pleasure and had no further ado with fleshly lusts.

Soon the noise of this marriage was spread abroad, even to the court of King Arthur in England. There was a knight from Brittany that came to Sir Lancelot and told him what Sir Tristram had done.

'Fie upon him,' said Sir Lancelot in disgust, 'that so noble a knight as Sir Tristram should be found false to La Beale Isoud. But tell him this: of all the knights in the world I loved him most, and had most joy of him, because of his noble deeds. Now let him know that the love between us is done forever. I give him warning that from this day forth he is my mortal enemy.'

Then this knight went into Brittany again, and told Sir Tristram that he had been in Arthur's court.

'Heard you anything of me?' asked Tristram.

'God help me, I heard Sir Lancelot speak of your great shame, because you are a false knight to your lady. He bad me tell you that he will be your mortal enemy wherever he may meet you.'

'I repent this,' said Tristram, 'for of all knights I loved to be in his fellowship most.' And then Sir Tristram made a great moan and was ashamed.

In the meantime, when La Beale Isoud heard of Tristram's marriage she made a letter to Queen Guenevere and complained bitterly of Sir Tristram. Then the queen answered her, and told her to be of good cheer, for Sir Tristram was famed to be such a noble knight that many ladies, by crafts or sorcery, would strive to wed such a man.

'But in the end,' Queen Guenevere wrote to Isoud, 'it shall be thus, that Sir Tristram shall hate her, and love you better than ever he did before.'

✤ Sir Tristram and the ✤ Unchristened Knight

When La Beale Isoud understood that Sir Tristram was wedded in Brittany, she sent to him by her maid Bragwaine as piteous letters as could be thought. She begged Tristram, if it pleased him, that he would come to her court, and bring his wife with him, and they should be kept as well as she herself.

Then Sir Tristram called unto him Sir Kehydius, the king's son in Brittany, and asked if he would go with him secretly into Cornwall. They ordained a little vessel and therein they went, with Dame Bragwaine and Gouvernail. But in the sea a contrary wind blew them onto the coasts of north Wales, nigh the Castle Perilous. Sir Tristram and Kehydius took horses and departed into the wild ways. And there by a well they saw a likely knight sitting with heavy countenance, and a strong horse tied to an oak, and this knight was Sir Lamorak de Gales.

Meanwhile there came Sir Palomides, the good knight, following the Questing Beast. This had in shape a head like a serpent, a body like a leopard, buttocks like a lion and feet like a hart. And it made a noise like thirty couple of hounds questing. This beast ever more Sir Palomides followed, for it was called his quest.

The beast came by Sir Tristram and Sir Lamorak, and as Palomides followed it he smote down both knights with one spear. And so he went on after the barking beast, wherefore these two knights were wonderful angry that Sir Palomides would not stop and fight afoot.

For honourable men may understand that at sometime the worse knight will put the better knight to rebuke. The man was never formed that at all times might stand, but sometime he may be put to the worse by misfortune.

Sir Tristram took up Kehydius and rode back to the coasts of Wales, determining in his mind that he would prove himself against Sir Palomides, whether he were the better knight. So they went into the ship and sailed unto Cornwall all wholly together. Then Dame Bragwaine went before to the court of King Mark and told the queen, La Beale Isoud, that Sir Tristram was nigh her in that country. When she heard this, Isoud swooned for pure joy. And when she might speak she said, 'Help that I might talk with him, or my heart will burst.'

Then Sir Dinas, the steward, brought Tristram and Kehydius privily unto a chamber that Isoud had assigned. And there no tongue can tell the joys betwixt Sir Tristram and La Beale Isoud, nor heart think it, nor pen write it.

But at the first time Sir Kehydius ever saw La Beale Isoud he was so enamoured upon her that he might never withdraw his love. Then privily he wrote her letters and ballads of the most goodly kind. And when Isoud read his letters she had pity of his complaint, and unadvised she wrote to comfort him.

By command of Isoud, Sir Tristram was all this while in a turret, where she came to him when she might. Then, on a day, King Mark played at chess under a window where Tristram and Kehydius and Isoud were within the chamber. And it mishapped that Sir Tristram found the letters that had passed betwixt Kehydius and La Beale Isoud.

'Alas, madam,' lamented Tristram, 'Now you are a traitress to me, which does me great pain. But as for you, Sir Kehydius, howbeit I wedded your sister of the White Hands for the goodness she did me, yet as I am true knight she is a clean maiden for me. But know well, for this treason you have done me, I will revenge it upon you.'

Then Sir Tristram drew his sword and cried, 'Sir Kehydius, save yourself'.

At this, La Beale Isoud swooned. But Kehydius saw no other help but to leap out at the bay window, even over the head of King Mark playing at chess. When the king saw one come hurling over his head, he shouted, 'Fellow, what are you that comes leaping from the window?'

'My lord king,' said Kehydius in haste, 'it fortuned that I was asleep in the window above your head, and as I slept I dreamt, and as I dreamt I fell.' And thus he excused himself.

Then Sir Tristram dreaded lest he were discovered unto the king. He armed himself, and took his horse and spear, and knightly he rode forth from the castle of Tintagel. He made great sorrow, and for days and nights he would have neither meat nor drink. Then by fortune he came near a castle where he was formerly known.

'Is he so nigh me?' said the lady of the castle. 'He shall have meat and drink of the best, and an harp I have whereupon he taught me, for of goodly harping he bears the prize in the world.'

She brought him meat and drink but he ate little. Upon a night he put his horse from him, unlaced his armour, and would go into the wilderness, breaking down trees and boughs. Sometimes he would harp, and the two wept together, he and the harp. And when the lady lost him in the wood, she would play upon the harp and he would come creeping and listening. Thus he endured a quarter of a year, till at last he ran away. And then he was naked and waxed lean and poor of flesh. He fell into the fellowship of herdsmen and shepherds, and ate what they gave him. When he was wicked they would beat him with rods, and so they clipped him with shears and made him like a fool.

Meanwhile a maiden went to Sir Palomides, the heathen knight, and told him all the mischief that Sir Tristram endured.

'Alas, it is great pity,' said Palomides, 'that ever so noble a knight should be so mischieved for the love of a lady. I will seek him, and comfort him if I may.'

So Sir Palomides rode into that country, and by adventure met with Sir Kehydius. Queen Isoud had commanded him out of the land of Cornwall, and he was departing with a dolorous heart. Then the two knights rode together, complaining one to the other of their hot love for La Beale Isoud.

'Now let us seek Sir Tristram,' said Palomides, 'that loves her as well as we. Let us prove whether we may recover him.'

They rode three days and nights into the forest without ever taking lodging, and they found not Sir Tristram. So Sir Palomides rode away into the realm of Logris, and Sir Kehydius went towards Brittany.

Now it was noised abroad that Tristram was dead, and that his cousin Sir Andred should become lord of his lands in Liones. King Mark wept false tears when he heard this. But Queen Isoud made such sorrow at these tidings that she was nigh out of her mind and thought to slay herself.

So she got a sword and pitched it through a plum tree up to the hilt so that it stuck fast, about breast high. Then she knelt and said, 'Sweet Lord Jesu, have mercy upon me, for I may not live after the death of Sir Tristram. He was my first love and shall be the last.'

She would have run upon the sword, but King Mark spied her and caught her in his arms and bore her away to a tower. And there he kept her, and watched her surely. After that, she lay long sick, nigh at the point of death.

Then upon a day a knight came out of the forest bearing a giant's head. When he came to the court of King Mark, the knight told the king that he had been rescued from the grim giant Tawleas by a naked man who had struck off the great head with one blow.

'Well,' said the king, 'I will see this wild naked man.'

So King Mark went with his knights and hunters and found lying by a well a fair man all naked, with a sword by him. They took and bound this naked Tristram and cast mantles upon him, and led him safely unto Tintagel. There they bathed him and washed him, and gave him hot suppings till they had brought him to his remembrance. But none who saw him knew him as Sir Tristram, nor what man he was, so much was he changed.

Thus it fell upon a day that Queen Isoud took Bragwaine and went to see this man brought naked from the forest. The man was in the garden, reposing himself against the sun. The queen looked on him but did not remember him surely. She said to Bragwaine, 'It seems I should have seen him heretofore in many places.' But Sir Tristram saw her and knew her well. He turned away his face and wept.

The queen had a little dog that Sir Tristram gave her the first time she came into Cornwall. As soon as this dog smelt Tristram, it leapt upon him and licked his cheeks and ears. It whined and barked and sniffed his naked body all over. Then said Dame Bragwaine to La Beale Isoud, 'Alas, my lady, I see by this dog that it is my own lord, Sir Tristram.'

When Isoud might speak, she cried aloud, 'My lord Tristram, blessed be God you have your life. But I fear King Mark, when he knows you, will banish you or else destroy you. For God's sake, draw you unto the court of King Arthur, for there you are beloved. And ever as I may I shall send unto you, and early and late I will be at your commandment, to live as poor a life as ever did a queen.'

'O madam,' Sir Tristram groaned, 'go from me, for much anger and danger have I escaped for your love.'

Queen Isoud departed, but the little dog would not go from him. And thus King Mark came by that garden with some of his knights.

'Sir,' said Sir Andred to the king, 'this is Sir Tristram. I see it by the dog.'

'Nay, I cannot suppose that,' said the king. 'But you, sir knight, say what is your name, upon your faith.'

'So God help me,' said he, 'my name is Sir Tristram de Liones. Now do by me what you wish.'

'I repent of your recovery,' muttered the king, and he turned away. Then he called his barons to judge Sir Tristram to death.

But many barons would not assent thereto. So by their advice Sir Tristram was banished out of the country for ten years, and took his oath upon it. The barons, both friends and foes, took him to his ship which he entered in the fellowship of Sir Dinadan, a knight of Arthur's court. And as they set upon the sea, Sir Tristram called to those on land.

'Greet well,' he called, 'King Mark and all my enemies, and say them I will come again when I may.' He spake thus, and forthwith he took to the sea.

At their landing, as they rode upon adventures, there came to Sir Tristram and Sir Dinadan a maiden seeking help for Sir Lancelot. By the treason of Queen Morgan le Fay, he was in danger from thirty knights that lay in wait for him.

'Fair maid,' said Tristram, 'bring me to the place.'

But Sir Dinadan protested, 'What will you do? It is not for us to fight with thirty knights, and I will not do so. It is enough to match two, or maybe three.'

'Fie, for shame,' said Tristram. 'Do but your part.'

'Nay, I will not,' replied Dinadan, 'except you lend me your shield. You bear a shield of Cornwall, and cowardice is expected from knights of Cornwall.'

'Not so, and I leave not my shield for her sake that gave it me. But one thing I promise you, Sir Dinadan. If you desert me I shall slay you. Knight, face but one enemy. And if your heart will not serve you, stand by and look upon the fight.'

'Sir,' said Dinadan, 'I promise to look and do what I may to save myself. But I would rather I had not met with you.'

Then Sir Tristram went at the traitorous knights, and he slew two with his spear and ten with his sword. At this Sir Dinadan also came in, and he did passing well, so that of the thirty knights but ten were left to flee away.

As they rested and blew for their wind, Dinadan said to Tristram, 'You fare like a madman that would cast himself away, and I curse the time that ever I saw you. In all the world there are no two knights as mad as Sir Lancelot and you. Once I fell in the fellowship of Sir Lancelot, as I have done now with you, and he set me a task that put me in bed for a quarter-year. Jesu defend me from two such knights.' Then he took his horse and his harness and departed.

Now, a great tournament was announced at the Castle of Maidens to which many knights came to win honour, both from Arthur's court and from many other countries. And Sir Tristram went among these knights. He commanded his man Gouvernail to ordain him a black shield, all otherwise plain. And on the first day Sir Tristram did such acts that kings marvelled what knight this was with the black shield, though some knew him and held their peace. So that day King Arthur and all the judges gave the prize to the knight with the black shield, and on the next day also. But of a sudden Tristram turned aside into the forest, and no man perceived where he went. Then King Arthur blew the retreat unto lodgings. And in all the field was a noise that might be heard two miles hence, as lords and ladies cried, 'The knight with the black shield has won the field'.

But Dame Bragwaine rode after Sir Tristram and on the way found a knight making like a madman, waving his sword. The dame fled and when she came up with Tristram told him of her adventure. So Sir Tristram took horse and sword and went to the place, where he heard a knight complaining to himself.

'I, woeful knight Palomides,' cried the man, 'what misadventure befalls me, that am defiled with falsehood. Why do I live so long?'

He got his sword and made many strange signs and tokens such as heathens use. And, raging, he threw his sword into a fountain. Then he wailed and wrung his hands for pure sorrow, but bethought himself again and plunged into the fountain over his belly to seek after his sword. Then Sir Tristram ran forwards and held Sir Palomides fast in his arms.

'What are you,' cried Palomides, 'that holds me so?'

'I am a man of this forest that would do you no harm.'

'Alas,' Palomides went on, 'I do this because I may never win honour where Sir Tristram is. Always he wins the prize above me. But if he be away, for the most part I have the prize, unless Sir Lancelot or Sir Lamorak be there. Once, in Ireland, Sir Tristram put me to the worse, and in Cornwall, and again in other paces.'

'What would you do,' asked Tristram, 'if you had Sir Tristram?'

'I would fight with him, and ease my heart upon him. Yet, to say truth, Sir Tristram is the gentlest knight in this world living.'

Then Sir Tristram said him such kind words that Sir Palomides went with him to his lodging. But Palomides could not sleep for anguish, and in the dawn he took his horse privily and rode away.

Upon the third morn, when more great deeds were done, Sir Palomides came hotfoot at Tristram of the black shield. They dashed together like thunder while kings, queens and lords beheld them. After long fighting Tristram smote Palomides three mighty strokes upon the helm, saying at every stroke, 'Take this for Sir Tristram's sake'. With that, Sir Palomides fell to the earth grovelling.

Then Sir Tristram took up his black shield and did such work among the knights, even unto King Arthur, that he was like a lion till Sir Lancelot, on Arthur's side, struck him and sore wounded him. Therewith Tristram departed from the field.

But Sir Palomides, though Tristram was hurt and had departed, still sought him in a rage. In his madness, he fell into a river and nigh drowned. Kind folk rescued him and took him to the castle of Sir Darras, the good old knight, and to this castle Sir Tristram and Sir Dinadan had also retired to rest. After a time Tristram was much amended of his wound, though he still looked not quite himself. Sir Palomides was not sure of his face, even though his mind played ever on Sir Tristram. Then he would say to Sir Dinadan, 'If ever I may meet with that knight Tristram, he shall not escape my hand.'

'I marvel,' answered Dinadan, 'that you boast behind Sir Tristram, for it is but late that he was in your hands, and you in his. Why did you not hold him when you had him? For I myself saw twice or thrice that you gained but little honour from meeting Sir Tristram.' And then Sir Palomides was ashamed.

Soon there came one to old Sir Darras and told him that three of his sons were slain at the tournament, and two others grievously hurt. And all this was done by the knight that bore the black shield.

'Well, sir,' said his steward, 'one of the knights within our castle bears the black shield.'

They searched the chambers and in Sir Tristram's found his black shield. Then without tarrying Sir Darras put Tristram, Dinadan and Palomides within a strong prison, where Sir Tristram was like to have died of sickness. And every day Palomides reproved Tristram for the old hatred between them. Sir Tristram spoke fair and said little. But when Palomides saw the falling of sickness upon Tristram, he was heavy for him and comforted him in the best wise he could.

For sickness is the greatest pain a prisoner may have. All the while he has the health of his body, he may endure under the mercy of God and in hope of good deliverance. But when sickness touches him he is bereft of all wealth, and then he has cause to wail and weep. Right so did Sir Tristram, for he took such sorrow that he had almost slain himself.

After a time the maid that attended to the prisoners found Sir Dinadan weeping and Sir Palomides weeping. So she went unto Sir Darras and told him how the mighty knight of the black shield was likely to die.

'God defend,' said Darras, 'that knights come to me for succour and I should suffer them to die. Therefore fetch that knight and his fellows.'

Then old Sir Darras said to Tristram, 'Sir knight, I repent of your sickness, for you are called a full-noble knight and so have proved yourself. It aggrieved me greatly that you slew three of my sons, but it shall never be said that I destroyed such a noble knight in prison. Your horses and harness have been kept fair and clean. Go, and your fellows with you. But tell me first your name.'

'My name is Sir Tristram de Liones, of Cornwall born, and nephew unto King Mark. As to your sons, know that I might not have done otherwise had they been my own next kin. But if I had slain them by treachery, then had I been worthy to die.'

'All that you did,' agreed Sir Darras, 'was by force of knighthood, and so I could not put you to death. But since you are Sir Tristram, the good knight, I pray you heartily to be good friend to me and to my sons.'

This Sir Tristram promised by the faith of his body, for he had done but as a natural knight ought to do. So he reposed him until he was big and strong. Then the three knights took horse and departed, and rode to the crossways, where Sir Tristram said, 'Now fellows, here we will go our sundry ways'.

At last Sir Tristram came to Camelot, and King Arthur ran unto Tristram and took him by the hand saying, 'Sir Tristram, you are as welcome as any knight that ever came to this court.'

Then came Queen Guenevere and many ladies, and many knights of the Round Table. With one voice they called, 'Welcome, Sir Tristram.'

'Welcome,' said Arthur again, 'for one of the best and gentlest knights of the world. Therefore, gentle knight, grant me a boon, and abide in my court.'

'Sir, thereto I am loath, for I have ado in many countries.'

'Not so,' said Arthur, 'you may not say nay.'

'Well, sir,' replied Sir Tristram, 'let it be as you wish.'

Then King Arthur looked about the seats of the Round Table that were void and lacked knights. And in the seat of Marhaus, the dead Irish knight, he saw these words: 'This is the seat of the noble knight, Sir Tristram'. And with great ceremony and feast King Arthur made Sir Tristram a knight of the Round Table.

But King Mark felt great despite of the renown of Sir Tristram. He had chased Tristram out of Cornwall, yet he still had suspicion. It seemed to him that there was too much love between his queen, Isoud, and Sir Tristram. So King Mark took his way into England, intending to slay Sir Tristram.

As King Mark rode forwards, he came upon adventures that did him no honour. Sir Lamorak reproved him for a cowardly knight of Cornwall, and knocked him end over his horse's tail. And Sir Dinadan reproved him also, when King Mark would have unworthily slain a knight upon the road.

'You knights of Cornwall,' Dinadan taunted him, 'are no men of honour. You govern yourselves shamefully. I see you are full of cowardice, and you would be a murderer. That is the greatest shame that a knight can have.'

And as fast as worthy knights rode forwards to the joust, King Mark rode backwards like a servant boy. When, upon a time, Sir Lancelot came fast at King Mark with a spear, the king made no defence, but tumbled to the earth like a sack and cried Sir Lancelot mercy.

'Arise, recreant knight and king.' shouted Lancelot.

'I will not fight,' said Mark humbly, 'but will go as you wish.'

'Alas, alas,' said Sir Lancelot, 'that I may not give you one good buffet, for the love of Sir Tristram and La Beale Isoud.'

So he brought King Mark to King Arthur, and there Mark threw his helm upon the ground, and his sword, and fell flat on his face at the feet of Arthur.

'God help me,' said King Arthur, 'you are welcome in a manner, and in a manner you are not welcome. You have been ever against me, and a destroyer of my knights. Now, how will you acquit yourself?'

'Sir, as your Lordship will require me, unto my power, I will make large amends.' For King Mark was always a fair speaker, and false thereunder.

'Well,' said Arthur, 'give me a gift that I shall ask you. Grant me that you will be a good lord unto Sir Tristram. Take him with you into Cornwall. Let him see his friends, and there cherish him for my sake.'

So King Mark swore it upon a book, and he and Tristram took each other by the hands hard knit together. Soon after, the two made ready to ride into Cornwall, whereat most of the Round Table were angry and heavy. And in especial Lancelot, Lamorak and Dinadan were angry out of measure, for they feared the false king would slay or destroy Sir Tristram.

Therewith Sir Lancelot came to King Mark and said, 'Sir king, beware, I warn you, of treason. For if you mischief Sir Tristram by any manner of falsehood, by the faith I owe to God and to the order of knighthood, I shall slay you with my own hands.'

Then, with the lamenting of the court, King Mark and Sir Tristram rode together. For it was Tristram's will that he go with the king. And all was for the intent to see La Beale Isoud. Without the sight of her, he might not endure.

After this was done, when the knights of the Round Table were going their ways, King Arthur let make a joust at a priory, whereat there was great despite betwixt Sir Lamorak and Sir Gawain and his brethren. There was a cry: 'Beware the knight with the red shield.' Thereupon Sir Lamorak came in red and overthrew three of Gawain's brethren. Then he smote Sir Gawain from his horse and hurt him sore. All the brethren were wonderful angry that they had been put to dishonour that day. So Gawain said privily to his brothers, 'Know well, my fair brethren, this Sir Lamorak will never love us. We slew his father, King Pellinore, for we deemed that he had slain our father, the King of Orkney. In revenge for Pellinore, Sir Lamorak did us a shame to our mother, whom he did lie with. Therefore I will be avenged.'

'You shall find us ready,' replied his brethren.

'Then hold you still,' said Gawain, 'and we shall espy our time.'

They sent for their mother, Queen Morgause, to come to a castle fast by Camelot. And Sir Lamorak, when he knew this, made a night assigned when he should come to her. In darkness, Sir Lamorak tied his horse to a privy gate, unarmed himself and went unto the queen's bed. They had great joy, for each loved the other.

But Sir Gaheris, brother to Gawain, was aware of this. He saw his time. He came to the bedside all armed, with his sword naked, and of a sudden he got his mother by the hair and struck off her head. When Sir Lamorak felt the blood dash upon him all hot, he leapt from the bed in his shirt as a knight dismayed.

'Ah, Gaheris,' he cried, 'knight of the Round Table, foul and evil have you done. Alas, why have you slain the mother that bore you? With more right, you should have slain me.'

'Because you are unclothed, I am ashamed to slay you. But for you to lie with our mother is too much dishonour for us to suffer. So in what place I may get you henceforth, I shall slay you. Now my mother is quit of you. Take your armour and get you gone.'

When it was known that Gaheris had slain his mother, King Arthur, brother unto the slain queen, was mighty angry and banished Gaheris from out of the court. Sir Gawain also was angry that Gaheris had let Sir Lamorak escape. There was trouble in Camelot, wherefore Sir Lancelot said to the king, 'Now we shall lose the good knight Lamorak, and that is great pity.'

'God defend,' said Arthur, 'that I should lose Sir Lamorak, or Sir Tristram, for then twain of my chief knights were gone.'

'Nay, sir,' replied Lancelot, 'I am sure you shall lose Sir Lamorak. Sir Gawain and his brethren have sworn to slay him by one mean or other.'

About this time, Sir Tristram in Cornwall sent a letter privily unto La Beale Isoud. He prayed her to be his good lady, to make ready a vessel for her and him, and he would flee with her back into Logris, which is the realm of England. Thus it was done by the help of Sir Dinas, the steward. Sir Tristram was secretly delivered out of prison, and in all haste he and Isoud departed.

They came by water unto this land of Logris, and there Sir Lancelot met with them. He brought them unto Joyous Gard, that was his own castle, a place garnished and furnished as for a royal king and queen.

And Sir Lancelot charged all his people to honour them and love them, as they would himself. Then King Arthur and Queen Guenevere were glad that Sir Tristram and La Beale Isoud had returned.

So those two made great joy daily, with all manner of mirths. And every day Tristram would ride out hunting, for he was called the best chaser of the world, and the noblest blower of a horn. Daily he rode out armed, for he was in a strange country, with many perilous knights. And who knew what treason King Mark might do?

So a little before the month of May, as Sir Tristram was chasing a hart most eagerly, he alighted in his heat to drink of the burbling water of a well. Right then he heard and saw the Questing Beast come to the well. Then he put on his helm quickly, for he deemed that Sir Palomides would be close behind, for that beast was his quest. Withal came the noble Palomides, the Saracen, and either saluted the other warily and in haste. For Sir Palomides would not turn from his quest, but expected to meet Sir Tristram again for the tournament at the Castle Lonazep.

Soon Sir Dinadan, the merry knight, came into that forest, and when he saw Sir Tristram following the hart he called him to halt, saying, 'I saw but late a foolish knight lying by a well. And there he lay like a fool grinning, and would not speak. His shield lay by him, and his horse stood still, champing the grass. And I knew well that he was a lover.'

'Fair sir,' said Tristram, 'are you not a lover?'

'Fie on that craft.'

'But that is evil said, for a knight may never be of prowess except he be a lover.'

Anon, as they spoke a knight came riding, and Sir Dinadan knew him for that same doting fellow who lay by the well.

'By his shield of azure,' said Tristram, 'he is Epinogrus. I know him well as a great lover. If you require him he will joust with you. Then we shall prove whether a lover or no lover be the better knight.'

Therewith Sir Dinadan called out, 'Sir knight, make you ready to joust with me, for this is the custom of knights errant.'

'Is it the rule of you knights errant,' answered Epinogrus, 'to make a knight joust whether he will or not?'

'As for that,' said Dinadan, 'make ready, for here is me.'

They spurred forwards and met like the noise of winter storm, so hard that Epinogrus smote Sir Dinadan to earth. Then Sir Tristram pulled Dinadan up by the hand, and said smiling, 'How now? It seems to me that the lover has sped well. But take your horse and let us go hence.'

Sir Dinadan mounted grumbling. 'Fie on you,' he groaned. 'God defend me from your fellowship, for I never sped well since I met you.'

They rode until evening, and when they came to Joyous Gard La Beale Isoud asked of Sir Tristram his adventure.

'But is not Sir Dinadan,' she said, 'he who made the song against King Mark?'

'The very same, for he is the best jester and japer, and the best fellow I know. All good knights love his fellowship.'

Then Isoud went unto Dinadan. Either saluted the other, and they spoke together.

'Madam,' said Sir Dinadan, 'I marvel of Sir Tristram and other lovers, what ails them to be so mad and so besotted upon women.'

'Why, sir,' said she, 'are you a knight and be no lover? It is your shame. You may not be called a good knight except you make a quarrel for a lady.'

'God defend me, for the joy of love is too short, and the sorrow that comes thereof lasts over long.'

'Now I pray you,' said Isoud, 'tell me, will you fight for my love with three knights that do me great wrong? As you be King Arthur's knight, I require you to do battle for me.'

'Madam,' replied Sir Dinadan, 'you are as fair a lady as ever I saw, and much fairer than is my lady Queen Guenevere. But in a word, I will not fight for you with three knights. Jesu defend me.'

So La Beale Isoud laughed, and had good game with him, with all the good cheer they might. And on the morn early Sir Tristram armed himself, and Isoud gave him a fine helm. Then the two knights got ready to ride to the tournament at Lonazep.

Thus riding, they met Sir Palomides on the way and together they went to the castle, where they saw four hundred tents and pavilions, and marvellous great command from many nations.

'God help me,' said Tristram, 'yonder I see the most noble knights that ever I saw.'

'Nay, sir,' said Palomides, 'there was as great a gathering at the Castle of Maidens, where you won the prize. And also in Surluse, where the Haut Prince made the tournament that lasted seven days.'

'Who there was the best?' said Sir Tristram.

To this, Sir Gareth gave answer, who had come with his brother Gaheris unto the company: 'It was Sir Lancelot du Lake, and then the noble knight Sir Lamorak de Gales.'

Then Sir Tristram looked upon him and sighed, 'Ah, Sir Gareth, the death of Sir Lamorak was over great pity. I dare say he was the cleanest-mighted man, the biggest and the best-winded of his age, except for Sir Lancelot. I heard say that Sir Gawain, and you his brethren, slew him among you, a better knight than ever you were. It is shame that all you who come from such great and kingly blood be now called the destroyers and murderers of good knights. Had it pleased God, I would I had been by Sir Lamorak at his death.'

'Then should you have gone the same way,' said Gaheris with contempt, and he spurred his horse away.

'It is for such things done treasonably,' said Tristram full of thought, 'that I fear to draw unto the court of my lord Arthur. I would have you know this.'

'Sir, I blame you not,' said Gareth. 'Well I understand the vengeance of my brethren Gawain, Agravaine, Gaheris and Mordred. As for me, I meddle not. Therefore there is none of them that loves me. As they be murderers, so I left their company.'

'You say well,' replied Tristram. 'But I had rather been there than have all the gold betwixt here and Rome.'

'Iwis, and so would I,' said Sir Palomides. 'Yet I never had the prize at any joust where Sir Lamorak was, but he put me to the worse. That day he was slain, he did the most deeds of arms that ever I saw in all my life days. And when my lord Arthur gave him the prize, Sir Gawain and his brethren Agravaine, Gaheris and Mordred set upon Sir Lamorak in a privy place. First they slew his horse and then they rushed upon him on foot, both before and behind. Sir Mordred gave him the death-wound in his back, and then all hewed him apart. So I heard from one of his squires that saw it.'

'Fie upon treason,' said Sir Tristram, 'for it kills my heart to hear this tale.'

'So does it mine,' said Sir Gareth. 'Though they be my brethren, I shall never love them for that deed.'

'Now speak we of other things,' said Palomides sadly, 'and let him be, for his life you may not get again. Sir, let us leave off this matter and see how we shall do at this tournament. Let us four hold together against all that will come.'

'Not by my counsel,' said Sir Tristram, 'for I see by their pavilions that there will be four hundred knights, and many good men among them. Be a man never so valiant, nor so big, yet he may be overmatched. So have I seen knights do many times. And when they thought best to have won honour, they lost it. For manhood is not worth, except it be mixed with wisdom. And as for me, I shall keep my own head as well as another.'

So they rode on through woods and fields to the place, fast by Lonazep, where Sir Tristram had sent his two pavilions. There La Beale Isoud awaited them. But when Sir Palomides heard of this, his heart was ravished out of measure and he would not go in, till Sir Tristram took him by the finger and led him. And when Palomides saw Isoud, he could scarcely speak, but looked and looked and was silent.

On the morn, as they came to the fighting, it happened that Sir Palomides looked up towards La Beale Isoud as she lay in a window, and he espied how she laughed. Therewith he took such a rejoicing that he smote down all he met. His strength began to double and he did so marvellously that all men had wonder of him, and ever he cast up his eye unto Isoud. Then he fared like a lion, and all the kings gave him the honour for that day.

That day, Sir Tristram was not foremost in battle, and he fought only in disguise so that few knew him. Then Sir Dinadan railed with Sir Tristram to provoke him to do well, saying, 'What the devil is upon you this day? Sir Palomides' strength never feebled, yet you fared all day as if you had been asleep, and therefore I call you coward.'

'Listen, Dinadan,' said Tristram, 'I was never called coward in my life. And though Sir Lancelot gave me a fall, I except him from all knights, for he is too over good for any living. Of his sufferance, largess, bounty and courtesy, I call him knight peerless.'

Sir Tristram was angry. But Sir Dinadan said all this language to cause him to wake his spirits and to be angry. For well Dinadan knew that if Tristram were thoroughly wroth, Palomides should not get the prize upon the morn.

'Truly, as for Sir Lancelot,' Sir Palomides said, 'I know not his peer. This day I did full uncourteously unto him, for I smote his horse's neck with my sword, and a cry went up huge and great, "See how the infidel Saracen has smitten down Sir Lancelot's horse." Then were many angry with me, because it was unknightly done to kill a horse wilfully. But Sir Lancelot was full courteous unto me. And had he been as ungentle to me as I to him, this day I would have won no honour.'

This talking was in the houses of kings. But all kings, lords and knights said, of clear knighthood, of pure strength, of bounty, of courtesy, Sir Lancelot and Sir Tristram bore the prize above all that ever were in Arthur's days.

On the morn Sir Tristram rode out with Sir Palomides and La Beale Isoud, and they were all in green as fresh as May, and they left Sir Dinadan sleeping in his bed. And it happed that King Arthur and Sir Lancelot stood at a window and saw Isoud. She was so fair that the king had a great desire to go and see her. So the king beheld her, and liked her wonderly well. But Sir Palomides said to Arthur, 'Uncourteous knight, what seek you here? Why do you come upon a lady thus suddenly? Therefore withdraw.'

In anger he took a spear and came hurtling upon King Arthur, and smote him down, though he knew not whom he struck.

Then Sir Lancelot put the king on horseback, and as they departed Sir Tristram said unto Palomides, 'You did yourself great shame when you smote that knight. He came of his gentleness to see a fair lady, and that is every good knight's part, to behold a fair lady. It will turn to anger, for know well that you struck King Arthur, and the other good knight with him was my lord Lancelot.'

'I may never believe,' said Palomides, 'that King Arthur will ride so privily as a poor errant knight.'

'Ah, you know not my lord Arthur. All knights may learn knightly deeds from him. Therefore be sorry for your unkindness to so noble a king.'

'What is done,' said Sir Palomides, 'may not be undone.'

Then Sir Palomides began to remove himself from Sir Tristram.

'How feel you today?' asked Tristram. 'May you do as you did yesterday?'

'Nay,' said Palomides, 'I feel myself so weary and so sore bruised of the deeds of yesterday that I may not endure as I did then.'

'Well, shall I lack you this day?'

'Trust not to me, for I may not do as I did.' All this Palomides said to beguile Sir Tristram. Then Sir Palomides rode by himself. He disguised himself with the harness and shield of another, and changed to the other side, and tried all he might do to shame and to dishonour Sir Tristram. And when, after seven nights, Sir Bleoberis and Sir Ector went to Queen Guenevere, who had been sick, to give account of the tournament, they told her how Sir Palomides had won the prize at the first day, and the second day Sir Tristram and the third Sir Lancelot.

'But who,' said the queen, 'did best all three days?'

'My lords Lancelot and Tristram,' they answered, 'had least dishonour. Sir Palomides did mightily. But he turned against the party he began with, which caused him to lose some of his honour. For it seemed that Sir Palomides is envious.'

'Then he shall never win honour,' said Guenevere, 'for all men of honour hate an envious man, and will show him no favour. But he that is courteous, kind and gentle has favour everywhere.'

After that tournament Sir Palomides departed and rode as adventures would guide him. On a day, at high noon, he saw a fair wounded knight lying on the earth, and his horse bound by him, and he weeping as though he would die.

'Knight, why wail you so?' said Palomides mildly. 'Let me lie down and wail with you, for my sorrow is a hundredfold more than yours. Such as I am, be it better or be it worse, I am Sir Palomides, son and heir unto King Astlabor. I was never christened, though my two brothers are truly so. What woe I endure! I love the fairest queen and lady that ever bare life, and her name is a Beale Isoud.'

'That is great folly,' replied the wailing knight, who was named Epinogrus, 'for Sir Tristram, one of the best knights of the world, loves Queen Isoud.'

'That is truth.'

'But did La Beale Isoud ever love you?' said Epinogrus. 'Or did you rejoice her ever in any pleasure?'

'Nay, by my knighthood, I never espied that she loved me more than all the world, nor ever had I pleasure with her. But the last day she gave me the greatest rebuke that ever I had, the which shall never go from my heart. Yet I well deserved that rebuke, for I did not knightly. Alas, now I have lost all the honour that ever I won, for I never had such prowess as I had in the fellowship of Sir Tristram.'

Then Sir Palomides rode on. In a little time he came to a manor where an old man sat at the gate, saying his prayers and his beads, and within the gate were many goodly men weeping. Anon one of the men beheld Sir Palomides and knew him, crying out, 'Fellows, here is the same knight that slew our lord at Lonazep.'

At once they went to harness, to the number of threescore, and rushed freshly upon Palomides with many great strokes, and took him and put him in a strong prison. Twelve knights passed judgment on him, and found him guilty of their lord's death. On the morn, they bound the legs of Palomides under an old steed's belly and they took him to the castle of the slain knight, and there Sir Palomides should have justice.

But as they were riding fast by the castle of Joyous Gard, there came a man from the castle that knew Sir Palomides and he called out, 'Saracen knight, for what cause are you led so?'

'Ah, fair fellow,' replied Palomides, 'I ride towards my death for the slaying of a knight at the tournament of Lonazep. If I had not deserted my lord Tristram there, as I ought not to have done, now I might be saved. But I pray you, sir, recommend me unto Sir Tristram, and unto my lady Queen Isoud. Ask them forgiveness.'

Then that knight wept for pity of Sir Palomides, and rode in haste to Joyous Gard to try to arrange his rescue. Thus it befell that Sir Lancelot took the rescue upon himself, for he deemed it shame to suffer such a noble knight as Sir Palomides to die. Sir Lancelot took arms and rode out, and made those men loose Sir Palomides, and returned again with him to Joyous Gard, where Sir Tristram and La Beale Isoud were also residing.

When they were come within the gate, and unarmed and unhelmed, then Sir Tristram took Sir Lancelot in arms, and so did Queen Isoud. And Palomides knelt on the bare earth and thanked Sir Lancelot. Then there was joy among them, for Tristram and Isoud forgave Sir Palomides, whatever his faults. But the oftener that Sir Palomides saw La Beale Isoud, the heavier he waxed day by day.

So upon a day, in the dawning, Sir Palomides went into the forest by himself. There he rested by a well. Looking in the water he saw his own visage, how he was disturbed and faded, nothing like he was.

'What may this mean?' he sighed. 'Ah, Palomides, why are you faded, you that was wont to be called one of the fairest knights of the world? I will lead this life no more, for I cannot get she whom I love.'

Therewith he laid him down by the well and began to make a rhyme and song of Isoud and himself. And Sir Tristram, who was in the forest to chase the fat deer as was his wont, heard this singing so loud and plaintive. He rode softly thither and saw that it was Sir Palomides. Tristram tied his horse to a tree and came near, and listened to the complaints that were of the noble Queen Isoud, all most wonderfully well said and full piteously made. He listened from beginning to end, and the song troubled him sore.

When Palomides had finished Sir Tristram was angry out of measure, and thought to slay Palomides as he lay. But he remembered him that Sir Palomides lay all undefended and unarmed, and that he had a noble name. So he stirred Palomides with his foot and said, 'Sir Palomides, I have heard your complaint concerning La Beale Isoud. This treason you have owed me over long. Know therefore you shall die. But tell me, how will you acquit yourself?'

'Thus I will acquit me,' said Palomides. 'Know well that I love La Beale Isoud above all other ladies. And I know it shall befall me as befell to Sir Kehydius, that died for the love of Queen Isoud. O my lord Tristram, I have loved Isoud many a day, and she has been the causer of my honour, or else I had remained the most simple knight in the world. By her, and because of her, I have won whatever honour I have. I never had reward nor bounty of her, and yet I have been her knight without recompense. So Sir Tristram, I dread not any death, for now life and death are the same to me.'

'Have you uttered your treason?' said Sir Tristram.

'I have done you no treason,' answered Palomides. 'Love is free for all men. Though I have loved your lady, she is my lady as well as yours. But you rejoice her, and have your desire of her, which I never had nor am like to have. And yet shall I love her to the uttermost of my life.'

'Then I will fight with you,' said Sir Tristram, 'for life or for death.'

A day was set for the battle, but before it Sir Tristram was sore hurt in the chase of the deer, and lay in his bed with a wound in his thigh six inches deep. When Sir Palomides heard this he was not sorry, for death is still a hard thing, and Sir Tristram was the biggest knight in battle then living, except Sir Lancelot.

So Sir Palomides departed where fortune might lead him. And within a month, when Sir Tristram was cured of his wound, he also took horse and rode from country to country, inquiring for Palomides and seeking strange adventures, whereby he won much noise and fame.

Now when Sir Tristram was come home unto Joyous Gard from his adventures, La Beale Isoud counselled him to go to the court for the great feast of Pentecost. So Sir Tristram took leave of Isoud and within a few miles it happed by fortune that he saw before him Sir Palomides, going also to the court. Then Sir Tristram repented him that he was not armed. But Palomides saw Tristram and cried on high, 'Sir Tristram, now we be met. Before we depart we will redress our old sores.'

Yet at this time they might not fight, for Sir Tristram was unarmed. So Palomides said, 'Therefore ride on your way'.

'I may as I choose,' replied Tristram, 'to ride or abide. But Sir Palomides, I marvel at one thing, that you who are so good a knight will not be christened, though your brother Sir Safer has been christened many a day.'

'Howbeit in my heart,' said Palomides, 'I believe in Jesu Christ and his mild mother Mary, I may not yet be christened. For I vowed I have one battle to do, and then I will be baptized with a good will.'

'By my head,' protested Tristram, 'that one battle you shall seek no longer. For God defend that you shall remain a Saracen through my default. Look, yonder is a wounded knight. Now help me to arm in his armour, and I shall soon fulfil your vows.'

'As you will,' said Sir Palomides, 'so shall it be.'

Sir Tristram put on the armour of the wounded knight Sir Galleron, who was a knight large of flesh and bone. He got Sir Galleron's spear, mounted his own horse, and then were both he and Sir Palomides ready. At once they came together as two wild boars, lashing, feinting and crossing, as noble men that oft had been well proved in battle. Thus they fought for many hours, till Palomides cut away great pieces of Tristram's shield. So he wounded Sir Tristram, for Palomides was a well-fighting man.

Then Sir Tristram was sore mad, and gave such strong, sad strokes that by fortune he hacked the sword from Palomides' hand. Palomides stood and beheld his fallen sword with a sorrowful heart. He knew that had he stooped for it, he had been slain.

'How now,' cried Sir Tristram. 'I have you at advantage, but never shall it be said that I slew a weaponless knight. Take up your sword, and let us make an end of it.'

But Sir Palomides stood quiet and held his arms wide. Then he said, 'Sir, I have no great lust to fight any more. My offence to you is not so great but that we may be friends. All that I have offended is and was for the love of La Beale Isoud. I dare say she is peerless above all ladies, and I never proffered her any dishonour. My offence was against your own person, and for that you have given me this day many sad strokes, and some I have given you again. Wherefore I require you, my lord, forgive me all that I have offended unto you. And this same day have me to the next church. First let me be clean confessed and after see that I be truly baptized. Then we will all ride together to the court of King Arthur, that we be there at the high feast.'

'Now take your horse,' replied Sir Tristram, 'and as you say so shall it be. All your evil God will forgive, and I do also.'

Thus they rode, and within a mile they came to the suffragan Bishop of Carlisle. He let fill a great vessel of water, and when he had hallowed it he confessed clean Sir Palomides, the Saracen knight, and then baptized him. So they rode on towards Camelot, where King Arthur and Queen Guenevere, and all the court, were glad out of measure that Sir Palomides was christened.

Then was the high feast of Pentecost held most solemnly. After this feast, all the knights of the Round Table broke up their company and went upon the tasks of their adventures. And Sir Tristram de Liones returned again to La Beale Isoud at the castle of Joyous Gard. But Sir Palomides, the christened Saracen knight, followed ever after the Barking Beast, for that was his quest.

✦ The Quest of the ✦ Holy Grail

At the vigil of Pentecost, when all the fellowship of the Round Table were come unto Camelot and had heard their Mass, and the tables were set ready for the meat, there entered into the hall a fair gentlewoman full fast on horseback, for her horse was all besweated.

She alighted before the king and said, 'Sir, for God's sake say me where Sir Lancelot is.'

Then she went unto Sir Lancelot and said, 'I salute you on behalf of King Pelles, and I require you come with me hereby into a forest.'

'What will you with me?' said Lancelot.

'You shall know,' she said, 'when you come thither.'

'Well,' said he, 'I will gladly go with you.'

Right so departed Sir Lancelot with the lady and rode to a great valley, where he saw an abbey of nuns. They entered and a fair fellowship welcomed them and led them unto the abbess's chamber, where Lancelot unarmed him. In the meantime there came twelve nuns that brought with them Galahad. And he was fair and well made, so that men might not find his match in all the world. And all the nuns wept.

'Sir,' they said, 'we bring you this child we have nourished, and we pray you to make him a knight, for he could not receive the order of knighthood from a more worthy man's hand.'

122

The Holy Grail appearing in a vision before the knights of the
Round Table

Sir Lancelot and Queen Guenevere

King Arthur setting out on his quest for the Holy Grail

Above: King Arthur with his advisors

Below: King Arthur laying siege to Sir Lancelot's castle

The young squire looked seemly and demure as a dove, with all manner of good features. Sir Lancelot thought he had never seen a young man so fair of form.

'Comes this desire of himself?' he asked. And they all said yea.

So on the morn, at the hour of prime, Sir Lancelot made Galahad a knight and said, 'God make you a good man, for of beauty you have as much as any living. And now, fair sir, will you come with me unto the court of King Arthur?' But Galahad would not go with him at that time.

So Sir Lancelot returned unto Camelot. And when the king and all his knights were come from their service in the minster, the barons espied in the seats of the Round Table, writ with golden letters, 'Here ought to sit he,' and 'He ought to sit here'. Thus they went about till they came to the Seat Perilous, where they found new-written letters that said:

Four hundred and fifty-four winters have passed from the passion of Our Lord Jesu Christ. Now ought this seat to be fulfilled.

'This is a marvellous and adventurous thing,' they all said.

Then Lancelot accounted the years and said, 'This very feast of Pentecost is the time when this seat ought to be fulfilled. Let us ordain a cloth of rich silk to cover these letters till he be come that ought to achieve this adventure.'

They would now have hastened unto dinner. But Sir Kay, the steward, reminded the king of his old custom not to sit at meat before he had seen some adventure. Right so, as they stood speaking, in came a squire, saying to the king, 'Sir, I bring a marvellous tidings. Beneath, at the river, is a great stone floating above the water, and therein I saw sticking a sword.'

All the knights went with Arthur and they found in the river a stone floating, as it were of red marble, and therein stuck a rich sword with a pommel wrought with precious stones and lettered in gold:

Never shall man take me hence, but only he by whose side I ought to hang. And he shall be the best knight of the world.

Then said the king unto Sir Lancelot, 'Fair sir, this sword ought to be yours, for I am sure you be the best knight of the world.'

'Certes sir,' Lancelot answered full soberly, 'it is not my sword. I have no hardiness to set my hand to it, for it longed not to hang by my side.

Also, whoever assays to take the sword and fails shall be woefully wounded by it. Therefore know that this same day shall begin the adventures of the Holy Grail, that which is called the holy vessel.'

'Now, nephew,' said Arthur unto Sir Gawain, 'assay it, for my love.'

'Sir, save your good grace, I shall not do that.'

'Nay,' said the king, 'take the sword at my command.'

'Sir,' replied Gawain, 'your command I will obey.'

Therewith he took the sword by the handles but might not stir it.

'My lord Gawain,' Lancelot warned him, 'now this sword shall touch you so sore that you will wish you had not done it for the best castle of this realm.'

'Sir,' Gawain lamented, 'I might not gainsay my uncle's command.'

Then King Arthur repented much his command, so Sir Percival assayed the sword, only to bear Sir Gawain fellowship. But he also might not move it. Then there were no more that durst to be so hardy.

So the king and all went unto dinner. And when they were served, and all seats fulfilled save only the Seat Perilous, anon there befell a marvellous thing. All the doors and windows of the palace shut by themselves, yet the hall was not greatly darkened. While they were thus abashed, in came a good ancient man, clothed all in white, and with him he brought a young knight on foot, in red arms, without sword or shield, save a scabbard hanging by his side.

And the old man said unto Arthur, 'Sir king, I bring here a young knight who is of kings' lineage, and of the kindred of Joseph of Arimathea, whereby the marvels of this court, and of strange realms, shall be fully accomplished.'

The king bade them welcome. Then the young man unarmed himself, and he was in a coat of fine red cloth, with a mantle furred with ermine upon his shoulder. And the old man led the young knight to the Seat Perilous, beside Sir Lancelot. Then the ancient lifted up the cloth and found these letters: 'This is the seat of Galahad, the High Prince'.

So the old man set him down surely in that seat, saying, 'Young sir, know you well that this place is yours.'

With that the good old man departed, and all the knights of the Round Table marvelled greatly of Sir Galahad, that he durst sit in the Seat Perilous, though so tender of age. And they knew not whence he came, but all only by God, and they said, 'This is he by whom the Sangrail shall be achieved.'

Sir Lancelot looked upon the young man and beheld his son. Then he had great joy of him, while Sir Bors told his fellows, 'Upon pain of my life, this young knight shall come unto great honour.'

In a little time the king took Sir Galahad by the hand to show him the adventure of the stone with the sword. And Queen Guenevere also heard thereof, and came with many ladies to see where the stone hoved on the water.

'Look, sir, on this marvel,' said Arthur to Galahad. 'Right good knights have assayed the sword and failed.'

'That is no marvel,' said Galahad, 'for this adventure is not theirs but mine. Here by my side hangs the scabbard, for the surety of this sword.'

At once he laid his hand on the sword. He lightly drew it out of the stone and put it in the sheath, and said to the king, 'Now it goes better than it did beforehand. This sword sometime belonged to the good knight Balin le Savage. With it he slew his brother Balan through a dolorous stroke, the same that Balin gave unto my grandfather King Pelles, who is not yet whole, nor shall be till I heal him.'

As they spoke, there came riding down the river a lady on a white palfrey who said weeping to Sir Lancelot, 'How changed is your great doing since this day in the morn.'

'Maiden, why say you so?' asked Lancelot.

'You were this day,' she replied, 'the best knight of the world. But now there is one better than you, as is well proved by the adventure of this sword that you durst not set to your hand. Therefore remember, henceforth think not yourself the best knight of the world.'

'I know well,' said Sir Lancelot, 'I was never the best.'

'Yea,' said the maiden, 'that you were, and are yet of any sinful man of the world. And now, my lord Arthur, the hermit Nacien sends word that you shall have the greatest honour that ever befell king in Britain. For this day the Holy Grail will appear in your house, and feed you and all your fellowship of the Round Table.' And so she departed.

'Now,' said King Arthur, 'all you of the Round Table will depart on this quest of the Sangrail, and never shall I see you again all whole together. Therefore, let you joust in the meadow of Camelot, so that men may speak of such a day after your death.'

But this moving of the king was to see Sir Galahad proved. So Galahad put on his helm and a noble coat of mail, but he would take no shield, not even at the king's asking. Then he took a spear and dressed him in the midst of the meadow, when the queen was in a tower to behold him with all her ladies. And he began to break spears marvellously, so all men had wonder of him, for he surmounted and defouled all other knights save twain, Sir Lancelot and Sir Percival.

After he had done great deeds, Sir Galahad alighted at the queen's request and unlaced his helm, that the queen might see his face. She beheld him long, and said, 'Truly, I dare say Sir Lancelot begat him, for never two men resembled more in likeness. Therefore, his prowess is no marvel. For he is come of the best knights in the world, of the highest lineage. Sir Lancelot is of the eighth degree of Our Lord Jesu Christ, and thus Sir Galahad is of the ninth degree.'

When the tourney was finished, the king and all estates went home unto evensong in the minster, and after that to supper. Then anon they heard cracking and crying of thunder. In the midst of this blast there entered a sunbeam seven times clearer than any seen before, and of a sudden they were alighted by the grace of the Holy Ghost. Then every knight looked one to another, and each looked fairer than ever before, so that all were struck dumb.

At this there entered into the hall the Sangrail, covered with rich silk of white and gold. And all the hall was filled with good odours, and every knight had such meats and drinks as he best loved. And when that Holy Grail had been borne through the hall, though none saw who bore it, suddenly the holy vessel departed. Then all had breath to speak.

So the king yielded thanks to God, and after a while Sir Gawain said unto all the company, 'Now one thing still beguiles us. We could not see the Holy Grail, it was so preciously covered. Wherefore I will make here a vow: that tomorrow I shall labour in the quest of the Sangrail, and never shall I return again unto the court till I have seen it more openly.'

When they of the Round Table heard Sir Gawain say so, they arose up and made such vows as he had made. But King Arthur heard this and was greatly displeased, for he knew well that they might not gainsay their vows.

'Alas,' said he to Gawain, 'you have nigh slain me with your promise. Through this you have bereft me of the fairest fellowship and the truest of knighthood that was ever seen. When all depart from hence they shall never meet more in this world, for many shall die in the quest. I have loved you all as well as my life, therefore it shall grieve me right sore, the loss of this fellowship.' Therewith the tears fell in Arthur's eyes.

'Ah, comfort yourself,' said Sir Lancelot. 'For it shall be unto us a great honour, and much more than if we died in any other place. As to death, that we are sure of.'

'I say these doleful words out of my love,' replied the king. 'For never Christian king had so many worthy men as I have had this day at the Round Table, and that is my great sorrow.'

When the queen and the ladies knew these tidings they all had much heaviness, and many of those ladies that loved knights would have gone with their lovers. But an old knight in religious clothing prevented them and said, 'None in this quest may lead lady nor gentlewoman in so high a service. I warn you plain, he that is not clean of his sins shall not see the mysteries of Our Lord Jesu Christ.'

At last the knights went to their rest. And in honour of the highness of Sir Galahad, he was led into King Arthur's chamber and there rested in the king's own bed.

On the morn, after the service in the minster, King Arthur accounted those who had undertaken the quest of the Sangrail. He found they were a hundred and fifty, and all were knights of the Round Table. So all these knights put on their helms and departed, and recommended them all wholly unto the queen. Then there was weeping and great sorrow among the rich and the poor, even in the streets of Camelot. When he saw this, King Arthur turned away and could not speak for tears.

Now, Sir Galahad rode four days without a shield. At the fourth day he came to an abbey where behind the altar hung a shield as white as any snow, with a red cross in its midst. There were two knights there of the Round Table who would have assayed for this shield. But one of the monks told them, 'Sirs, this shield should be hung only about the neck of the worthiest knight of the world. Therefore I counsel you knights to be well advised.'

But one of the knights, King Bagdemagus, still assayed the shield, and bore it from the church. He had not gone two miles when a white knight on a white horse rode on to him and burst his mail, and pierced him through the right shoulder, and took the white shield from him, saying, 'Knight, you have done yourself great folly, for this shield is only for him that shall have no peer.'

Then the white knight said to the squire of Bagdemagus, 'Take this shield unto the good knight Galahad that you left at the abbey, for it behoves unto no man but Sir Galahad.'

Galahad received this shield and blessed his fortune, commending himself to God. He hung the white shield about his neck and rode onwards to a hermitage where by adventure he met and saluted the white knight.

'Sir,' asked Galahad, 'be many marvels fallen by this shield?'

'Thirty-two years after the Passion of Jesu Christ,' said the knight, 'Joseph of Arimathea, he who took down Our Lord off the Holy Cross, went from Jerusalem with a great party of his kindred. So they journeyed till they came to a city called Sarras, where King Evelake made war against the Saracens, and in especial against his cousin King Tolleme. On a day, when the kings faced each other in desperate battle, Joseph told Evelake that he should surely be slain except he leave the old law and believe upon the new law.

'Then he showed King Evelake the right belief of the Holy Trinity, which the king agreed to with all his heart. And this shield that you have was made for King Evelake. When he won the battle, he was gladly baptized, and the most part of his people with him. Soon after, Joseph wished to depart, and Evelake went with him, even unto this land called Great Britain. Not long after, Joseph was laid on his deathly bed. Then Evelake made much sorrow and said, "For love of you I have left my country. Give me now some token that I may think on you."

'So Joseph, who was sore bleeding at the nose, took the king's shield and made on it a cross of his own blood. "Now may you see a remembrance that I love you," said Joseph, "and you shall think on me whenever you see this shield. And the last of my lineage, the good knight Galahad, shall finally have this shield about his neck, and shall do many marvellous deeds." Thus in years this shield came to Nacien, the holy hermit, till this day when I gave it unto Sir Galahad.'

He told all this, and then the white knight vanished away.

Then Galahad rode a long time into a waste forest, and there it happed that he met with Sir Lancelot and Sir Percival. But they knew him not, for he was newly disguised. When they met, they dressed themselves each to other and jousted before a hermitage where a recluse lived. But when this holy woman saw Sir Galahad, she cried out, 'God save you, best knight of the world'. Then she looked towards Lancelot and Percival and said further, 'Certes, if yonder two knights had known you as well as I do, they would not have encountered with you.'

But Sir Galahad was adread to be known. So he smote his horse with his spurs and sped away. Then the other two got up on their horses and rode fast after him, but soon he was out of their sight. With this, Sir Percival would turn again to the recluse with heavy cheer.

Sir Lancelot would not go now with Percival, for he was too sad. So he rode far and wide in a wild land, following no path but as strange adventure led him. At last he came to a marble stone by a stony cross-roads, though it was so dark he knew not what it was. Nearby was an old chapel where Lancelot tied his horse, did off with his helm and hung his shield on a tree. The chapel door was wasted and broken. Within he found an altar richly arrayed with cloth of clean silk and a silver candlestick bearing six great candles. Then Sir Lancelot had great will to enter the chapel, for he was heavy and dismayed. He put off his harness and ungirt his sword. He took his shield from the tree and laid himself down upon it, to sleep before the cross.

So he fell into half-waking and half-sleeping, and thus he saw come by him two white palfreys bearing a sick knight on a litter, which rested before the cross.

'O sweet Lord,' the sick knight sighed, 'when shall this sorrow leave me? And when shall I be blessed by the holy vessel? For I have endured thus long, and for little trespass.'

With that Sir Lancelot saw the great candlestick come before the cross, though nobody brought it. Also there was a table of silver, and the holy vessel of the Sangrail. Therewith the sick knight sat up and held out both hands and said, 'Fair sweet Lord, present in this holy vessel, make me whole of this malady.'

On hands and knees he crawled to touch the holy vessel. When he had done this, he was whole again. 'Lord God,' he said most humbly, 'I thank you, for I am healed.'

Then the holy vessel went into the chapel, and Lancelot knew not where it had gone. For he was so overtaken with sin that he had no power to rise. But the once-sick knight dressed himself and kissed the cross, and said to his squire who brought him his harness, 'Certes, I thank God I am right well. But I marvel of this sleeping knight here, who had no power to wake when the holy vessel was brought herein.'

'I dare say,' said the squire, 'that he dwells in some deadly sin yet unconfessed.'

So the knight went on to dress himself, save helm and sword, which he took from Lancelot. And when he was clean armed, he took also Lancelot's horse, for it was better than his. Thus he departed.

Soon Sir Lancelot awaked and wondered whether he dreamt or not. Right so he heard a voice saying, 'Sir Lancelot, harder than is stone, more bitter than the wood, and more naked and barer than the leaf of the fig tree. Go from hence, and withdraw from this holy place.'

These words went to his heart, for he knew not wherefore he was called so. He knew not what to do and departed sore weeping, and he cursed the time that he was born. For he deemed that he would never have honour more. He went to the cross and found his helm and sword and horse taken away. He called himself a very wretch, and said to himself thus: 'My sin and wickedness have brought me into great dishonour. When I sought worldly adventures for worldly desires, I always achieved them. And never was I discomfit in any quarrel, were it right or wrong. Now I take upon me the adventures of holy things and I see that my old sin hinders and shames me, so that I had power neither to stir nor speak when the holy blood appeared before me.'

Thus he sorrowed till it was day and he heard the fowls sing. With the rising of the sun he was somewhat comforted. But when he remembered that his horse and harness were gone, he knew truly that God was displeased with him. So he went on foot. By prime he came to a high hill with a hermitage, and knelt wearily before the hermit and cried mercy from Our Lord for his wicked works. And when the hermit had said his Mass, Lancelot prayed him for charity to hear his life.

'My name is Sir Lancelot du Lake,' he said unto the hermit, 'that has been right well spoken of. But now my good fortune is changed, and I am the most wretched of the world.'

The hermit beheld him and marvelled how he was so abashed.

'Sir,' said he, 'there is no knight living now that ought to give God so great thanks as you. For He has given you beauty, seemliness, and great strength above all others. Therefore you are beholden unto God more than any other, to love Him and dread Him. For your strength and manhood will little avail you if God be against you. And for your presumption to be in His presence, where His flesh and blood were, when you were in deadly sin that caused you to be blind with worldly eyes. For He will not appear where such sinners be, except unto their great hurt.'

'Now,' Lancelot wept, 'I know well you say truth.'

'Sir,' said the good man, 'hide none old sin from me.'

And then Sir Lancelot told that good man all his life, how he had loved a queen unmeasurably and long. 'And all my great deeds of arms

I did the most part for that queen's sake, were it right or wrong. Never did I do battle all only for God, but to win honour and cause me to be better beloved. Now counsel me, good father, I pray you.'

'Ensure me that you will forbear that queen's fellowship as much as you may.'

And Lancelot promised him so, by the faith of his body.

'Look then,' said the hermit, 'that your heart and your mouth accord, and you shall have more honour than ever you had.'

'But, good father, I wonder of the voice that said to me marvellous words.'

'Marvel not, for it seems God still loves you well. A stone is hard, like unto your obduracy, my lord Lancelot, for you will not leave your sin. And never would you be made soft, neither by fire nor by water, nor by the heat of the Holy Ghost that may not enter you. And the voice called you bitterer than wood, for where overmuch sin dwells there may be but little sweetness, wherefore you are likened to an old rotten tree.

'And now I shall show you why you are more naked and barer than the fig tree. When Our Lord preached in Jerusalem on Palm Sunday, he found all hardness in the people where none in the town would harbour him. And in the midst of the way there was a fig tree, well garnished of leaves, but fruit it had none. Then Our Lord cursed the tree that bore no fruit, which betokened Jerusalem. So you, Sir Lancelot, when the Holy Grail was brought before you, were found to have no fruit, nor good thought, nor good will, but all defouled with lechery.'

'Certes,' lamented Sir Lancelot, 'all is true. From henceforth I cast me, by the grace of God, never to be so wicked again, but to follow knighthood and do feats of arms.'

Then the good hermit gave Sir Lancelot penance and enjoined him to pursue knighthood, and afterwards he absolved him.

At that time, when Sir Galahad had sped away so fast and Sir Lancelot had ridden alone in the wild ways, Sir Percival turned again unto the recluse. He knelt at her window and gave her his name, and begged her help to find the knight with the white shield and the red arms.

'Truly, madam,' he said, 'I shall never be at ease till I may fight with him, for I have the shame of his blows yet.'

'Ah, Percival,' said she, 'I see you have a great will to be slain, as your father was, through outrageousness.'

'Madam, it seems by your words that you know me.'

'Yea, well I ought to know you, for I am your aunt, though I be now in a religious place. Sometime I was called the Queen of the Waste Lands, the queen of most riches in the world. But my riches never pleased me so much as does my poverty now.'

Then Sir Percival wept for very pity to find his aunt, so she asked him, 'Nephew, when heard you tidings of your mother?'

'Truly, I heard none of her,' he said, 'but I dream of her much in sleep. Therefore I know not whether she be dead or alive.'

'Certes, nephew, she is dead. After your departing she took such a sorrow that anon she died.'

'Now God have mercy on her soul. I regret it sore. We must all change from life into death. But, fair aunt, tell me what is that knight? Be he the one that bore the red arms on Whit Sunday?'

'That is he,' she replied, 'who went in red arms. That same knight has no peer, for he works all by miracle, and he shall never be overcome by earthly man's hand.'

'Well, madam,' said Percival, 'now that you tell me this I will never have ado with Sir Galahad but by way of kindness. But for God's love, fair aunt, teach me some way where I may find him, for much would I love his fellowship.'

'Then you must ride unto his cousin-german, at the castle called Goothe. And if he can tell you no tidings, ride straight unto the Castle of Carbonek, where the maimed king is lying, for there shall you hear true tidings of him.'

With sorrow they departed one from the other, and Sir Percival rode till evensong. Then he heard a clock smite, and was aware of a house well closed in with walls and deep ditches. He knocked at the gate and was led unto a chamber where he had right good cheer that night.

On the morn, at Mass, he saw a pew closed with iron. And behind the altar was a rich bed clothed with silk and gold, and on it a man or woman, for the face was covered. At the consecration, the one on the bed rose up uncovered and Sir Percival saw an old man with a golden crown upon his head, and his body naked unto his navel. This body was full of great wounds. And ever he held up his hands towards Our Lord's body, crying, 'Sweet Father, Jesu Christ, forget me not.' And so he lay down, still mumbling his orisons, and he seemed to be of the age of three-hundred winters.

'What is this man?' said Percival to the priest of the Mass.

'Sir,' he replied, 'you have heard how Joseph of Arimathea brought the good King Evelake into this land from the city of Sarras. And ever Evelake sought the Holy Grail, coming so close to it that God was displeased with the king and struck him almost blind. Then the king cried mercy, saying, "Lord, let me not die till the good knight of my blood of the ninth degree be come, so that I may see him and kiss him, when he shall achieve the Sangrail." And this prayer was granted, for he heard a voice that said, "When that knight shall come, the clearness of your eyes shall be restored and your wounds shall he healed." Now this same man you see here is King Evelake, who has lived three-hundred winters this holy life. And, sir, men say that the knight is even now in the court that shall heal him.'

Therewith Sir Percival departed, and met about noon some twenty men of arms that carried in a bier a knight deadly slain.

'From whence are you?' they asked Sir Percival.

'Of the court of King Arthur,' he answered.

Then they cried all at once, 'Slay him!'

So they rushed together, giving many sad and fierce blows. Percival's horse was slain under him. And he also might have suffered thus had not, by adventure, Sir Galahad, bearing the red arms, come unto those parts. And when he saw all those men upon one knight he cried, 'Save me that knight's life'.

Then Galahad smote out on the right hand and on the left hand, and it was a marvel to see how he put those men to a rebuke. After a time they fled into the thickness of the trees, and Sir Galahad followed them hard.

When Sir Percival saw him chase them so, he knew well it was Sir Galahad, and made great sorrow that he had no horse. 'Fair knight,' he called loudly, 'abide and suffer me to thank you. You have done much for me.' But Galahad rode so fast he soon was out of sight.

Still Percival followed after on foot, calling out. Soon came a knight riding, clean armed and on a black horse, and behind him pricked a yeoman on a hackney as fast as he might, crying out, 'Woe is me, he has stolen my horse, wherefore my lord will slay me. Sir, take my hackney and pursue him as best you may, and I will follow on foot.'

Sir Percival mounted on the hackney and followed the black horse, that went but at an ambling pace. Soon Sir Percival overtook the knight and they fell to words, and then to battle. The knight dressed his spear and smote the hackney dead, giving Percival a great fall, and then rode on his way.

'Abide, wicked knight,' roared Sir Percival in mad anger. 'Coward and false-hearted knight, turn again and fight with me on foot.'

But he answered not and went his way. Then Percival cast his helm and sword on the earth and sorrowed till night, when he laid him down and slept.

He waked at midnight and saw a woman who said unto him right fiercely, 'Sir Percival, what do you here?'

'Truly, I do neither good nor great ill,' he replied.

'If you fulfill my will,' said she, 'I shall lend you my own horse that will bear you wherever you wish.'

Thus it was agreed, and she came soon with a horse that was inky black. Percival marvelled that it was so large and well apparelled, but hardily he leapt upon it and spurred into the forest where the moon shone clear.

Within an hour the horse had carried him four days' journey to a rough, roaring water. The horse would have borne him into it. But when he saw the water so boisterous, Percival made a sign of the cross on his forehead. At once the horse shook him off and dashed into the water neighing and bellowing, and it seemed that the water burnt. Then Sir Percival perceived that the horse was a fiend, which would have brought him to his perdition. So he got on his knees and commended himself unto God, and prayed all the night to keep him from such temptation.

On the morn, in the clearness of the light, he saw he was in a wild mountain closed around by the sea, with wild beasts all about. As he looked into a valley he saw a serpent bring a young lion by the neck. With that came a great lion roaring after the serpent to do battle. Sir Percival thought to help the lion, for it was the more natural beast of the two. Percival gave the serpent a deadly wound, then he did off his helm to gather his wind, for he was greatly heated with the serpent. And the fierce lion went about him fawning as a spaniel, before it took its little whelp and bore it away.

Then Sir Percival was alone, but comforted himself in Jesu Christ. For in those days there were but few people that believed in God perfectly. In those days the son spared not the father no more than a stranger. But Sir Percival was not one of them. Thus, when he had prayed, he saw the lion come again and lie down at his feet. All that night, the lion and he slept together.

In the morn, he arose and blessed himself, though he felt himself feeble. Then as he looked towards the sea he saw a ship come sailing covered in a rich silk, with an old man therein in the likeness of a priest.

'God keep you,' said the old man, 'but of whence be you?'

'I am of King Arthur's court,' replied Percival, 'a knight of the Round Table. I and many fellows are in quest of the Sangrail. But here I am in great duress, and never like to escape out of this wilderness.'

'Doubt not,' said the old man, 'if you be as true a knight as the order of chivalry requires, and of good heart, no enemy shall slay you. But I am come to comfort you.' He spoke this and departed.

While Sir Percival sat upon the rock thinking upon this, and stroking the lion that ever kept him company, he saw another ship come as if all the wind of the world had driven it. It was covered with the blackest silk, and in it was a lady of great beauty.

'I have come out of the waste forest,' said this lady, 'where I found the red knight with the white shield.'

'Ah, madam,' said Percival, 'with that knight I would gladly meet.'

'Sir knight,' she replied, 'if you shall do my will, I shall bring you unto that knight.'

So Percival promised to fulfill her desire, and then she asked him if he had ate any meat of late.

'Nay truly, madam,' he said, 'none this three days. But late I spake with a good man that fed me his good and holy words, and refreshed me greatly.'

'Beware, sir,' she replied, 'that same man is an enchanter and a multiplier of words. If you believe him you shall plainly be shamed, and die on this rock for pure hunger. But if you be a young and goodly knight, I shall help you.'

'What are you that proffer me such kindness?'

'Sir, I dwelt with the greatest man of the world and he made me so fair and clear that there was none like me. And of that great beauty I had a little pride more than I ought. So he drove me from his company, and from my heritage, and never had pity of me. As you are a good knight, I beseech you to help me. And as you are a fellow of the Round Table, you ought not to fail a gentlewoman who is disherited.'

Then Sir Percival promised her all help. As the weather was hot, she called forth a pavilion from the ship, saying, 'Sir, now rest you in the heat of the day.' She put off his helm and put her cool hand upon his brow, and so he slept.

When he awoke there was all manner of meat set upon a table, and he drank the strongest wine he ever knew. Therewith he was a little heated. So he beheld the lady and thought she was the fairest creature ever seen. He proffered her love and prayed that she would be his. But she refused him, in a manner so that he would be the more ardent on her. Then when she saw him very well heated, she gave herself to him, on understanding that he should do whatever she commanded.

'Now shall you do with me,' she said, 'whatsoever it pleases you.'

She unclothed and lay in a bed of the pavilion, and Sir Percival laid him down by her naked. As he lay, by adventure and grace he saw his sword on the ground with a red cross on the pommel. Then he bethought him on his knighthood and his promise unto the good old man. He signed the cross on his forehead, and therewith the pavilion turned upside down and changed into a black cloud of smoke.

'Sweet Father, Jesu Christ,' Sir Percival cried out adread, 'I am nigh lost, but let me not be shamed.'

And from the ship came a voice of Despair, saying, 'Ah, Sir Percival, you have betrayed me.' With that she went with the wind and the gale, and it seemed that all the water burnt after her.

Then in sorrow Sir Percival drew his sword and said, 'Since my flesh shall be my master, I shall punish it.' And he thrust himself through the thigh, so that the blood started about him as he cried, 'O good Lord, take this in recompense for what I have done against you.'

Therewith he clothed and armed him, and wrapped a piece of his shirt to staunch his bleeding, and said to himself the while, 'Wretch that I am, how near I was to have lost my virginity, that which may never be recovered once lost.'

As he made this moan, he saw coming from the Orient the ship of the good old man. When he was landed, Sir Percival went unto him weakly and told him what had passed.

'O knight,' said the good man, 'you are a fool. That gentlewoman was the master fiend of hell, that has power above all devils. Now beware, lord Percival, and take this for an example.'

Then the good man vanished way. So Sir Percival took arms and entered into the ship, and departed from thence.

✢ The Way to the ✢ Spiritual City

When Sir Gawain first departed on the adventure of the Holy Grail he rode many journeys forwards and backwards, but nothing worth the name did he discover. At last he came to the abbey where Galahad had found the white shield, and he asked of the monks the way to pursue after Sir Galahad.

'Certes,' Gawain told them, 'I am unhappy that I took not the way he went. If I meet him I will hold fast to him, for all marvellous adventures come to him.'

'But what, sir, are you?' asked a monk.

'Truly, I am a knight of King Arthur that am in the quest of the Sangrail, and my name is Sir Gawain.'

'Well, sir,' said the good man, 'we know the noise of your fame. Sir Galahad will not be of your fellowship, because you are wicked and sinful and he is full blessed. But tell me, sir, how stands it betwixt God and you at this time?'

So Sir Gawain showed his life to that good man. And the monk reproved him, saying, 'When you were first made knight you should have taken to knightly deeds and virtuous living. But you have done the contrary, and have lived mischievously many winters. Yet Sir Galahad is a maid, and a sinner never. And for that reason he shall achieve wherever he goes, which neither you nor none of your fellowship shall attain. For you have lived the most untrue life that ever I heard. So now, Sir Gawain, you must do penance for your sins.'

'Sir, what penance shall I do?'

'Such as I will give,' said the good man.

'Nay,' replied Gawain, 'I may do no penance. For we knights adventurous often suffer great woe and pain.'

'Well,' said the good man. And then he held his peace.

So Sir Gawain departed and rode long. But he found not the tenth part of adventure as he was wont to do. He rode from Whitsuntide until Michaelmas and found nothing that pleased him. So it befell on a day that Gawain met with Sir Ector de Maris, and after either made great joy of the other they complained that they could find no adventure.

'Truly,' said Sir Gawain, 'I am nigh weary of this quest, and loath to follow further in strange countries.'

'I marvel,' said Sir Ector, 'that I have met with twenty knights, all fellows of mine, and they all complain as we do.'

'But I wonder,' said Gawain, 'where is Sir Lancelot, your brother?'

'Truly, I hear nothing of him, nor of Galahad, Percival nor Bors.'

'Let them be,' said Gawain, 'for they four have no peers. And if they fail of the Sangrail, it is a waste for all the remnant to try to recover it.'

Ector and Gawain rode eight more days. Then they came to a wasted empty chapel, all broken, and there they set their spears by the door and made their orisons a great while, till for heaviness they fell asleep. Within a while they awoke yawning and Sir Ector said, 'Truly, I shall never be merry till I hear tidings of my brother Lancelot.'

As they sat talking they saw a hand showing unto the elbow, covered with a red silk cloth. Upon that hung a bridle, and held within the fist was a great candle that burned clear. It passed before them into the chapel and vanished away.

Anon came a voice that said, 'Knights full of evil faith and poor belief, for this reason you have failed. Therefore you may not come to the adventures of the Holy Grail.'

'Ector,' cried Gawain, 'heard you those words?'

'Yea, I heard all. Now let us go to some hermit that will tell of this vision, for it seems to me we labour all in vain.'

So they inquired of a squire on the path to know where there was a hermit. He told them of a poor house on a little mountain where Nacien was, the holiest man in the country. They rode till they came to the rough mountain and could ride no further. Then they went on foot to a poor house by a chapel where, in a little courtyard, Nacien gathered the plants and herbs that were his meat. When the hermit saw the knights errant he saluted them and made ready to confess them. After they had told him much, he knew well what they were. And he thought to counsel them.

'I will tell you,' he said, 'what betokens the hand with the candle. That is the Holy Ghost, where charity is ever. And the bridle signifies abstinence. For when a Christian man's heart is bridled in, he falls not in deadly sin. And the clear candle signifies the right way of Jesu Christ. And this voice has warned you that you have failed in these three things: in charity, abstinence and truth. Therefore you may not attain the high adventure of the Sangrail.'

'Good sir,' said Gawain, 'it seems by your words it will not avail us to travel in this quest.'

'Truly,' replied Nacien, 'there be a hundred such as you that never shall prevail but to have shame. And as to you, Sir Gawain, it is a long time since you were made knight, and never have you served your maker. Now you are so old a tree, there is neither leaf nor fruit in you. Therefore bethink you that you yield to Our Lord the bare rind, since the fiend has the leaves and the fruit.'

'Sir, had I leisure I would speak with you,' said Gawain. 'But my fellow here, Sir Ector, is gone and awaits me yonder beneath the hill.'

'Better that you were counselled,' warned the hermit. But Sir Gawain rode away with Sir Ector and dropped quickly off that mountain. And still they rode long and far before they could find any adventure.

As these two knights were going about and about seeking strange things, Sir Bors also had departed from Camelot in the quest of the Holy Grail. Soon he met a religious man, riding on an ass, and sought counsel of him. For Sir Bors knew that he who brought the quest of the Sangrail to an end would have much earthly honour. So they rode together to a hermitage and prayed. Then Sir Bors clean confessed, and they ate bread and drank water together.

'Now,' said the good man, 'eat none other till you sit at the table where the Sangrail shall be.'

'That I agree to,' said Bors, 'but how do you know that I shall sit there?'

'Yea, I know it, though there shall be but few of your fellows there with you.'

'All is welcome,' said Sir Bors, 'that God sends me.'

Then Bors took his leave. As he rode on a little from thence he looked into an old tree and saw a great bird on a dry branch without leaves. Below the bird were chicks dead for hunger. So the bird smote itself with a sharp beak and bled until it died among its chicks. And suddenly the young birds took life by the spent blood of the great bird. When Sir Bors saw this, he knew well that it was a great tokening. He went on his way in heaviness and thought, and so by evensong he came to a high tower where he gladly lodged.

On the morn, further into the forest, at a parting of the paths, Bors saw approaching a small company of knights. As they came closer he saw two knights that led Lionel, his brother, all naked and bound upon a stout hackney. And these knights beat Lionel with thorns so sore that the blood trailed down more than a hundred places of his body. But Lionel said never a word, and in his great heart suffered all that they might do.

At once, Sir Bors dressed himself to rescue his brother. But as he was ready he looked on the other side and saw a knight riding off with a fair gentlewoman towards the thickest place of the forest, and she was crying out, 'Saint Mary succour your maid.'

Sir Bors saw and heard all this, but he knew not what to do.

'Must my brother be slain?' he lamented. 'Or shall this maid lose her virginity?'

Then he lifted up weeping eyes and prayed, 'Sweet Jesu Christ, whose liegeman I am, keep safe Lionel, my brother, while for Mary's sake I shall succour this maid.'

By great strength Bors beat down the knight and rescued the lady. But he could not stay for thanks, so he commended her to God and rode fast after Lionel, following the trace of his horse. In a while he overtook a man in religious clothing, riding a horse blacker than a berry. Sir Bors called out to him, 'Sir, I seek my brother. Have you seen a misfortunate, naked man beaten by two knights?'

'Ah, Bors, discomfort you not,' said the man, 'nor fall into despair, for I tell you sad tidings that he is truly dead.'

The man took him to a new-slain body lying in a bush, and it seemed well that it was the body of Lionel. So Sir Bors wept his sorrow over the body. 'Fair brother,' he cried, 'now that you have left me I shall never have joy in my heart.' Then he took the body lightly in his arms and put it upon his sadlebow. And when he came to a chapel by a tower, he placed the body into a fair tomb of marble.

As he mourned, Bors said to the one in religious clothes who was still with him, 'Good man, I have dreamt some dreams. Sir, tell me the meaning of my visions.' When he heard these dreams the man warned Lors that they betokened danger to Sir Lancelot, he that was the cousin of Sir Bors.

'My lord Lancelot,' said the man, 'might die by your default, just as you let Sir Lionel die.'

'I hear and understand your exposition,' replied Bors humbly.

'That maid was nothing to you,' said the man in black clothing, 'yet you chose to rescue her while Lionel died. So it will be in your default if your cousin Sir Lancelot shall die.'

'Alas, that I am loath, for I dread more than anything in the world to see Sir Lancelot die by my default.'

Then the man in black led Sir Bors into the tower nearby, where ladies made him welcome and unarmed him. When he was in his doublet they brought him a mantle furred with ermine, and they made him such good cheer that he forgot all his sorrow and anguish. He set his heart on delights and dainties and took no more thought on Lancelot or Lionel. Anon came a fair lady with soft words, and she was more beautiful than Queen Guenevere. She said she loved him, though when he understood that language he was abashed. He was right ill at ease and would not break chastity, so he knew not how to answer her.

'Alas,' she sighed, 'shall you not do my will? I have loved you long for your great beauty and hardiness. Grant me, I pray you Bors, that you lie by me this night.'

'Nay,' said he, 'in no wise shall I do it.'

Therewith she took him by the hand and said most sweetly, 'Now you shall see how I die for your love.' So she stood him at the foot of the tower and went with her twelve gentlewomen unto a high battlement. Then a voice cried from above, 'Sir Bors, have mercy on us all and do my lady's will. Or we must suffer death with our lady, falling together from this high tower.'

He looked upwards and saw them, all ladies of great estate, and he had great pity for them. Then at once they fell down unto the earth, and he was all abashed. Anon he heard a loud noise, as though all the fiends of hell had been about him. And looking on every side he saw neither tower, nor lady, nor gentlewomen, nor even the chapel where he thought he had brought his brother Lionel.

'Fair Father God,' he said, lifting hands to heaven, 'I am grievously escaped.' And with haste he took arms and horse, and rode away at a gallop.

After he had journeyed some days, Sir Bors went towards a castle where he was advised of a great tournament. So he rode in that way, hoping to meet with his brother Lionel or any other of his fellowship in the quest of the Sangrail. At the entry of a forest he found a knight sitting all armed and he saw that it was Lionel, abiding the start of the tourney. Bors greeted his brother with great joy. But Lionel drew back from him and said, 'Ah brother, as for you I might have been slain. You left me in peril of death to succour a gentlewoman. That was as great an untruth as ever brother did to brother. For that misdeed I owe you death, and well you have deserved it. Therefore, save you if you may.'

When Sir Bors understood his brother's anger, he knelt and cried him mercy, holding up both his hands. But Lionel would have no pity. 'I make my vow to God,' he said, 'you shall have death for it.'

Right so he took his harness and mounted upon his horse. Then Sir Bors saw that he must fight or die, but still he knew not what to do, so still he knelt at the horse's feet. Whereupon Lionel rushed his horse over him, and the horse's feet smote Bors unto a sore distress so that he swooned. Then Lionel alighted and would have rent the helm from the head of Bors for to kill him, had not a good hermit of great age come running from his nearby hermitage and thrown himself across Sir Bors.

'Ah gentle knight,' the hermit cried, 'have mercy upon me and your brother. If you slay him you shall be dead of sin, and that were most sorrowful.'

'God help me, sir priest,' said Lionel, 'leave or I slay you.'

'Certes,' replied the good man, 'I had rather you slay me than him.'

'Well, I am agreed,' said Lionel, and he struck him so hard with his sword that the hermit's head flew off backwards. Then Lionel took his brother by the helm and unlaced it to have slain him without fail.

Now it happed that the knight Colgrevaunce, a fellow of the Round Table, was at that time travelling to the tournament. When he beheld the death of the good man, he marvelled at it. But he took Lionel strongly by the shoulders and pulled him back from Sir Bors. Then Lionel defied him and gave him a great stroke on the helm, and thus they began to fight. And while they fought long Sir Bors awoke and rose up anguished, full sorry and heavy that either man might be slain.

Bors would have risen to depart, but his feet were all unsteady. So he abode till Colgrevaunce had the worse, for Lionel was of great chivalry and right hardy, and he pierced Colgrevaunce so that he was nigh to death for loss of blood. 'Ah, Bors,' he called out weakly, 'why come you not to save me from peril of death? Did I not come to your succour?'

'That shall avail you nothing,' said Lionel, 'but you shall both die of my hand.'

Then Sir Colgrevaunce called again unto Bors, 'Why will you let me die here for your sake? It will please me better if you save a worthy man.'

But he could not escape, and Lionel smote him dead to the earth. With that, Lionel ran upon his brother like a fiend and gave him a stroke that made him stoop.

So Sir Bors drew his sword, all weeping, and said, 'Fair brother, you have done full evil this day, to slay a holy priest and a gentle knight that was one of your fellows. Know well that I am not greatly adread of you, but I fear the wrath of God. This is an unkindly war, therefore God show miracle upon us both.'

Right so a cloud came betwixt them in the likeness of a fire, so that both their two shields burnt. And they heard a voice that said, 'Flee Bors and touch him not, or else you shall slay him.'

Then they were sore afraid and they both fell to the earth. Again they heard a voice say, 'Bors, go hence, and bear your brother no longer fellowship. Take your way right to the sea, for Sir Percival awaits you there.'

So the brothers with many tears forgave each, the one and the other, and Sir Bors rode the next way to the sea. On the strand he found a ship covered all in silk of white and gold. As soon as he entered, the ship departed and went so fast it seemed like flying. But darkness came on and Sir Bors slept till day.

When he awaked he saw a knight all armed save his helm, and he knew it was Sir Percival. Then said Sir Percival, 'We lack nothing but Galahad, the good knight.'

After Sir Galahad had rescued Sir Percival from the twenty knights, he began to take his way to the sea. As he journeyed it befell that he saw a great battle before a castle. Those without were slaying the defenders at the gate without mercy, and those within were at a great mischief. Then Galahad put forth a spear and thought to help them.

Now it happed that Sir Gawain and Sir Ector were with the men outside. And when they espied the white shield with the red cross, one said to other, 'Yonder is Sir Galahad. He that would meet with him in fight should be a great fool.'

Then by adventure Galahad came upon Gawain, and felled him to the earth with a stroke that split his helm and his cap of iron into his head, and also carved his horse's shoulder in two. Thus with great hardiness Sir Galahad helped those within. At last the defenders issued from the gates and chased their enemies all about. But when Galahad saw all these knights flee, he stole away privily so none knew where he went.

'By my head,' said Gawain woefully to Ector, 'now is the wonder come true, as Sir Lancelot said, that the sword stuck in the stone should give me such a buffet that I would not have it for the best castle in the world.'

'So, sir,' replied Sir Ector, 'it seems your quest is done.'

'Mine, but not yours,' said Gawain. 'I shall seek no further.'

Meanwhile Sir Galahad rode a long time towards the Castle of Carbonek. That night there came to him a maiden who bade him follow her and promised him the highest adventure that ever knight saw. So she led him to a castle by the sea, where her lady was. He ate and slept a while, and then the maid called him by torchlight to go with her lady to a ship by the shore. They went aboard, he and the lady, and heard voices greet them.

'Welcome, Sir Galahad,' called out Bors and Percival from within that ship. 'We have abided you long.'

'As for you, good knights,' answered Galahad, 'I never thought to find you in these strange countries.'

'If only,' said Bors, 'Lancelot, your father, were here, then were we all at ease, and would nothing fail.'

The wind arose and drove them through the sea away from the land of Logris, till they sailed betwixt two great rocks where a whirlpool roared. Their ship might not go there, but another awaited them. Thither the lady took them, saying unto Percival, 'Know well, sir, that I am your sister, daughter unto King Pellinore. And this I must tell you: if you be not in perfect belief of Jesu Christ, enter not this ship, or else you shall perish.'

Therewith Sir Percival answered her gladly, 'Fair sister, I shall enter therein, for if I be an untrue knight I shall willingly perish.'

Then they entered all, one by one, and in the midst of the ship was a most rich bed and at the foot was a sword of divers rich fashion, half-drawn out of the sheath.

'Sir,' said Percival's sister, 'there was a king called Pelles, the Maimed King, who supported much Christendom and Holy Church. Once, in hunting, he drove towards the sea so fiercely that he lost his hounds and his knights save only one. The two went then towards Ireland, and there they found this ship. They entered, for the king was right perfect of his life, but his knight was not beyond sin. The king found this sword and drew it out as much as you see now. But therewith a spear came suddenly, none knew whence, and smote him through both his thighs. And never since might he be healed till we shall come before him. So tell me, Sir Galahad, was not King Pelles your grandsire, maimed for his hardiness?'

'Yea, in the name of God,' replied Galahad. 'But as to this sword now, where shall we find the gentlewoman to make new girdles for it?'

Then the lady opened a box and took out girdles that were seemly wrought with golden threads and set with precious stones and a buckle of gold.

'Lo, lords,' she said, 'here is a girdle for the sword. The greatest part of this girdle was made of my hair, which I loved while I was a woman of the world. But as soon as this adventure was ordained for me, I clipped off my hair and made this girdle in the name of God.'

So she took the girdle and set it about the sword and said, 'The name of this weapon is the Sword with the Strange Girdle, and the sheath is the Mover of Blood.'

Then they all said to Sir Galahad, 'In the name of Jesu Christ, we pray you that you gird yourself with this sword, which has been so much desired in all the realm of Logris.'

'Well,' said Galahad, 'now let me begin to grip this sword to give you courage.'

He gripped about it and held it fast in his fingers. Then the sister of Percival took it and girt it about his middle, saying 'I care not if I die, for now I hold me one of the blessed of the world, who has become the worthiest knight of the world.'

'Maiden,' answered Galahad, 'you have done so much that I shall be your knight all the days of my life.'

Soon the wind blew hard and they went a great pace in the sea, and drove upon rocks in the marshes of Scotland. And then they were in much danger. But they recked it not and trusted in God to deliver them. Safely they came out of those wastes and rode upon the way, seeking the Maimed King who had abided so long to be healed.

As they journeyed, there came a knight all armed after them and said, 'Lords, hark what I say. This lady that you lead, is she a maid?'

'Sir,' she replied, 'a maid I am.'

In the meantime twelve knights came from the castle, and with them was a gentlewoman who held a silver dish. As they came near, one of the knights said, 'Sirs, each maid that passes hereby shall give this dish full of blood.'

'Blame unto him who brought up such a custom,' said Sir Galahad. 'I assure you this lady will not fulfill it while I live.' And so also said Bors and Percival.

Therewith the two parties ran at each other and began to meddle together. Galahad drew the sword with the strange girdle and slew on the right hand and on the left hand, so that all who saw him thought him no earthly man but a monster. And his two fellows helped him passing well. When this prowess was seen from the castle, an envoy came humbly at nightfall and offered them safe lodging, saying, 'Sirs, when you know the custom of this castle, we daresay you will accord.'

So they entered and had some welcome, though they looked over the shoulder right and left. Then it was told them that the lady of the castle had a sickness beyond any doctor, that might only be cured if she were anointed with the blood of a clean virgin.

Then was Percival's sister sad. 'Fair knights,' she said, 'I see now that this gentlewoman is like to die.'

'Certes,' said Galahad, 'but if you shall bleed for her as much as a dish you may die.'

'Truly, if I die to heal her I shall get great honour and soul's health, and worship to my lineage. Let there be no more battle. On the morn I shall yield to the custom.'

In the dawning, after Mass, the sick lady was brought forth. Then Percival's sister bled of her body a full dish, and the lady blessed her for it. But the maid said to her weakly, 'Madam, I feel my life spirit drain away, and I am come to the death to make you whole. For the love of God, pray for me.' With that she fell in a swoon.

At once Galahad and his fellows sprang to her and staunched her. But she had bled so much that she might not live. Between swooning and waking, she whispered to Sir Percival, 'Fair brother, bury me not in this country. Put me in a boat and let me go as adventure will lead me. And when you three come to the city of Sarras, to achieve the Holy Grail, you shall find me arrived there. For I say to all you that you also shall be buried in the same place.'

Then she received from the priest the body of her Saviour, and her soul departed.

Forthwith there fell a sudden tempest, thunder, lightning and rain, as if all the castle would have broken, and all was turned upsodown. This lasted until evensong. And when, in the darkening air, Galahad and Percival went about to see what was fallen, they found in the castle neither man nor woman left alive.

With that they heard a voice that said, 'This vengeance is for bloodshedding of maidens.'

'Now,' said the three knights one to another, 'we must depart each our way. Let us pray Our Lord that we meet together in short time.' Then they did off their helms, and kissed, and wept, and departed.

At this time Sir Lancelot was also come nigh the sea, by the waters of Mortaise. He felt himself in peril and knew not what to do. So he lay down to sleep, and took the adventure that God would send him.

As he slept there came a vision that said to him, 'Lancelot, arise up and enter into the first ship you shall find.' So he started up and saw great clearness about him. He took his arms and came to a strand where he found a ship without sail or oar. He went within and of a sudden felt the most sweetness he ever knew, and he was fulfilled of all desires.

'Sweet Father,' he prayed, 'Jesu Christ, what is this joy? For it passes all earthly joys that ever I felt.'

Then he lay on the ship's boards and slept till daylight. When he awoke, he saw a rich bed, and on it was a lady dead, who was the sister of Sir Percival. In her right hand was a writ, and when Lancelot had read it he understood all her adventure and her lineage.

147

So Sir Lancelot went a month on this barge with this dead lady. And as to how he lived, he was fed as did He who fed the people of Israel with manna in the desert. He said his prayers, and he was sustained with the grace of the Holy Ghost.

One night as the boat drifted to shore, Sir Lancelot went out of the barge to play by the waterside. He heard a knight come riding. This knight came softly unto the barge and alighted, and put his horse from him and went into the boat. As he went on the boards, Sir Lancelot saluted him and the knight replied right gladly, 'But what, sir, is your name? For much my heart gives unto you.'

'Truly,' he said, 'my name is Sir Lancelot du Lake.'

'Sir,' answered the knight, 'then you are welcome. For you were the beginner of me in the world.'

'Are you Galahad?'

'Yea, forsooth.' And so Galahad knelt and asked him blessing, and there was more joy between them than tongue can tell. And always, beside them, was the dead lady in the bed. Then Sir Galahad looked upon her face and he knew her well. Her death, so he said, was the greatest pity.

Lancelot and Galahad dwelt within that ship half a year, and served God with all their power. One time, on a Monday, it befell that they saw by the shore a knight armed all in white and leading a white horse. He beckoned them and saluted them and said, 'Galahad, you have been long enough with your father. Come out of the boat and start upon this horse, and go where the adventures shall lead you in the quest of the Holy Grail.'

Sir Galahad made him ready. He kissed his father and said, 'Sweet father, shall I not see you more, till at last I see the body of Jesu Christ?'

With that he took the horse. And then they heard a voice sound in the air: 'Think for to do well, for the one shall never see the other before the dreadful day of doom.'

'Now, son Galahad,' said Lancelot, 'since we shall depart and never see other again, I pray to the High Father to conserve me and you both.'

'Sir,' said his son, 'no prayer avails so much as yours.'

Then Sir Galahad rode away. Lancelot turned back to the boat and the wind blew fresh, driving the barge a month through the sea. By adventure, on a night at midnight, he landed before a castle, on the back side, and saw a gate opened towards the sea, with two lions keeping it. And the moon shone clear.

Soon a voice called, 'Lancelot, enter into the castle, where you shall see a great part of your desire.'

He ran to his arms and went to the gate with drawn sword. But a dwarf at the gate struck his arm suddenly so that his sword fell. Again a voice was heard, saying, 'O man of evil faith, why trust you more in your arms than in your Maker?'

'Father Jesu Christ,' Lancelot replied, 'I thank you that you reprove me. Now I see that you hold me for your servant.'

So he entered the castle with his sword in its sheath, and found all doors open till he came to the last chamber. He set his hand on the door thereto, but he could not open it.

He struggled much with the door. Then he heard a voice singing so sweetly that it seemed no earthly thing. So Sir Lancelot knelt before the chamber, for he knew then that the Holy Grail was within.

'O Jesu,' he prayed, 'sweet Father, if ever I pleased you hold me not in despite for my sins, but show me something of what I seek.'

With that the door opened and there came out a great clearness, so that the house was as bright as all the torches of the world. Then he would have entered, but again a voice spoke and said, 'Flee, Lancelot, and enter not.'

At once he withdrew aback right heavy. He looked into the chamber and saw the holy vessel, covered with red and gold silk on a silver table, with many angels about it. And a priest, at the consecration of the Mass, held up his hands so heavy, and it seemed the very body of Christ was betwixt them. Lancelot marvelled, for he thought the priest would fall to earth, so greatly charged of the figure was he. When none would help him, Lancelot came swiftly forwards and cried, 'O Jesu Christ, take it as no sin if I give needful help to this good man.'

Right so he entered the chamber. But as he came nigh to the silver table, he felt a hot breath intermeddled with fire that scored over his face. Therewith he fell to earth. He could not rise, for he had lost the power of his body, and his hearing and his seeing. Then he felt many hands about him. They bore him out of the chamber, and left him seeming dead to all the people.

On the morrow, when it was fair day, the folk found Sir Lancelot lying before the chamber door. So they took him up and placed him in a rich bed, hid far from all people, and one said he was alive and the other said nay. Then spoke a wise old man and said, 'He is not dead, but so full of life as the mightiest of you. I counsel you that he be well kept until God send him breath and spirits again.'

In such manner they kept Sir Lancelot four-and-twenty days and nights. And on the twenty-fifth, after midday, he opened his eyes.

'Why have you awaked me?' he lamented to the folk. 'I was more at ease among marvels of secretness than I am now.'

'Well, my lord,' they said unto him, 'how stands it with you?'

'Forsooth, I am whole of body,' said he, 'thanked be Our Lord. But sirs, for the love of God tell me where I am.'

'This, sir, is the Castle of Carbonek.'

Therewith came a gentlewoman with a shirt of small linen cloth. Sir Lancelot would not change to it but took the hair shirt again, as he had vowed to the hermit before. Then the people said to him, 'Sir, now the quest of the Sangrail is achieved for you. You shall see no more.'

'I thank God,' he said, 'for it suffices me. In seeing this, I suppose no man in this world has been more fortunate than I.'

So he put on the hair shirt, and above that a linen shirt, and then a robe of scarlet, fresh and new. When he was so arrayed, all the folk marvelled at his comeliness and knew him for what he was, the good knight.

'O my lord Sir Lancelot,' they cried out, 'be that you?'

And he answered, 'Truly I am he.'

In the meantime, word came to King Pelles within the castle that the knight thought dead was Sir Lancelot. Then was the king right glad, and gladly they met together. Thus they had much talking, at the end of which the king gave Lancelot sad tidings. The king's daughter, fair Elaine, was dead.

'Sir, 'tis the greatest pity,' said Lancelot, 'for she was a full beauteous lady, fresh and young. And she bore the best knight that is now on earth, or that ever was since God was born.'

After a time, when they had feasted and had great joy together, Lancelot departed from King Pelles, for he said that he would see the realm of Logris again, which he had not seen in a twelvemonth. He travelled far. And on a bright day in the morn he turned unto Camelot, where he found King Arthur and Queen Guenevere. But more than half of the knights of the Round Table were slain and destroyed. Sir Ector, Sir Gawain and Sir Lionel were three that came home. But of Sir Galahad at that time there were no tidings.

Meanwhile Sir Galahad rode many journeys in vain. Then by adventure he came into a perilous forest where a well boiled with great waves. But as soon as Galahad set his hand to it, it burnt no more. For the heat was a sign of lechery, which was at that time much used. But that heat might not abide his pure virginity. And for this miracle the place was called ever after Galahad's Well.

Then Sir Galahad went on towards the Maimed King, and after five days he met with Sir Percival. They journeyed on together, traversing the wild ways, through tangles and bushes, till they happed to see Sir Bors riding alone. He was full of gladness to meet them and said, 'In more than a year and a half I have not lain ten times where men dwell, but only set my head on stones and earth, amid forest and mountain, where God alone was my comfort.'

All rode together many a mile until they came to the Castle of Carbonek. When they were entered into the castle, King Pelles knew them. And then there was great joy, for every man knew well by this arrival that the quest of the Holy Grail was fulfilled.

Therewith it seemed that there came four angels bearing up in a chair a man in the likeness of a bishop, with a cross in his hand. They set him down in the chamber where the Sangrail was, by the table of silver, and on his forehead he showed these letters:

See you here Joseph, the first bishop of Christendom, whom Our Lord succoured in the city of Sarras, in the spiritual place.

The knights marvelled much, for that bishop had been dead more than three hundred years. But the bishop said, 'O knights, marvel not, for I was sometime an earthly man.'

Then they saw angels bearing candles and a towel, and another carried a spear that bled three drops into a box. The bishop began to say the Mass, even to the consecration, and took an oblation in the likeness of bread. But when he lifted it up, there appeared one like a child with a face as red and bright as any fire. So this child made himself into the bread, and they all saw that the bread was formed of a fleshly man.

With that the priest went to Galahad, and kissed him, and bade him kiss his fellows, Percival and Bors. And anon the priest said, 'Now, servants of Jesu Christ, you shall be fed at this table with sweet meats that never knights tasted.'

151

Then the bishop vanished away. They came to the table in great dread, and made their prayers. And when they would dare look up, they saw a man come out of the holy vessel, and this man had all the signs of the passion of Jesu Christ, bleeding all openly from his wounds.

'My knights, and my servants, and my true children,' the man said, you are come out of deadly life into spiritual life. Now shall you see a part of my secrets and my hidden things. Now hold and receive this high meat that you have so much desired.'

He took the holy vessel and came to Sir Galahad, who knelt and received his Saviour. And after him so received both his fellows, Bors and Percival. Then said the man to Galahad, 'Son, know you what I hold betwixt my hands?'

'Nay, but if you will tell me.'

'This is the holy dish wherein I ate the lamb at Easter. Now you have seen what you most desired, but not so openly as you shall see it in the city of Sarras, in the spiritual place. Therefore go hence and bear with you this holy vessel, that shall never more be seen in the realm of Logris. And for why? They of this land have turned to evil living. Therefore I shall disinherit them of the honour I have done them. So, you three, go tomorrow unto the sea, and take with you the sword with the strange girdle. But first take the blood of this spear and anoint the Maimed King, that he might be whole.'

He gave them his blessing and vanished away.

Therewith Sir Galahad went to the spear that lay upon the table. He touched the blood with his fingers. Then he came to Pelles, the Maimed King, and anointed his legs with the blood. At once, the king started upon his feet as a whole man and thanked Our Lord for his health. And soon, in recompense to Jesu Christ, he cast himself out of the kingship and took himself to a place of the white monks, where he joined with their fellowship as a full holy man.

Right so departed Galahad, Percival and Bors unto the ship that awaited them, and they found on board the silver table and the Sangrail covered with rich silk of red and gold. Thereto they made great reverence, and fell long time in prayer. In especial, Sir Galahad asked of Our Lord that He might permit His servant to pass out of this world what time it might please him. But when Sir Percival heard this, he said to Galahad, 'I pray you, of your fellowship, wherefore ask you this?'

'It is,' said Galahad, 'to taste a joy of heart that never earthly man had. When my body is dead, my soul shall see the Blessed Trinity every day, and the majesty of Jesu Christ.'

Then Sir Galahad slept amid the rocking of the waves. When he awaked he looked about him and saw the city of Sarras. And as they came to land they saw the ship wherein Percival had put his sister.

'Truly,' said Percival, 'in God's name, well has my sister kept her covenant.'

The three knights took her from the boat and brought her unto the palace, and buried her as solemnly as a king's daughter ought to be.

At the year's end it befell that the king of Sarras lay sick and felt that he would die. Now, he had done wrong to the three knights that came from afar to his city, for he came from a line of paynims and wished to put those Christians in deep prison. But feeling death upon him he cried them mercy, and they forgave him goodly. And soon he died.

Then by all the assent of the whole city, they made Galahad, the good knight, king of Sarras. When he had beheld the land, he made a chest of gold and precious stones, and in this he placed the silver table and the holy vessel of the Sangrail. And every day early the three fellow knights came before it to make their orisons. One time, on such a day, as they came in the morning light to the holy vessel, they saw a man like a bishop begin to say a Mass of Our Lady. When he came to the sacrament of the Mass, and accomplished it, he called to Sir Galahad, 'Come forth the servant of Jesu Christ, and you shall see what you have so much desired.'

Then Sir Galahad began to tremble right hard, as the deadly flesh began to behold the spiritual things. He held his hands towards heaven and said, 'I thank you, for now I see what has been my desire for many a day. Now I would no longer live, if it may please you, Lord.'

Therewith the priest took Our Lord's body in his hands, and proffered it to Galahad, and he received it most gladly and meekly.

'Know you what I am?' said the priest.

'Nay,' answered Galahad.

'I am Joseph, son of Joseph of Arimathea, whom the Lord has sent here to bear you fellowship. I came because you resemble me in two things: you have seen the marvels of the Holy Grail, and you have been a clean maiden, as I have been and am.'

Then Sir Galahad kissed Sir Percival and commended him to God, and likewise he kissed Sir Bors and commended him to God.

'Fair knights and fellows,' he said to them, 'salute me to my lord, Sir Lancelot, my father. When you see him, bid him remember of this unstable world.'

He knelt before the table and made his prayers. And suddenly a multitude of angels bore his departed soul up to heaven.

This his fellow knights saw. Then they saw a hand come from heaven, which caught up the holy vessel and the spear and carried them also up to heaven. And since that time no man has been so hardy as to say that he had seen the Holy Grail.

Sir Gawain and Sir Lancelot in mortal combat

Camelot

The death of Perceval's sister

la place. Enli q̃ j gn̄t mortalite del
roi artu et de mordres son fil la v il
furent tout destruit.

vant li rois ar tus voit
celui cop si dist trop do
lans. ha: dieu por quoi
me laissies vos tant abaissier de

King Arthur's last battle

✤ Lancelot and Guenevere ✤

hen Sir Percival and Sir Bors saw Galahad dead, if they had not been good men, they might easily have fallen in despair. As soon as Galahad was buried, Percival retired him to a hermitage and took a religious clothing. And Bors was always with him, but unchanged in habit, for he purposed at some time to go again into the realm of Logris.

Thus for a year and two months Sir Percival lived a full-holy life. Then he passed out of this world, and Bors buried him by his sister and by Galahad in the spiritual city. Then Sir Bors saw that he was in a far country, as far even as Babylon, and he departed from Sarras. So it befell him by good adventure that he came over the sea unto Logris. And once he was on the land he rode as fast as he might to Camelot, where King Arthur was.

Now after the quest of the Holy Grail was fulfilled, all knights that were left alive came again unto the Round Table. Their number was not so many as had been, and so King Arthur and the queen made great joy of this remnant. And in especial they were glad of Sir Bors and Sir Lancelot, for they had been a weary long time away in the search of the Sangrail.

Then Sir Lancelot began to resort unto Queen Guenevere again, and forgot the promise and the perfection that he had made in the quest.

Ever his thoughts were privily on the queen, and so they loved together hotter than they did before. They had such secret close meeting one with the other that many in the court spake of it, and in especial Sir Agravaine, Gawain's brother, for he was ever open-mouthed.

At this time also many ladies and maidens resorted to Sir Lancelot, beseeching him to be their champion. And Lancelot applied him daily in such matters of right, in the name of Jesu Christ. Thus he tried to withdraw himself somewhat from the company of Queen Guenevere, to eschew the slander and noise. Then the queen waxed angry with him, and sent for him unto her chamber.

'Sir Lancelot,' she said, 'I feel daily that your love begins to slake. You have no joy in my presence, but ever you are out of this court, concerning the quarrels of other ladies. You were never wont to do this beforehand.'

'Ah madam,' replied Lancelot, 'hold me excused. I was but late in the quest of the Sangrail and I saw great mysteries, as much as ever saw sinful man. I may not lightly forget that high service. Also, madam, many speak of our love in this court, as Sir Agravaine and Sir Mordred. Madam, I dread them more for your sake than for mine. If you fall in any distress through wilful folly, then there is none other remedy but by me and my blood. For know you well that our boldness may bring us to a great shame and slander, and I am loath to see you dishonoured. That is why I take upon me more ado for maidens than ever I did, so that men should understand my joy is elsewhere than only with you.'

The queen stood still. But when she had heard all this she burst out weeping and might not speak for a while.

At last she spoke sobbing and said, 'Lancelot, now I see you are a false recreant knight and a common lecher. You love and hold other ladies, and scorn me. I shall never love you more. Be not so hardy as to come into my sight. Right here I discharge you from this court. Upon pain of your head, see me no more.'

Right so Sir Lancelot made ready to depart with such heaviness that scarcely might he sustain himself. He called unto his kin and fellows and told them how the queen had forbad him the court, and so he was in mind to leave his own country. Then Sir Bors advised him to be not hasty, for women will ofttimes sore repent them later. 'By my advice,' said Bors, 'ride to the good hermit Sir Brastias, here beside Windsor, and there abide till I send you word of better things.'

'You say well, and I will do by your counsel,' said Lancelot. 'But, fair brother, I pray you get me the love of my lady Queen Guenevere, if you may.'

Then the noble knight Lancelot departed suddenly, so that none earthly creature but Sir Bors knew where he was become.

When Sir Lancelot was gone, the queen made a privy dinner in London unto the knights of the Round Table, to show outwardly that she had as great joy in other knights as in Lancelot. Sir Gawain and his brethren came there, and twenty others, all good fellows of the Round Table. And among them was Sir Pinel le Savage, cousin unto Sir Lamorak, that good knight slain by Gawain and his brothers.

The queen made a great feast with all manner of dainties, and in especial fruits of apples and pears. For Sir Gawain loved these well and ate them daily, and whoever feasted Gawain would commonly purvey for him such good fruits.

Now this knight Pinel, because of his kinsman Sir Lamorak, hated Sir Gawain, who was a hot knight by nature. So out of pure envy and hate Sir Pinel poisoned certain apples, hoping thereby to poison Gawain. But it befell by misfortune that a knight called Patrise, cousin unto Sir Mador, took a poisoned apple. When he had eaten it, he swelled till he burst and suddenly fell dead among them. Then every knight leapt from the board in shame and anger. They were aghast at the queen. For since Queen Guenevere had made that dinner, they all had suspicion of her.

'My lady,' said Gawain unto her, 'this dinner was made for me. All folk that know me understand well that I love fruit, and now I see how I had near been slain. Therefore, madam, I dread me lest you will be shamed.'

The queen stood sore abashed and knew not what to say.

'This shall not be so ended,' said Sir Mador, 'for here I have lost a noble knight of my blood. Therefore, upon this despite, I will be revenged to the utterance.' And there openly he accused the queen of the death of his cousin Sir Patrise.

Then was there so much cry and noise that King Arthur came in to them at the dinner. And ever Sir Mador stood before the king, and ever he accused the queen of that shameful death he called treason.

'Fair lords,' said Arthur, 'I may not have ado in this matter, for I must be a rightful judge. I repent that I may not do battle for my wife, for I deem this deed never came from her. But I suppose some good knight will put his body in jeopardy for my queen rather than she shall be burnt in a wrong quarrel. Therefore, Sir Mador, be not so hasty. Name your day for battle and some good knight shall answer you for her, or else it were to my great shame and to all my court.'

'My gracious lord,' replied Mador, 'be not displeased. There is none knight here but all have great suspicion of the queen. What say you all, my lords?'

And all answered one and another that they could not excuse the queen, for she had made the dinner.

'Alas,' wept the queen, 'I made this dinner for a good intent, and never for no evil, so Almighty God help me in my right.'

'Well,' said the king heavily to Sir Mador, 'in fifteen days be ready armed on horseback in the meadow beside Winchester. If any knight will encounter with you there, do your best and God speed the right. But if there be no knight at that day, then must my queen be burnt, and there she shall be ready for judgement.'

'Sir, I am answered,' said Sir Mador.

Therewith the knights departed. And when the king and queen were alone together, he asked her how this case befell. Then she answered, 'So help me God, I know not how or why.'

'But where is Sir Lancelot?' said Arthur. 'If he were here he would not grudge to do battle for you.'

'I know not where he is. His kinsmen deem that he is not within this realm.'

'That I repent,' said the king, 'for he would soon stint this strife. But upon my life, Sir Bors will not refuse you, if only for Sir Lancelot's sake. Of other knights that were with you at dinner, none will say well of you, and that shall be a great slander for you in this court.'

'Alas,' said Guenevere, 'now I miss Sir Lancelot. He would put me soon at my heart's ease.'

'What ails you,' asked the king, 'that you cannot keep Sir Lancelot upon your side? Now go your way, and require Sir Bors to do battle for you, for Sir Lancelot's sake.'

So the queen sent for Bors unto her chamber and besought him of his help.

'Madam,' said he, 'I was at that dinner and so I may not with honour have ado in this matter, for dread that many of those knights would have me in suspicion. Also, madam, now you have driven Sir Lancelot out of this country, I marvel how you dare for shame require me to do anything for you.'

'Alas, fair knight,' said she, 'I put me wholly in your grace, and all that is done amiss I will amend.' Therewith she knelt and besought Sir Bors to have mercy on her. Right so came King Arthur and discovered her kneeling.

'Madam, you do me great dishonour,' said Bors, and pulled her up.

'Ah, courteous knight,' said the king, 'have mercy upon my queen, for I am certain she is untruly defamed. Therefore promise, gentle knight, to do battle for her. This I require you for the love of Sir Lancelot.'

'My lord,' replied Bors, 'you require of me the greatest thing that any man may. But for my lord Lancelot's sake, and for your sake, I will be the queen's champion, unless there come by adventure a better knight to do battle for her.'

Then Sir Bors departed secretly and rode unto Sir Lancelot at the hermitage and told him of all this adventure.

'Ah Jesu,' said Lancelot, 'this is come happily as I would have it. I pray you make you ready to do battle, but tarry as long as you may till you see me arrive.'

So it was agreed between them. But when the noise went about the court that Sir Bors should do battle for the queen, many knights were displeased with him. They deemed that the queen had done that treason. Then Sir Bors answered his fellows of the Round Table.

'My lords,' he said, 'should we suffer the most noble queen of the world to be shamed openly? Consider King Arthur, her lord and our lord. He is the man of most worship in the world, the most christened, and he has ever honoured us in all places.'

'As for our most noble king,' they replied, 'we love him and honour him as well as you do. But we love not Queen Guenevere, because she is a destroyer of good knights.'

The day for the battle came on fast. On that morn, when the king was come with the queen unto the meadow beside Winchester, the queen was put in the constable's ward and a great fire was made about an iron stake. If Sir Mador had the better of the battle, she should be burnt. For it was the custom in those days to show neither favour, nor love, nor affinity, but none other except righteous judgment, as well upon a king as upon a knight, as well upon a queen as upon any poor lady.

Then Sir Mador called unto Sir Bors, 'Make you ready, and we shall prove whether you of the queen's party be in the right or I.'

Therewith either departed to his tent and made ready. And anon Sir Mador came into the field fully armed and cried unto King Arthur, 'Bid your champion come forth, if he dare.'

But as Sir Bors took his horse and came to the lists' end, he was aware of an armed knight riding fast from a wood upon a white horse, with a strange shield of strange arms. All in most great haste he clattered up to Sir Bors and said, 'Fair knight, I pray you withdraw, for a better knight must have this battle and so it ought to be mine. And with all my heart I thank you for your good will.'

'What knight is that?' called out the king.

'I know not,' said Bors. 'But now, my lord, here am I discharged.'

'Will you fight for the queen?' said Arthur to the knight.

'Therefore came I hither,' said he, 'so tarry no longer, for I have ado many matters elsewhere. But know that it is dishonour to all knights of the Round Table to see so noble and courteous a queen thus to be rebuked and shamed amongst you.'

Then they all marvelled what knight that might be, for none but Sir Bors knew him.

So they couched their spears, and hurtled together so strongly down the lists that it seemed as if the earth shook. And they did mighty battle for nigh on an hour. At last the knight smote Sir Mador grovelling upon the ground. But Mador was a well-proved knight, and rising suddenly he struck an upwards blow that cleaved the knight through the thick of the thigh, and the blood ran out fiercely.

When he felt himself wounded and saw the blood, this knight in wrath gave such a buffet on the helm that Mador fell flatling, and the knight strode to him to have off his head. But Sir Mador cried him mercy and prayed for his life, and yielded and released the queen of his quarrel.

Therewith King Arthur, seeing all this, stooped down from his seat to the knight and thanked him, and likewise did the queen.

'I pray you, fair sir,' said the king, 'put off your helm and repose you, and take for your pains a sop of wine.'

Thus did the knight. And when he put off his helm to drink, every person knew that it was Sir Lancelot du Lake. At once, the king took the queen by the hand and went to Sir Lancelot and said, 'Gramercy, sir, for your great travail this day for me and for my queen.'

'My good lord,' said Sir Lancelot, 'I ought of right to be ever in your quarrel, and in my lady the queen's. You are the man that gave me the high order of knighthood. And on that same day, when through my hastiness I lost my sword, my lady the queen found it and lapped it in her train and gave it me, or else I had been shamed among all knights. Therefore I promised her to be her knight in right or wrong.'

'I thank you,' said Arthur, 'for this journey. And know well that I shall acquit your goodness.'

And ever Queen Guenevere beheld Sir Lancelot and wept so tenderly she sank almost to the ground for very sorrow, for that he had shown such goodness to her who was unkind.

Then it befell that Nimue, the Maiden of the Lake, she that had wedded the good knight Pelleas, came to the court to do as ever great service unto the court through her sorcery and enchantments. And when she heard of the death of Sir Patrise, she told it openly that the queen was never guilty. Then she named Sir Pinel, and how he had done it and for what cause. Thus was the queen excused, and Sir Pinel fled into his own country.

So was there much gladness in the court, and games, and entertainments. And after Our Lady Day the king let cry a tournament at Camelot, that is also called Winchester. But the queen would not ride at that time, for she was sick. And many deemed that she stayed for the sake of Sir Lancelot, who was not yet whole from Sir Mador's wound.

Then the king was heavy and angry as he lodged towards Winchester with his fellowship in a town called Astolat, in English named Guildford. And for this cause, the queen sent unto Sir Lancelot and said, 'Sir, what will your enemies and mine say and deem? "See how Sir Lancelot holds him ever behind the king, so that he and the queen may have pleasure together." Thus will they say.'

'Madam,' replied Lancelot, 'of late you become wise. I will be ruled by your counsel, and tomorrow betimes I will take my way towards Camelot.'

On the morrow early, as Sir Lancelot rode into Astolat for to take his lodging, King Arthur espied him from the garden and then knew well that Lancelot would come to the tournament and do marvels at the jousts. So the king smiled and went his way. But Sir Lancelot, who did not wish to be openly known, asked of his host Sir Bernard for the loan of a shield. Though this knight was unknown to Sir Bernard, he agreed to lend him the shield of his elder son. And since his younger son, Sir Lavaine, was also on the way to the tourney, in most courteous manner Lavaine would ride with Lancelot unto Camelot.

Beside these sons, the old baron Sir Bernard had a daughter called the Fair Maiden of Astolat. And when she beheld Sir Lancelot she cast such a love unto him that she might never withdraw it. And her name was Elaine le Blank. In the heat of this love she went to Sir Lancelot and asked him to wear for her a token at the jousts.

'Fair maiden,' he answered, 'that is more than ever I did before for lady or maid.' But then he remembered him that he wished to be disguised, and none fellow or kinsman would ever know him under a token. Thus he granted it to her, and she showed him a sleeve of scarlet, embroidered with great pearls, for him to wear upon his helm.

'Never before,' he said smiling, 'did I do so much for a maiden.'

Then Lancelot and Lavaine rode unto Camelot, that was also called Winchester, with a great press of kings, dukes, earls, barons and many noble knights. But when the trumpet for the jousting sounded, Sir Lancelot drew him somewhat apart to a little leafy wood to see how went the field.

'See yonder,' said Sir Lancelot to Sir Lavaine, 'there is a company of good knights, and they hold together as boars that were worried with dogs.'

Then these two knights came in at the thickest of the press, and those on their side that had gone fast backwards soon went fast forwards.

'O mercy Jesu,' cried Sir Gawain, 'what knight is yonder doing such deeds of arms? I would say it were Sir Lancelot by his riding and his buffets, but he bears a red sleeve upon his helm, and I never knew Sir Lancelot bear any token of lady or gentlewoman.'

'I know what he is,' said Arthur. 'But let him be. He will do more and be better known before ever he depart.'

After long time, and many grievous battles, the king blew unto lodging, and the heralds gave the prize unto the knight with the white shield that bore the red sleeve.

But in that day's fighting Sir Lancelot was sore hurt, with a spear that broke its shaft still in his side. So he took no account of the prize but, groaning piteously, rode a great gallop nigh on a mile, till he came privily to a little hidden wood. And with him rode Sir Lavaine to do him service. In the safety of the trees, Lancelot said with a high, weak voice,

'Gentle Lavaine, help me take this shaft from my side. It sticks so sore that it nigh slays me.'

At this asking, Sir Lavaine gripped the shaft and pulled it out. Therewith Lancelot gave a shriek and a marvellous grisly groan, and near a pint of blood burst from him, so he sank upon his buttocks and swooned pale and deadly. Lavaine turned him into the wind, but still Lancelot lay as if dead. At last he cast open his eyes and begged Lavaine to help him to his horse, for to ride him but two miles to a hermitage where lived Sir Baudwin, some time a noble knight, but now in wilful poverty, and a surgeon and a good doctor.

When Sir Baudwin beheld the wounded knight as he leant upon his saddlebow, ever bleeding, he would have known him had he not been so pale and grimly for loss of blood. Then the hermit came closer and saw by a scar on the cheek that he was Sir Lancelot, and so he greeted him.

Then Baudwin called servants and lightly unarmed Sir Lancelot, and laid him in bed. And anon he staunched the blood, and made him drink good wine, so that Lancelot was well refreshed and knew himself. For in those days the guise of hermits was not as it is now. In those days hermits had been men of worship and prowess, and held great household, and refreshed people in distress.

Meanwhile, after the tournament, King Arthur and all the fellowship turned unto London again. And it happened that Sir Gawain rode by way of Astolat and lodged with Sir Bernard, to whom he gave tidings of the jousts, and of the mighty deeds of arms done by the knight that bore the red sleeve.

'Now I thank God,' said fair Elaine when she heard all this, 'that the knight sped so well. For he is the man in the world that I first loved, and truly he shall be the last.'

'Fair maid,' said Gawain, 'is that good knight your love?'

'Certainly sir, he is my love.'

'Then know you his name?'

'Nay truly, I know not his name nor from whence he comes, but I love him.'

Then Sir Bernard told Sir Gawain how it was that this knight had changed his shield for to be disguised, and how he left his own shield in the household. Then that shield was fetched out by Elaine and Sir Gawain knew it at once, that it was Sir Lancelot's shield.

'Ah Jesu mercy,' said Gawain, 'now my heart is heavy. Is the knight that owns this shield your love?'

'Yea, truly, he is my love. God would I were his love.'

'Well, God grant you fair grace,' said Gawain. 'But know you well, he is grievously wounded, by all manner of signs. And know you also that he is the noble knight Sir Lancelot, for by this shield I find him out.'

Then, at once, fair Elaine desired to seek her love, or else she would go out of her mind. And Sir Bernard gave her leave to ride in this search. Therewith Sir Gawain departed from Astolat and came unto the court in London, and openly disclosed that the knight who jousted best was Sir Lancelot.

'All this I knew beforehand,' said King Arthur. 'But I marvel that ever he would bear a token for any maiden, for I never knew or heard say that he ever bore any token of earthly woman.'

'By my head,' said Gawain, 'this Fair Maiden of Astolat loves him marvellously well. But what it means I cannot say.'

But when word came to Queen Guenevere that Sir Lancelot had carried the red sleeve of Elaine, she was near slain for wrath. She sent in all haste for Sir Bors and lamented Lancelot's falsehood.

'Alas, madam,' said Bors, 'I fear he has betrayed himself and us all.'

'No matter though he be destroyed,' replied the queen, 'for he is a false traitor knight that he should bear the red sleeve. Fie on him!'

In the meantime fair Elaine had clamoured unto her brother Sir Lavaine to take her to the hermitage where Sir Lancelot lay. Then Lavaine brought her to that place, and when she saw Lancelot so sick and pale in his bed, she fell suddenly in a swoon. After a long while she waked and cried, 'My lord, Sir Lancelot, alas why be you in this plight?' And then she swooned again.

When she came to herself, Sir Lancelot kissed her most gently and said, 'Fair maiden, why fare you thus? You put me to pain, more so than this little hurt from which I shall be right hastily whole, by the grace of God. But I repent me that my name is known, for I am sure it will turn unto anger.'

Then this maid Elaine never went from Sir Lancelot, but watched him day and night with such attendance that there was never woman more kindlier of man than she.

After a little time Sir Bors was also sent thither by the word of Lavaine. He leant upon the bedside and told Sir Lancelot what passed in the court, and how the queen was angry with him beyond telling for bearing the red sleeve upon his helm.

'But is this she,' Bors went on, 'that is so busy about you, whom men call the Fair Maiden of Astolat?'

'She it is,' answered Lancelot, 'and by no means can I put her from me.'

'Why should you?' said Bors. 'She is truly a fair maiden, well beseen and well taught. You could love her, but as to that I dare not counsel you. She is not the first lady that has lost her pain upon you, and that is the more pity.'

And ever Elaine did her diligent labour unto Sir Lancelot night and day, that there was never child nor wife more meek to father or husband than was this Fair Maiden of Astolat.

At last came the time when Sir Lancelot was ready to depart the hermitage. Upon that morn, fair Elaine came with her father and her two brothers to see him ride his way.

'Now fair and courteous knight,' she said to him with tears in her eyes, 'have mercy upon me and suffer me not to die for your love.'

'What would you that I did?' said Lancelot gently.

'I would have you to my husband,' replied Elaine.

'Fair maiden, I thank you,' said he, 'but truly I cast me never to be a wedded man.'

'Then, fair knight,' she said, 'will you be my paramour?'

'Jesu defend me, for then I reward your father and your brother full evil for their great goodness.'

'Alas, then must I die for your love.'

'Nay, you shall not so,' said Sir Lancelot. 'Because you love me as you say you do, to whatsoever good knight that will wed you, I shall give you together a thousand pound yearly to you and to your heirs.'

'Of all this I will none,' answered Elaine. 'Except you wed me, or be my paramour at the least, know well, Sir Lancelot, that my good days are done.'

'Fair madam,' replied he, 'of these two things you must pardon me.'

And so he took his leave and turned again unto King Arthur and the court whole and sound. Then the king made great joy of him, and so did all the knights of the Round Table except Sir Agravaine and Sir Mordred. But Queen Guenevere was mad angry with Sir Lancelot, and estranged herself from him. He made all means to speak with her, but she would not have it.

Meanwhile fair Elaine sorrowed day and night, and never slept, nor ate, nor drank. Thus she endured ten days, growing so feebled that she needs must pass out of this world. In this despair she shrived her clean, and received her Creator. But still and ever she complained upon Sir Lancelot, till her ghostly father bade her leave these thoughts.

'Why should I?' she answered. 'Am I not an earthly woman? While I have breath I may complain, for I believe I do none offence though I love an earthly man. I take God to my record that I loved none other but Sir Lancelot du Lake. And I am a clean maiden for him and for all others. Sweet lord Jesu, have mercy upon my soul, for I loved this noble knight out of measure, and I cannot withstand this fervent love whereof I have my death.'

Then she wrote a letter and prayed her father to put it in her hand when she was dead, and to place her in her richest clothes within a little barge, and thus to have her body rowed upon the Thames unto Westminster.

Anon she died. So by fortune the king and queen were speaking by a window when they espied this black barge upon the river, and they knew not what it meant. The king took the queen by the hand and went to the riverbank. They looked within the barge and saw the fairest woman lying dead, covered in clothes of cloth of gold, and she lay as though she had smiled. The queen espied a letter in her right hand, and the king took it to his chamber and made a clerk to read it, and thus said the letter:

Most noble knight, Sir Lancelot, now has death made us two at debate for your love. I was your lover, she whom men called the Fair Maiden of Astolat. Therefore I make my moan unto all ladies. Yet pray for my soul and bury me at least, and offer my Masspenny. This is my last request.

Sir Lancelot was sent for, and the letter read to him. And he and all the court wept for pity. Nor was he accounted blameless, for the queen rebuked him.

'You might, sir,' said she, 'have showed her some bounty and gentleness that may have preserved her life.'

But Sir Lancelot rehearsed for her all the causes of this love, and what he had offered to her. 'For, madam,' he added, 'I wish not to be constrained for love. It must arise of the heart, and not by constraint!'

'That is truth,' said the king. 'A knight's love is free and never will be bounden, for where he is bounden he loses himself. But, my lord Lancelot, for your honour see that she be interred worshipfully.' Upon the morn Sir Lancelot buried her richly, and offered her Mass-penny. Then the queen repented her of her rebuke and prayed him mercy for her anger, that was without cause.

"Tis not the first time,' Lancelot replied, 'that you have been displeased with me without cause. Ever must I suffer you, but I take no account of the sorrow I endure thereby.'

So passed on all that winter, with all manner of hunting and hawking, and jousts and tourneys made betwixt many great lords. Then there were fine feasts unto kings and dukes, and revel, game and play, and all manner of noblesse was used. And he that was courteous, true and faithful to his friend was at that time cherished.

And so went the year from Candlemas until after Easter. Then the month of May was come, when every lusty heart begins to blossom and to bring forth fruit. For it gives unto all lovers courage, that lusty month of May. All herbs and trees renew both men and women, and all lovers call again to mind old gentleness and old service, and many kind deeds that were forgotten by negligence.

Therefore, like as May month flowers and flourishes in many gardens, so let every man of honour flourish his heart in this world, first unto God and next unto the joy of those to whom he has promised his faith. Honour in arms may never be foiled, but first reserve the honour to God, and second the quarrel must come of your lady. And such love is called virtuous love.

So it befell in the month of May, Queen Guenevere called unto her knights of the Round Table that early upon the morrow she would ride on Maying into the woods and fields beside Westminster. 'Be well horsed,' she commanded, 'and be all clothed in green, some in silk and others in cloth. And I shall bring with me ten ladies, and every knight shall have a lady behind him, and a squire and two yeomen.'

Then ten knights made them ready in the freshest manner and rode on Maying with the queen in woods and meadows as it pleased them, in great joy and delight.

There was a knight called Meliagaunt, a son unto King Bagdemagus, and he had a castle within seven mile of Westminster. For many long years this knight had loved Queen Guenevere. Oft he plotted to steal away the queen, but forbore because of Sir Lancelot, for in no wise would he meddle if she were in his company. But at this time Sir Meliagaunt had espied the queen well. He saw that Sir Lancelot was not with her, and she had but ten knights all arrayed in green for Maying. So he got him twenty men of arms and a hundred archers for to take the queen and destroy her knights.

As the queen went Maying with her knights, all were bedashed with herbs, mosses and flowers in the freshest manner. Right so came Sir Meliagaunt riding out of a wood with eight score men well harnessed.

'Abide,' Meliagaunt shouted to the queen and her knights, 'abide, or guard your heads.'

'Traitor knight,' replied the queen, 'what think you that you do? Will you shame yourself? Bethink you how you are a king's son, and a knight of the Round Table. You shame all knighthood and yourself. But you shall never shame me, for I had rather cut my own throat in twain than that you should dishonour me.'

'Let that language be,' said Meliagaunt. 'I have loved you many a year without advantage as I have now. Therefore I will take you as I find you.'

At this the ten knights with the queen drew their swords and the two parties ran fiercely together. But the queen's men were dressed for Maying, and greatly out-numbered. So when Queen Guenevere saw her knights dolefully wounded, and like to be slain at the last, for pity she cried to Sir Meliagaunt and offered to go wheresoever he might lead if he would but spare her knights.

Thus by the queen's command her knights left off the battle and put the wounded on horseback, some sitting, some slung athwart, so that it was pity to see them. And Meliagaunt gathered them one with another all close with the queen, for full sore he dreaded that word of this might come to Sir Lancelot.

All this the queen espied. Privily she called unto her a child of her chamber that was swiftly horsed, and commanded him to go to seek Lancelot. 'Spare not your horse,' she said in low and urgent voice, 'neither for water nor for land.'

The boy sped away, setting spurs to the horse. And Sir Meliagaunt, seeing the child flee, sent armed men in chase to shoot at him, but all was in vain. When he saw this, Meliagaunt said to the queen, 'Madam, you are about to betray me. But I shall ordain for Sir Lancelot so that he shall not come lightly to you.'

Then in all haste he rode with her and her knights to his castle, and for Sir Lancelot he laid in ambush about the path thirty of the best archers. Meanwhile the child had sped to Westminster and delivered the queen's message. He told Sir Lancelot what had passed, and how Sir Ironside and Sir Brandiles and Sir Persant of Inde had fought for the queen strongly, but Sir Pelleas in especial had done marvellous deeds.

'Alas, that most noble lady,' cried Lancelot, 'that she should be so destroyed. I had rather than all France that I had been there, and well armed.'

Sir Lancelot rushed unto his horse, and told the child to warn Sir Lavaine to hie after him. Then Lancelot plunged his horse over the Thames into Lambeth, and rode as fast as he might. Within a mile he found the mark of the battle, and followed the track through a wood. And there, in a strait way, thirty archers waylaid him in ambush.

'By what command,' Sir Lancelot demanded of them, 'do you cause me, a knight of the Round Table, to leave my right of way?'

'Turn aside,' said they, 'or else go on foot, for surely we shall slay your horse.'

Then did Sir Lancelot try to force onwards, but they slew his horse with many arrows, for they durst not slay the noble knight himself. Lancelot leapt from the dying horse and went at them on foot, but he might not meddle with them for the many ditches and hedges betwixt him and them.

'Alas for shame,' he cried, 'that a knight should be so betrayed. But it is an old saw, "A good man is never in danger but when he is in the danger of a coward."'

So Sir Lancelot struggled on on foot, foul encumbered of his armour, his shield and his spear. He was full-sore annoyed, but loath to leave anything that belonged to him, for he must meet with arms the treason of Sir Meliagaunt. Then by fortune he met a cart coming to fetch wood.

'Tell me, carter,' he said, 'what shall I give you to suffer me to leap into your cart, and you to bring me unto a castle within this two mile?'

'This cart is not for you,' replied the carter. 'I am sent to fetch wood for my lord Sir Meliagaunt.'

At this, Sir Lancelot leapt on him and gave him such a buffet that he fell stark dead. The second carter was all afeared and cried, 'Fair lord, save my life. I shall bring you where you will.'

'Then I charge you,' said Sir Lancelot, 'drive me as fast as you might, even unto Sir Meliagaunt's gate.'

So the carter whipped up a great gallop and drove on towards the castle, where Queen Guenevere was waiting an hour or more in a bay window with her ladies. Soon they espied an armed knight standing in a cart.

'See, madam,' said a lady, 'a goodly armed knight rides there in a cart. I suppose he rides unto hanging.'

The queen looked on the man in the cart, and saw coming after it a horse shot with arrows that trod its guts and its paunch under its feet. And by the shield of the knight in the cart she knew him to be Sir Lancelot. 'Alas, I see you have a trusty friend,' she said in her breath, as if to Lancelot. 'But, sir, you are hard beset when I see you ride thus in a cart.'

At the gates of the castle, Sir Lancelot descended from the cart and cried so loud that all the castle rang of it, 'Where are you, false traitor, Sir Meliagaunt? Come forth here with your fellowship. For here I am, Sir Lancelot du Lake, he that shall fight with you.'

Therewith he flung the gate wide open upon the porter and smote him under the ear with his gauntlet and burst his neck in sunder.

When Sir Meliagaunt heard Sir Lancelot, he was deathly afeared. He ran unto the queen and fell upon his knee and said, 'Mercy, madam, now I put me wholly into your grace.'

'What ails you now?' she answered. 'I see you fear revenge. But what would you that I did?'

'No more,' he said, 'but that you would take all in your own hands, and rule my lord Lancelot. My body and all that I have, I shall put in your rule.'

'You say well,' replied Guenevere. 'Better is peace than ever war, and the less noise of this the more is my honour.'

So the queen and her ladies went down unto Sir Lancelot. He was angry beyond measure, and stood roaring for Meliagaunt in the inner court.

'Sir Lancelot,' she asked most softly, 'why be you so moved?'

'Ha, madam, you ask me that? Meseems you ought to be more angry than I, for you have the hurt and the dishonour.'

'Truly,' said she, 'and heartily I thank you. But you must come in with me peaceably. The knight Meliagaunt repents him, and all thing is put in my hand.'

'Well, madam,' said Lancelot, 'let this accord be, though Sir Meliagaunt has done full shamefully and cowardly to me. But madam, had I known you would accord with him so soon, I would not have made such haste.'

'Why, sir, do you regret your good deed? Know well that I make peace not out of favour or love unto him, but to lay down every shameful noise.'

'As to that,' replied Lancelot, 'I was never glad of shameful slander, and you know it right well. But there is no king, queen, nor knight living, except my lord King Arthur and you madam, but that I would make Sir Meliagaunt's heart full cold before ever I departed from hence.'

Right so the queen took Lancelot by the bare hand and led him to her chamber, where he viewed the ten good knights that were sore wounded. Then they had great joy of his coming, and he great dole of their hurts. After he had given them comfort, he went with Queen Guenevere and had good cheer with her. And he made her a promise that the same night he would come to a window leading on the garden. Though this window was barred with iron, there he promised to meet her when all folks were asleep.

The knights that were hurt had soft salves laid to their wounds, but in no wise would the queen suffer them to be from her. She ordained that they be laid in the rooms next by her chamber, upon beds and pillows, that she herself might see to them.

In the night Sir Lancelot called unto him Sir Lavaine, the good knight that had followed him from Westminster, and told him that he must go and speak with his lady, Queen Guenevere, and none should go with him. Then Sir Lancelot took his sword and privily went to a place where he had espied a ladder beforehand. He bore it through the garden and set it up to the window, and there anon the queen came softly to meet him. As they talked most fondly, he wished that he might come in to her chamber.

'I would be as glad as you,' she sighed, 'that you might come in to me.'

'Madam, with your heart would you that I were with you?'

'Yea, truly,' answered the queen.

So he set his hands to the bars of iron and pulled at them with such might that he burst them clean out of the stone walls, though one of the bars cut the brawn of his hand through to the bone. Then lightly he leapt into the chamber of the queen.

'Make no noise,' whispered the queen, 'for my wounded knights lie here fast by me.'

Then Sir Lancelot went unto bed with the queen. He took no account of his hurt hand, but took his pleasance and his liking until it was the dawning of the day. When he saw the sun peep and knew that he might tarry no longer, he departed by the window and put it together after him as well as he might.

Sir Lavaine awaited him in his own chamber, and Lancelot told him how his hand was hurt while Lavaine dressed it and staunched it. Then Sir Lancelot put a glove upon it, so that it should not be espied.

That morn the queen lay long in her bed, till it was nine of the clock. At last, to discover where she was, Sir Meliagaunt went to her chamber and found her ladies there ready clothed.

'Jesu mercy,' said Meliagaunt, opening the curtain for to behold her, 'what ails you, madam, that you sleep so long?'

As she lay, he saw that all the sheet and pillow were gored with blood from Lancelot's hand. Then Sir Meliagaunt deemed that she was false to the king, and that one of the wounded knights had lain by her in the night.

'Ah, madam,' said Meliagaunt, 'now I have found you a false traitress unto my lord King Arthur. Not for nought did you lay these wounded knights within the bounds of your chamber, for I see a wounded knight has this night lain with you.'

When the ten knights within heard these words they were in a rage, and spake all in one voice against Sir Meliagaunt. But when they saw the blood on the bed, they were ashamed and silent. And Meliagaunt was glad that he now had the queen at such an advantage, for he deemed in this way to hide his own treason. Then, with noise and rumour loud in the castle, Sir Lancelot came in, saying, 'What array is this?'

Therewith Sir Meliagaunt showed him the queen's bed all blooded. 'Truly,' said Sir Lancelot, 'you did not knightly, to touch a queen's bed while the curtain was drawn and she within. I dare say my lord Arthur himself would not have done it, unless it had pleased him to have lain with her. Therefore you have done dishonourably and most shamefully.'

'Nay,' answered Meliagaunt. 'I will prove with my hands that she is a traitress unto my lord Arthur. And as to you, Sir Lancelot, beware what you do. Though you are never so good a knight, be not advised to do battle in a wrong quarrel, for God will have a stroke in every battle.'

Then Sir Meliagaunt cast his glove that she was a traitress, and Sir Lancelot received that glove. So they were sealed with their signets and agreed to battle together in eight days, in the field beside Westminster.

'But now,' said Meliagaunt, 'I pray you await me with no treason before the time that we must fight. Let us go to dinner, and while dinner is got ready will it please you to see all of this castle? It has a pleasant air.'

They went together from chamber to chamber, and Sir Lancelot dreaded no perils. A man of honour and prowess dreads perils least, since he thinks every man is as he is. So it befell that Sir Lancelot, as he went easily, trod on a trap. A board rolled, and there Lancelot fell down more than ten fathoms into a cave full of straw from which he could not go out. After a while he was missed, but it was deemed by all that he had departed suddenly, as he was wont to do. For Meliagaunt had secretly put aside Sir Lavaine's horse, as if Lancelot had taken it, lacking his own that was killed with arrows.

When Sir Lancelot was not found, Sir Lavaine ordained litters for the wounded knights and he and the queen carried them back to Westminster. Then King Arthur was told of Meliagaunt's treason against the queen, and how he had accused her, and how Sir Lancelot had received the glove to do battle in the queen's quarrel.

'By my head,' said the king, 'I am afeared Sir Meliagaunt has taken upon him a great charge. But where is Sir Lancelot?'

'Sir, we know not,' they answered, 'but we deem he is ridden to some adventures, as is ofttimes his wont.'

'Let him be,' said the king. 'He will be found, except he be trapped with some treason.'

Meanwhile, when Sir Lancelot was in the cave below the castle, every day a lady brought him meat and drink. And each time she came in she wooed Sir Lancelot to have lain with her. And ever the noble knight said her nay.

So came that same day when the battle should be, and she said again to him, 'Sir Lancelot, methinks you are too hardhearted. Give me but a kiss and I shall deliver you, and your armour, and the best horse in Sir Meliagaunt's stable.'

'As for a kiss,' he replied, 'I may do that and lose no honour.' Then he kissed her and she brought him free from the cave, and she got him his armour, and the best horse in the stable, and the best saddle of war. He took his spear in his hand and his sword by his side, and commending the lady to God he went swiftly away.

At this time, as Sir Lancelot was galloping all that he might, Queen Guenevere was brought to the fire ready to be burnt. And ever Sir Meliagaunt cried upon King Arthur to do him justice, or else bring forth Sir Lancelot to do battle. Then were king and court full sore abashed and shamed that the queen should be burnt in the default of Sir Lancelot.

'My lord king,' said Sir Lavaine, 'all is not well with Sir Lancelot. Surely he is sick or in prison, or else he would be here. Therefore, my lord, I beseech you give me licence to do battle on behalf of my master, and for to save my lady the queen.'

'Gramercy gentle Lavaine,' said the king, 'for I dare say my queen is hereby wronged. I have spoken with the ten wounded knights, and there is not one of them, were he whole, but he would prove this falsehood upon Sir Meliagaunt's body. Therefore I give you leave, and do your best, for some treason has detained Sir Lancelot.'

Therewith Sir Lavaine hastily took arms and horse, and rode of a sudden to the end of the lists. But right as the heralds should cry *Lesses les aler* to begin the battle, right so came in Sir Lancelot, driving forwards his courser with furious pace.

'Ho,' cried Sir Lancelot. 'Abide!'

At once Sir Lancelot was called on horseback before King Arthur. There he told the king openly how Sir Meliagaunt had served him first and last. Then there was no more to say, but Sir Lancelot and Sir Meliagaunt dressed them unto battle. They couched their spears and came together like thunder. But Sir Lancelot bore so heavily upon Meliagaunt that he drove him over his horse's croup. Then Lancelot dashed him to the earth, and gave him such a buffet on the helm that all his head did ring and tears of woe did start from his eyes. At this he cried aloud, 'Most noble knight, Sir Lancelot, save my life.'

Sir Lancelot knew not what to do. He would rather have been revenged upon Sir Meliagaunt than have all the good of the world. In doubt, he looked towards Queen Guenevere for a sign. Then the queen wagged her head as though she would say, 'Slay him'. And full well Sir Lancelot knew that she would have Meliagaunt dead.

Therefore he said to Sir Meliagaunt, 'Rise, sir, for shame, and perform this battle to the utterance.'

'Nay,' he replied. 'I will never arise until you take me as yielded and recreant.'

'Well then, look what I shall proffer you,' said Lancelot. 'I shall unarm my head and my left quarter, and bind my left hand behind me. Right so I shall do battle with you.'

Therewith Sir Meliagaunt started up on his legs and called up on high, 'My lord Arthur, take heed of this proffer, for I will accept it.'

'What say you,' asked the king doubtfully to Lancelot, 'will you abide by this?'

'Yea, my lord, once said then I shall never go back.'

So the parters of the field disarmed Sir Lancelot and bound his left arm behind his back, without shield. And when the onlookers saw this, many a lady and knight marvelled that he would jeopardy himself in such a wise.

When Lancelot was trussed in this way Sir Meliagaunt came at him with sword all on high, and Lancelot showed him openly his bare head and side. Thus he brought him to the over-hasty stroke. Sir Lancelot, by sleight and dexterousness, avoided the blow and turned it back with such greater force that the head of Sir Meliagaunt was carved in two parts. Without more ado Meliagaunt was drawn dead out of the field. Queen Guenevere was released from the quarrel, and she and the king made more of Sir Lancelot du Lake, and more was he cherished, than ever beforehand.

Now at this time there came into the realms of Britain a knight from the land of Hungary, and his name was Sir Urré. Some years before, at a tournament in Spain, he had slain a good knight, but in this battle he had received seven great wounds, three on the head and four on the body. The Spanish knight that he slew had a mother, and she was a great sorceress. When she saw her son dead, by her subtle crafts she wrought that Sir Urré should never be whole of his wounds, but ever they should fester and bleed, until the best knight of the world had searched these wounds.

Then Sir Urré was put on a horse-litter with two palfreys, and his mother and his sister, the fair Felelolie, led him through many countries. Seven years did they take him through all lands christened, and never could they find a knight to ease him.

At the end of this time they came by fortune unto Scotland and then they roamed into the bounds of England just nigh the feast of Pentecost, when King Arthur and all his court were met together at Carlisle for the satisfaction of that feast. And when the king heard that these strangers were come, he sent unto the mother of Sir Urré to know of their adventure.

'You are right welcome,' said the king. 'If ever Christian man may heal him, here shall it be. And to give all other honourable men courage, I myself will assay to handle your son, and then by my command will others follow me, kings, dukes and earls.' And the king commanded all those of the Round Table present, to the number of a hundred and ten, to make ready themselves for an assay in the healing of Sir Urré.

Therewith the Hungarian knight was brought unto King Arthur and taken off his litter, and laid upon the earth with a cushion of gold under him.

'Fair knight,' said Arthur, 'I repent me of your hurt. To courage other noble knights, I will pray you to suffer me softly to handle your wounds.'

'Most noble christened king,' said Urré, 'do as you wish. I am at the mercy of God, and at your command.'

Then King Arthur softly handled him, but still some of his wounds wept and bled. And so tried all the good nobles of the court, kings, barons and knights, to no end. Among these knights were many of Sir Lancelot's kin, but he himself was not there, being at that time upon his adventures. All these hundred knights and ten searched Sir Urré's wounds, by the command of King Arthur, but no cure was done thereby.

After their assay, as they stood talking of many things and knew not what further to do, they espied Sir Lancelot come riding home from his deeds of arms.

'Peace,' said the king, 'let no manner of thing be said till he is ready among us.'

Anon, as the maid Felelolie saw Sir Lancelot, she ran to Sir Urré and said, 'Brother, here is a knight unto whom my heart gives greatly.'

'Fair sister,' he replied, 'so does my heart light against him.'

When Sir Lancelot was descended from his horse and welcomed at court, King Arthur sent for him and told him what had passed with the Hungarian knight. 'You must search his wounds,' said the king, 'as we have done.'

'Jesu defend me,' answered Lancelot, 'when so many noble men have assayed and failed, that I should presume upon me to achieve it.'

'You shall not choose,' said Arthur, 'for I will command you.'

'My most renowned lord, you know I dare not disobey your command. But Jesu defend me from the shame that I should think to pass all other knights.'

'You take me wrong,' said the king. 'You shall not do it for presumption, but to bear us all fellowship as a knight of the Round Table. And know well, if you prevail not, then no knight in this land may heal him.'

At this Sir Urré sat up weakly and said, 'Courteous Knight, for God's sake heal my wounds, for methinks ever since you came here my wounds grieve me not so much.'

So Sir Lancelot knelt down by Sir Urré and held up both his hands. He looked to the east and said secretly, 'Blessed Father, Son, and Holy Ghost, I beseech You of your mercy that my simple worship and honesty be saved. And You, blessed Trinity, give power to heal this sick knight by Your virtue and grace, but never of myself.'

Still kneeling, devoutly Sir Lancelot ransacked the wounds. They bled a little, then forthwith healed fair, as if they had been whole all seven years. When they saw this, King Arthur and all the court knelt and gave thanks and lovings unto God and to His blessed Mother. And ever Sir Lancelot wept as if he had been a beaten child.

King Arthur looked on Sir Urré, and saw that he was well made and big. Then he asked him how he felt himself.

'My good lord, now I feel myself never so lusty.'

'Will you joust and do deeds of arms?'

'Sir,' said Sir Urré, 'if it might please me to joust, I would be soon ready.'

✢ The Greatest Mortal War ✢ betwixt Arthur and Lancelot

Welcome merry May again, when every heart flourishes and burgeons. Winter with his rough winds and blasts causes a lusty man and woman to cower and sit fast by the fire; but man and woman rejoice and make glad when summer comes with his fresh flowers.

But in this season in the month of May there befell a great anger and unhappiness that stinted not till the flower of chivalry of all the world was destroyed and slain. And all was for the cause of two unhappy knights who were named Agravaine and Mordred, brethren unto Sir Gawain. For these knights had ever a privy hate unto Queen Guenevere and Sir Lancelot, and day and night they watched upon Sir Lancelot.

At this time it mishapped that Sir Gawain and all his brethren were in King Arthur's chamber when Sir Agravaine said thus openly, that many knights might hear it, 'I marvel that we all be not ashamed to see how Sir Lancelot lies daily and nightly by the queen, and we all know it so.'

'Brother Agravaine,' said Sir Gawain, 'I charge you move no such matter before me. I will not be of your counsel.'

And so said Sir Gaheris and Sir Gareth. Then Sir Mordred said, 'But I will'.

'Well I believe that,' said Gawain, 'for, brother Mordred, ever you work for unhappiness. I would that you left all this and made you not so busy, for I know what will fall of it.'

'Fall of it what fall may,' said Sir Agravaine, 'I will disclose it to the king.'

'Raise not war and wrack betwixt Sir Lancelot and us,' warned Sir Gawain. 'The best of us all had been full cold at the heart-root had not Sir Lancelot been better than we. For my part, I will never be against Sir Lancelot since he rescued me from the Dolorous Tower and saved my life. Your lives also he saved from Sir Turquin. Methinks, brother, such kindness should be remembered. But hush you, here comes our king. Now brothers, stint your noise.'

'We will not,' said Agravaine and Mordred.

'Then God speed you, for I will not hear your tales.'

'No more will we,' said Gareth and Gaheris. And therewith they three sorrowfully departed, saying, 'Alas, now is this realm wholly mischieved, and the noble fellowship of the Round Table shall be dispersed.'

At once there came in King Arthur, and asked them what noise they made.

'My lord,' answered Agravaine, 'I may keep it no longer. We brethren all know that Sir Lancelot holds your queen, and has done so long. We be your sister's sons, and we may suffer it no longer. You are the king that made him knight, and therefore we will prove it, that he is traitor to your person.'

'If it be so,' said Arthur, 'I would be loath to begin such a thing but I might have proofs upon it. Sir Lancelot is a hardy knight, the best among us. Except he be taken with the deed, he will fight all accusers, and I know none that may match him. So, in truth, I would he were taken with the deed.'

But the king was full loath thereto. For Sir Lancelot had done so much for him and for the queen so many times that the king loved him exceeding well.

'My lord,' said Sir Agravaine, 'you shall ride tomorrow to hunting, and doubt not Sir Lancelot will not go with you. When it draws towards night, send the queen word that you will lie out that night, and send for your cooks. Then upon pain of death we shall take him that night with the queen, and we shall bring him to you quick or dead. My brother Mordred and I will take with us twelve knights of the Round Table.'

'Beware,' said the king, 'for I warn you that you shall find him stalwart.'

'Let us deal,' answered Agravaine and Mordred.

Next morn King Arthur rode on hunting, leaving word that he would be out that night. Then Sir Agravaine and Sir Mordred got them twelve knights and hid themselves in the Castle of Carlisle. And these knights were all of Scotland, some Gawain's kin and others well-willers to his brethren.

So when night came Sir Lancelot said unto his fellow Sir Bors that he would go and speak with the queen.

'Sir,' said Bors, 'go not this night, for I dread me ever of Sir Agravaine, who waits daily to do you shame. I mistrust that the king is out this night. Peradventure he has laid some watch for you and the queen, and so I dread me sore of treason.'

'Have no dread,' replied Lancelot, 'for I shall go and come again, and make no tarrying. The queen has sent for me, and I will not be so much a coward but I will see her good grace.'

'God speed you well,' said Bors, 'and send you sound and safe again.'

So Sir Lancelot went lightly unto the queen's chamber with his sword under his arm, and being thus in his mantle only he put himself in great jeopardy. Then they were together, the queen and Lancelot, and whether they were abed or at other manner of disports no man knows, for love at that time was not as it is nowadays.

Suddenly there came to the door the fourteen knights that hid for him, crying with loud voice, 'Traitor knight, Sir Lancelot du Lake, now you are taken!'

'Alas,' cried the queen, 'we are mischieved both.'

'Madam,' said Lancelot with great urgency, 'is there any armour within your chamber that I might cover my poor body? Give it me and I shall soon stint their malice, by God.'

'Truly, sir, I have none armour, sword, shield nor spear. I dread our long love is come to an end, for by their noise they be many, and surely armed. You are likely to be slain, and I shall be burnt.'

'In all my life,' said Sir Lancelot, 'thus was I never beset, that I should be slain shamefully for lack of my armour. O Jesu mercy, this shameful noise I may not suffer. Better were death at once than to endure this pain.'

Then he took the queen in his arms and kissed her, and said, 'Most noble Christian queen, I beseech you, as you have ever been my special good lady, pray for my soul if I here be slain. Whatsoever comes of me, go with Sir Bors, my nephew. He and my kin will do you all the pleasure that they may, that you shall live like a queen upon my lands.'

'Nay,' replied the queen, 'I will never live after your days, but I will take my death as meekly for Christ's sake as ever did Christian queen.'

'Well, madam, since our love must depart, I shall sell my life as dear as I may. But Jesu Lord, I would give all Christendom for my armour.'

There was a mighty noise at the door of the chamber, for the knights without had a great bench from the hall and with this they rushed at the door. Sir Lancelot wrapped his mantle surely about his arm, then unbarred the door. With his left hand he opened it a little, to let but one through at a time. And first there came striding into the door Sir Colgrevaunce of Gore, a much man and large. Sir Lancelot slashed him sorely from the side, and felled him grovelling dead. Then with mighty force, thrusting with his shoulder, he barred again the door. Lightly, with the help of the queen and her ladies, he took from Colgrevaunce his armour and armed himself in it.

'Traitor knight,' came the cry from without the door, 'come out of the queen's chamber.'

'Leave your noise,' Lancelot shouted back, 'and go from the door, and tomorrow we will all go before the king. Then let it be seen who shall accuse me of treason. There I shall answer you as a knight should, and make it good upon you with my hands.'

'Fie on you traitor!' cried Agravaine and Mordred. 'We will slay you if we wish, for we have the choice of King Arthur to save you or slay you.'

'Then keep yourself,' cried Sir Lancelot, throwing open the chamber door.

Mightily and knightly, well armed, he strode among them. At the first buffet he slew Sir Agravaine. And there was none of them that might stand more than one buffet, so one by one he laid twelve more knights cold to the earth. Sir Mordred alone escaped, and he fled wounded as fast as he might.

As he stood in corpses, Sir Lancelot turned woefully to the queen and said, 'Madam, all our true love is at an end, for now King Arthur will ever be my foe. Come with me, and I shall save you from all adventures dangerous.'

181

'That is not best,' replied the queen. 'Now you have done so much harm, it is best you hold still with this. If tomorrow they will put me unto death, then may you rescue me as you think best.'

'Have no doubt,' said Sir Lancelot, 'while I am living I will rescue you.' So he kissed Queen Guenevere and either gave the other a ring, and there he left her.

With much dole and sorrow Sir Lancelot returned to his chamber, where there awaited him Sir Bors and his fellows. Sir Bors was never so glad to see him. With this, Sir Lancelot told them what had happed that night. 'Therefore, my fellows,' said he, 'be of good heart in whatsoever need I stand, for now is war come to us all.'

'Take no discomfort,' cried all those good knights, 'we shall gather those that we love, and that love us, and we will take the woe with the weal.'

Before seven of the clock, Sir Bors had called unto him Sir Lionel, Sir Ector, Sir Blamor, Sir Bleoberis, Sir Lavaine, Sir Urré and others, all good men, to the number of twenty-two, armed and on horseback. And joined unto them were some of north Wales, for Sir Lamorak's sake, and some of Cornwall, for Sir Tristram's sake, and all to the number of four score knights.

'My fair lords,' said Lancelot unto them, 'this night I have slain Sir Agravaine and twelve of his fellows. Now I am sure of mortal war, for these knights were sent and ordained by King Arthur to betray me. In his heat and malice, the king will judge the queen to the fire, and that I may not suffer. I will fight for the queen, but I dread the king will not take me as I ought to be taken. And if I rescue my lady Queen Guenevere, where shall I keep her?'

Then said Sir Bors, 'How did the noble knight Sir Tristram, by your goodwill? Kept not he with him La Beale Isoud near three years in Joyous Gard, your own place? There you may keep her long enough till the heat of the king be past. And then might you bring again the queen to King Arthur with great honour.'

'Yet by Sir Tristram,' said Sir Lancelot, 'I may have a warning. For when Sir Tristram brought again La Beale Isoud unto King Mark from Joyous Gard, look what befell on the end. How shamefully that false traitor King Mark slew him as he sat harping before his lady Isoud. He thrust him from behind to the heart with a sharpened sword. It grieves me to speak of his death, for all the world may not find such a knight.'

'That is true,' said Sir Bors, 'but take courage, for you know well that King Mark and King Arthur were never like of condition. No man yet can prove King Arthur untrue of his promise.'

So they all consented that this should happen if the queen were brought to the fire. And they put themselves in an ambush in a wood near Carlisle, to wait and see what the king would do.

Meanwhile, when Sir Mordred escaped sore wounded from the queen's chamber, he rode in full haste unto King Arthur and told him all how it was, and how they were all slain save only himself.

'Jesu mercy,' cried the king. 'Took you him in the queen's chamber?'

'Yea, God help me,' said Mordred, 'we found him there unarmed. But he slew Sir Colgrevaunce and took his armour, and thus he fought and slew us all unhappily.'

Then King Arthur had amazement at Sir Lancelot and said, 'He is a marvellous knight of prowess. Alas that ever he should be against me. Now I am sure the noble fellowship of the Round Table is broken for ever. It is fallen so that I must for my honour make the queen suffer the death.'

Right so the king took the proofs and experiences told him by Sir Mordred, with the deaths of thirteen knights about the queen's chamber, and he commanded Queen Guenevere to the fire, there to be burnt.

Therewith Sir Gawain spake. 'My lord Arthur, be not over-hasty in this judgment. Though Sir Lancelot were found in the queen's chamber, yet might it not be that he came for no evil? For you know well, my lord, that the queen is much beholden unto Sir Lancelot. Ofttimes he has done battle for her and saved her life. And peradventure the queen sent for him for goodness and none evil, but to come privily and secretly, to eschew the dread of slander. Ofttimes we do many things that we ween it be for the best, and yet by chance it turns to the worst.'

'That I well believe,' said Arthur. 'But my queen shall have the law. And if I may get Sir Lancelot, he shall have a shameful death. As for you, Sir Gawain, forsooth you have no cause to love Sir Lancelot. This past night he slew your brother Sir Agravaine, and your two sons Sir Florence and Sir Lovel.'

'Howbeit I am sorry,' replied Gawain, 'of the death of my brother and my sons, they are the causers of their own death. I gave them warning what would fall in the end. As they would not do by my counsel, I will not meddle, nor revenge me nothing of their deaths.'

'Well, dear nephew,' the king then said unto Gawain, 'I pray you make you ready in your best armour, with your brethren Sir Gaheris and Sir Gareth, to bring my queen to the fire.'

'Nay, my most noble lord, that will I never do. My heart will never serve me to see her die. As to my brothers, they will be loath to be there present. But they are young, and full unable to say you nay.'

Then spake the brethren Sir Gareth and Sir Gaheris unto the king, 'Sir, you may well command us to be there, but it shall be sore against our will. Except by your straight command, you shall plainly hold us excused. And if we must be there, we will be in peaceable wise and bear no harness of war upon us.'

'In the name of God,' said Arthur in wrath, 'then make you ready, for she shall soon have her judgment.'

When he heard all this, Sir Gawain turned away and wept bitterly, and so he went into his chamber.

In short time Queen Guenevere was led forth without Carlisle, and there she was despoiled into her smock. Her ghostly father was brought to her to shrive her of her misdeeds. Among the people at that place of the fire there was much wringing of hands, and many lords and ladies wept and wailed. But none more than a few knights in armour guarded the queen to the fire.

Now there was a man put there midst the people to espy, and he ran to give Sir Lancelot warning. Then from the wood nearby there was spurring and plucking up of horses, and right so they drove down upon the place of judgment. Most suddenly and at once they slew all those that stood against them. For there was none that might stand against Sir Lancelot in his anger, so all that bore arms, many a noble knight, were slain. And in this rushing and hurling, as Sir Lancelot swang here and there, it mishapped to him to slay Gaheris and Gareth, for they were unarmed and unaware. Sir Lancelot smote them upon the brainpans, but in very truth he saw them not. So were they found dead among the thickest of the press.

When Sir Lancelot was done with slaying, he rode straight unto the queen and made a gown to be thrown about her. Then he plucked her up and set her behind him on the saddle, and prayed her to be of good cheer. She gave thanks of God and Sir Lancelot, and so he rode away with the queen unto Joyous Gard, and there he kept her as a noble knight should do.

But when the king saw that his queen was taken away, and that his good knights were slain, in especial Sir Gareth and Sir Gaheris, then was he nigh mad in sorrow and wrath.

'Alas,' he cried, 'that ever I bore crown upon my head! My good knights be slain away from me, and I have lost the noble fellowship of Sir Lancelot and the kin of his blood. Mercy Jesu, but why slew he Sir Gareth and Sir Gaheris? I dare say Sir Gareth loved Sir Lancelot above all earthly men. Fair fellows, I charge you that no man tells Sir Gawain of the death of his two brethren for I am sure, when he hears that Sir Gareth is dead, he will go nigh out of his mind.'

'But they were slain,' some said, 'in the hurtling as Sir Lancelot swang in the thick of the press. He knew not whom he smote.'

'Their death,' replied the king, 'will cause the greatest mortal war that ever was. When Sir Gawain knows their death, I am sure that I shall never have rest of him till Sir Lancelot is destroyed, or else he destroys me. My heart was never so heavy as it is now. Much more am I sorry for my good knights' loss than for the loss of my fair queen. Queens might I have enow, but such a fellowship of good knights shall never again be together. Ah, Agravaine, Agravaine, Jesu forgive your soul for the evil will that you and your brother Mordred had against Sir Lancelot.'

Even while the king spoke, there came one unto Sir Gawain and told him how the queen was led away with Sir Lancelot, and nigh twenty-four knights slain.

'O Jesu defend my brethren,' said Gawain, 'for full well I knew that Sir Lancelot would rescue her. But where are my brethren? I marvel I hear not of them.'

'Truly, sir, Sir Gareth and Sir Gaheris are slain.'

'Who slew them, and in especial my good brother Gareth?'

'Sir, Lancelot slew them both.'

'Nay, I may not believe it, that he slew Sir Gareth. I dare say my brother Gareth loved him better than me, and all his brethren, and the king both. Say not he slew my brother Gareth.'

'Sir,' said this man, 'it is noised that he slew him.'

Right so Sir Gawain ran unto the king, crying, 'O King Arthur, my uncle, my brethren be slain, two noble knights. My own good lord, I pray you tell me, how slew he my brother Sir Gareth?'

'Truly,' said the king, 'I tell you as it is told me, Sir Lancelot slew him and Sir Gaheris both.'

'Alas, they bore no arms against him, neither of them. Now, my king, my lord and my uncle, I promise you by my knighthood, from this day I shall never fail Sir Lancelot until the one of us has slain the other. Therefore, my lord, dress you to the war, for I will be avenged upon Sir Lancelot. Now haste you thereto and assay your friends, for I shall seek him throughout seven kings' realms.'

'No need to seek him so far,' said the king. 'I hear say that he abides us in the Joyous Gard, and much people draw unto him.'

Then the king sent letters and writs throughout all England, and drew unto him many knights, earls and dukes, so that he had a great host. And this host made ready to lay siege to Sir Lancelot within Joyous Gard.

Sir Lancelot also had many good knights, some for his own sake and some for the queen's sake. Both parties were well furnished in all manner of things that longed to the war. But the king's host was so big that Sir Lancelot would not await him in the field, for he was full loath to do battle against the king. So Lancelot withdrew within his strong castle with all manner of victuals, enough for town and castle. For fifteen weeks King Arthur laid siege to Joyous Gard, but in no wise would Sir Lancelot ride out.

It befell upon a day in harvest time that Sir Lancelot looked over the walls and spoke on high unto King Arthur and Sir Gawain, saying, 'My lords both, this siege is in vain, and by this you will win no honour. If it pleased me to come out with my good knights, I should full soon make an end of this war.'

'Then come forth,' cried Arthur, 'if you dare. I promise you I shall meet you in the midst of the field. I am your mortal foe, for you have slain my good knights. Also you have lain by my queen and held her many winters, and then like a traitor taken her from me by force.'

'Fie on you, false recreant knight,' shouted Sir Gawain up unto the walls. 'I let you know that my uncle the king shall have both his queen and you, despite your face, to slay you both if it pleases him. Tell me, traitor knight, for what cause slew you my brother Sir Gareth, that loved you more than all my kin?'

'Alas that ever I was so unhappy,' said Lancelot, 'but I had not seen Sir Gareth and Sir Gaheris.'

'You lie, recreant knight. You slew him in despite of me.'

'Not so. And you may say as you please, yet may it never be said of me that by forecast of treason I slew a good knight, as you have done, Sir Gawain.'

'Ah, false knight,' raged Sir Gawain, 'mean you Sir Lamorak?'

'You slew him not yourself,' said Lancelot in contempt, 'for it had been overmuch on hand for you to have slain one of the best knights of his age.'

'Well, well,' said Gawain, 'since you upbraid me of Sir Lamorak, know that I shall never leave you till I have you in my hands.'

When Sir Bors, Sir Ector and Sir Lionel heard this outcry, they went to Sir Lancelot upon the walls and begged him strongly to ride out into the field. 'For Sir Gawain,' they said, 'will not suffer you to be accorded with King Arthur, and therefore fight for your life and your right, if you dare.'

Full unhappily Sir Lancelot consented, for he did not wish to set his hand against his king nor Sir Gawain. 'Then I needs must unto battle,' said Lancelot. 'Now know you well, my lords Arthur and Gawain, you will repent it whensoever I do battle with you.'

On the morn, great purveyance was made on both sides. And when the sun was well up, about nine of the clock, King Arthur was ready in the field with three great hosts. Then came Sir Lancelot's fellowship out at three gates, in full good array. Thus they came in order and rule, noble knights all, but Sir Lancelot ordained always that none was to meddle in no wise with Sir Gawain or King Arthur.

Soon it happed that Sir Gawain met with Sir Lionel and proffered to joust. Sir Lionel was a fierce knight and big, but Gawain drove him throughout the body and left him near dead, so that his people must bear him into the castle. Then began a heavy skirmish, and many were slain. Sir Palomides and Sir Bors overthrew many of the king's party, for these two were deadly knights. But ever Lancelot did what he might to save Arthur's men. And when King Arthur came nigh about Sir Lancelot, with intent to slay him, Sir Lancelot suffered him and would not turn back the stroke.

Then, peradventure, in the hottest of the fight, Sir Bors encountered with King Arthur and smote him down. So Bors alighted with sword high and said unto Lancelot, 'Shall I make an end of this war?' Thus he purposed to kill the king.

'Not so hardy,' cried Lancelot. 'Upon pain of your head, touch him no more. I will never see the most noble king that made me knight either slain or shamed.'

Therewith Sir Lancelot alighted off his horse. He took up the king and horsed him again, and said, 'My lord Arthur, for God's love stint this strife, for you get here no honour. My lord, remember what I have done in many places, and now I am evil rewarded.'

When the king was on horseback he looked on Sir Lancelot and the tears burst from his eyes. Then the king might no longer behold him and rode his way, saying, 'Alas, that ever this war began.'

About the time of evensong, either party withdrew to repose. Each collected the dead and gave them burial, and the wounded had soft salves laid on them. So uneasily they endured all that night.

But on the morn all was as before, with many grim battles and good men slain. As the fight went to and fro the party of Sir Lancelot began to be hard beset. Then Sir Lavaine and Sir Urré prayed Sir Lancelot to do his pain, and fight as they had done. 'For we see,' they said, 'you forbear and spare, and that does much harm. We pray you, spare not your enemies.'

'Alas, I have no heart to fight against my lord Arthur,' said Sir Lancelot, 'for then it seems I do not as I ought to do.'

But Sir Palomides also made protest and said, 'My lord, though you spare them all this day, they will never thank you. And if they may get you at avail, you are but dead.'

Sir Lancelot understood that they said truth, and he began to strain himself. So by evensong time his party stood better, for their horses went in blood past the fetlocks, there were so many people slain. Then for pity Sir Lancelot withheld his knights and suffered his enemies to withdraw aside.

It befell after a time that this war was a scandal unto all of Christendom, and at last it was noised before the Pope. He considered the goodness of King Arthur and Sir Lancelot, and called unto him the noble clerk, the Bishop of Rochester, and gave him bulls under seal for King Arthur of England. Upon pain of interdicting all England, the king must take Queen Guenevere unto him again and accord with Sir Lancelot.

When the bishop was come to Carlisle and showed the king these bulls, King Arthur was full happy to receive the queen again. But in no wise would Sir Gawain suffer the king to accord with Sir Lancelot. Then the bishop went to Joyous Gard, and displayed the Pope's bulls, and told Lancelot what had passed.

'Now I thank God,' said Sir Lancelot, 'that the Pope has made my lady the queen's peace. I will be a thousandfold more glad to bring her to the king again than ever I was of her taking away, so long as I may be sure to come safe and go safe. And the queen must have her liberty as before, and never from this day stand in peril.'

'Needs not to dread so much,' said the bishop sternly, 'for know you well, the Pope must be obeyed. And it were not the Pope's honour nor my poor honesty to see you distressed nor the queen shamed.'

Then Sir Lancelot purveyed him a hundred knights, and all were clothed in green velvet and their horses had trappings to their heels. Every knight had a branch of olive in his hand, in tokening of peace. The queen had four-and-twenty gentlewomen following her and Lancelot had twelve young gentlemen on coursers, and all were arrayed in green velvet with chains of gold, and the horses also, with many gold clasps set with stones and pearls to the number of a thousand. And the queen and Sir Lancelot both were clothed in white cloth of gold tissue. Right so they rode in most stately wise from Joyous Gard unto Carlisle.

Thus they rode throughout all Carlisle to the castle, that all folk might behold, and there was many a weeping eye. They alighted at the castle. Sir Lancelot led the queen by the arm, and then he knelt down, and the queen also, before the king. At this, many a bold knight wept as tenderly as if they saw their own kin. But the king sat still and said no word. When Sir Lancelot saw the king's countenance, he arose and lifted up the queen with him, and spoke full knightly.

'My most redoubted king,' he said, 'by the Pope's command and yours I have brought you my lady the queen, as right requires. If there be any knight, except your person, that will dare say she is untrue and unclean to you, I here myself, Sir Lancelot du Lake, will make it good upon his body that she is a true lady unto you. But you have listened to liars, and that has caused debate betwixt you and me. And these liars, Sir Agravaine and Sir Mordred, called me traitor and recreant knight.'

'They called you right,' said Sir Gawain.

'My lord Gawain,' replied Lancelot, 'in their quarrel they proved themselves not in the right.'

'Well, well, Sir Lancelot,' said the king, 'I have given you no cause to do me harm. I have honoured you and yours more than any of all my knights.'

'My good lord, be not displeased. I and mine have done you oft better service than any other knights, in many diverse places. And where you have been full hard beset divers times, I have myself rescued you from many dangers. And ever unto my power I was glad to please you, and my lord Sir Gawain.'

'The king may do as he will,' answered Sir Gawain, 'but know well, Sir Lancelot, that you and I shall never be accorded while we live. For you have slain three of my brothers, and two of them traitorly and piteously, for they bore no harness against you.'

'Would God they had been armed,' said Lancelot, 'for then they had been alive. But this much I shall offer me, if it may please the king and you, Sir Gawain. I shall begin at Sandwich, barefoot and in my shirt. And at every ten miles' end I shall found a house of religion, with a whole convent to sing and read day and night, for the sake of Gaheris, and Sir Gareth in especial. This shall I perform from Sandwich unto Carlisle. And this, Sir Gawain, methinks were fairer, holier and better to your brethren's souls than for you to war upon me, for thereby shall you get no avail.'

All the knights and ladies within the chamber wept when they heard this offer, and the tears fell on King Arthur's cheeks.

'I have heard you right well,' said Sir Gawain. 'Let the king do as he please, but I will never forgive my brothers' death. And if my uncle the king will accord with you, he shall lose my service. But as for this season, we will follow the charge of the Pope, and therefore you shall go safe as you came, though thereafter in this land you shall not abide past fifteen days. Such summons I give you with the king's consent.'

At this, Sir Lancelot sighed and the tears fell on his cheeks.

'Alas, most noble Christian realm,' he cried, 'whom I have loved above all other realms, and where I have gotten a great part of my honour, now I must depart in this wise, shamefully banished, undeserved and causeless. But fortune is so variant, and the wheel so movable, there is no constant abiding. Thus found it noble Hector, and Troilus, and Alexander the mighty conqueror. When they were most in their royalty, they alighted lowest. And so fares it by me. But I may live upon my lands as well as any knight. And if you, most redoubted king, will come upon my lands with Sir Gawain to war upon me, I must endure you as well as I may. As to you, Sir Gawain, if you come there, I pray you charge me not with treason or felony, for I must answer you.'

'Do your best,' replied Gawain. 'Therefore, hie you fast that you were gone. And know well that we shall soon come after, and break your strongest castle upon your head. So make no more language, but deliver the queen from you and pick you lightly out of this court.'

Then Sir Lancelot said unto Queen Guenevere in the hearing of all, 'Madam, now I must depart from you and this noble fellowship for ever. I beseech you, pray for me and say me well. And if you be hard beset by any false tongues, lightly my lady send me word, and I shall deliver you.'

Therewith he kissed the queen and brought her to the king, and took his leave.

And when Sir Lancelot rode out of Carlisle, there was sobbing and weeping for pure sorrow of his departing. So he took his way unto Joyous Gard, but ever after he called it the Dolorous Gard.

After Sir Lancelot had departed from the court for ever, he called his fellowship unto him and asked them what they would do. They answered all wholly together with one voice, that they would do as he would do.

Then wholly a hundred knights that were accorded to go with Sir Lancelot departed with him at once, and made their vows never to leave him for weal nor for woe. So they shipped at Cardiff and sailed into Benwick, which some men call Bayonne and some call Beaune, where the good wine is. For to say truth, Sir Lancelot and his nephews were lords of all France, and of all the lands that longed unto France.

When he was come there, Sir Lancelot stuffed and furnished and garnished all his noble towns and castles. And all the people of those lands came to him on foot and hands, and shortly he called a parliament. Then Sir Lancelot advanced all his noble knights, and first he advanced them of his own blood.

Meanwhile King Arthur and Sir Gawain made a great host ready, to the number of three-score thousand, to go over sea to make war on Sir Lancelot. At last all thing was ready, and so they shipped at Cardiff.

And because Sir Mordred was King Arthur's son, the king made him chief ruler of all England, and put also Queen Guenevere under his governance. So the king and his host crossed the sea and landed upon France, and there he burnt and wasted, through the vengeance of Sir Gawain, all that they might overrun.

When word of this came to Lancelot there were many opinions among his party. First, Sir Lionel said, 'My lord, let us keep our strong walled towns until they have hunger and cold, and blow on their nails. Then let us freshly set upon them, and shred them down as sheep in a field, that aliens may take example how they land upon our lands.'

But King Bagdemagus spoke otherwise, saying unto Lancelot, 'Sir, your courtesy will disgrace us all. It has waked all this sorrow. If they ride thus over our lands, they shall by process bring us all to nought whilst we in holes do hide.'

At this, Sir Galihud with boldness spoke further. 'Sir, here be knights come of kings' blood that will not long droop, except they are within these walls. Therefore give us leave to meet them in the field and we shall slay them, so they shall curse the time that ever they came here.'

And then all said at once, 'For Christ's sake let us ride out with Sir Galihud, for we be never wont to cower in castles.'

But Sir Lancelot, master and governor, answered them and said, 'My fair lords, I am full loath to ride out for shedding of Christian blood. Howbeit we will at this time keep our strong walls, and I shall send a messenger unto my lord Arthur to make a treaty. Know you well, fair knights, better is peace than always war.'

Therewith Sir Lancelot sent forth a maiden on a palfrey, with a dwarf that ran by her side, to require King Arthur to leave his warring. As she rode, she met with Sir Lucan the Butler, and asked of him how might she speak with the king.

'Alas,' said Sir Lucan, 'my lord Arthur would love Lancelot, but Sir Gawain will not suffer him. But speed you well, fair maid, for all we that be about the king would that Sir Lancelot did best of any knight living.'

Sir Lucan led the maiden unto where the king sat with Sir Gawain. And when she had told her tale, the water ran out of every eye. All those lords would be full glad for the king to accord with Sir Lancelot, save only Sir Gawain. 'My lord uncle,' he said, 'what will you do? Will you turn again, now you are passed thus far? If so, all the world will speak of your villainy.'

'Nay, Sir Gawain,' said Arthur, 'I will do as you advise me. And yet meseems these fair offers are good. But since I am come so far upon this journey, I would that you give the maiden her answer, for I may not speak to her for pity.'

So the maiden brought answer to Sir Lancelot, that to sue for peace was waste labour. When he heard this, the tears ran down Lancelot's cheeks. But his noble knights strode about him and said, 'Wherefore make you such cheer? Think what you are, and what men we are. Let us match them in the midst of the field.'

'I may no further,' lamented Lancelot. 'I needs must defend me.'

Then they held their language, and that night they took their rest. In the dawning, as the knights looked out, they saw the city of Benwick besieged about. On a time in that day, Sir Gawain on a strong steed came before the chief gate with a spear in his hand, crying, 'Is there none of you proud knights dare break a spear with me?'

With this, Sir Bors rode forth. But Sir Gawain smote him from his horse, and almost had he slain him. Then came forth Sir Lionel, the brother to Bors, but Sir Gawain was so big and had such grace that Sir Lionel he also wounded most sorely. And thus came Gawain every day, champing at the gate, and every day he smote down one knight or other. So they endured half a year, and there was much slaughter of people of both parties.

Then befell a certain day when Sir Gawain roared loud at the gate as before, crying, 'Where are you now, you false traitor Sir Lancelot? Why hide you within holes and walls like a coward? Look out now, for here I shall revenge upon your body the death of my three brethren.'

'God help me,' said Lancelot when he heard this. 'I am right heavy of Sir Gawain's words, for now he charges me with a great charge. Therefore I must defend me, or else be recreant.'

Some saddled his strongest horse and some fetched his arms, and all was brought to the gate of the tower. Then Sir Lancelot called from the high walls unto King Arthur, 'Now, sir king, I have forborne half a year, and suffered you and Sir Gawain to do what you would. I may endure it no longer. Sir Gawain has accused me of treason, and needs must I defend myself.'

'Sir Lancelot,' cried up Sir Gawain, 'descend if you dare. Leave your babbling and come to battle, and let us ease our hearts.'

Then Sir Lancelot armed him and mounted, and got a great spear in his hand. Sir Gawain was ready. The host without stood still all apart, for the covenant was made that there should be no man nigh them, nor deal with them, till the one were dead or yielded.

They went each way a great pace in sunder, and turned, and rushed together like the falling of mighty trees. The knights were so strong, and their spears so big, that the horses might not endure the blows and fell to earth. Then lightly they avoided their steeds, and stood foot to foot, with shields before them, and gave many sad strokes on divers places, and blood burst out on all sides.

Now Sir Gawain had a grace and gift from a holy man that for three hours every day, from nine of the clock till high noon, his strength increased three times, and by this cause Sir Gawain had won much prowess and honour. Thus, when they fought, Sir Lancelot felt the increase of might, and he thought he did battle with a fiend and no earthly man. So he traced and traversed, and covered himself with his shield, and kept his might and his attack during these three hours. But as soon as it was past noon, Sir Gawain had no more than his own might. When Sir Lancelot felt his enemy so come down, he stretched himself up and spoke.

'My lord Gawain,' said he, 'now I feel you have done. And now I must do my part, for many great and grievous strokes have I endured you this day with great pain.'

With this, Sir Lancelot doubled his strokes and gave Sir Gawain so hard a buffet that he fell down flat on his side, and Sir Lancelot withdrew from him.

'Why do you withdraw?' Sir Gawain taunted him. 'Turn, false traitor knight, and slay me. If you leave me thus, when I am whole I shall do battle with you again.'

'I shall endure you, sir,' answered Lancelot, 'by God's grace. But know well, Sir Gawain, I will never smite a felled knight.'

So Sir Lancelot withdrew into his city, and Sir Gawain was brought softly unto doctors and healthful salves.

For three weeks Sir Gawain lay sick in his tent, with all manner of leechcraft that might be had. As soon as he was cured and might ride, he armed himself at all points and came to the chief gate of Benwick, and gave out in loud voice his challenge as before. All this language Sir Lancelot heard, and he answered, 'Sir Gawain, I repent of your foul saying. Cease your language. I know well your might, and all that you may do. And, Sir Gawain, you may not greatly hurt me.'

'Come down, traitor knight,' shouted Gawain, 'for I expect this day to lay you as low as you laid me.'

So they did battle again, with great pain and suffering, and blood flowing from many grievous wounds. And again Sir Lancelot felt the marvellous increase of Gawain's might, and with it so increased his wind and his evil will. But Sir Lancelot hardily endured the three hours. When noon was come and Sir Gawain returned to his own proper strength, Lancelot said to him, 'Now have I proved you twice, that you are a full dangerous knight and a wonderful man of your might. Now I feel that you have done your mighty deeds, and I must do mine.'

Then Sir Lancelot doubled his strokes again, and smote Sir Gawain on his old wound, so that his brain swooned and he fell to the earth. Anon he awoke and still he waved and thrust at Sir Lancelot, even as he lay on earth, daring him to perform this battle unto the uttermost.

'I will do no more than I have done,' said Sir Lancelot. 'I may not stand to smite a wounded man. God defend me from such a shame.'

He turned him and went his way towards the city, and ever after him came the voice of Sir Gawain, calling him traitor knight and threatening him new battle.

Thus the siege endured. This time, Sir Gawain lay sick near a month before he was well recovered and ready to fight again with Sir Lancelot. But right so tidings came unto King Arthur from England that made the king and all his host remove them out of France.

✢ The Death of Arthur ✢

ir Mordred, for the time ruler of all England, had letters writ as though they came from beyond the sea telling that King Arthur was slain in battle against Sir Lancelot. Wherefore Sir Mordred made a parliament and called the lords together, and there he made them choose him king. So was he crowned at Canterbury, and held a feast there of fifteen days.

Afterwards he drew him unto Winchester, and there he said plainly to Queen Guenevere that he would wed her, who was his uncle's wife and his father's wife. The day was set and the feast was ready, for which cause Queen Guenevere was exceeding heavy. But she durst not discover her heart, so she spake fair and agreed to Mordred's will.

She desired to go to London, to buy all manner of things for the wedding. And Sir Mordred, because of her fair speech, trusted her well and gave her leave to go. When she came to London, she took the Tower of London and suddenly, in all haste possible, she stuffed it with all manner of victuals, and well garnished it with armed men, and so kept it.

When Sir Mordred knew how he was beguiled, he was angry out of measure. He laid a mighty siege about the Tower, and made many great assaults, and threw great engines upon it, and shot large guns. But he did not prevail, and the queen, for fair or foul, would never trust herself to come in his hands again.

After a time the Bishop of Canterbury, that holy man, said unto Sir Mordred, 'Sir, will you first displease God and then shame yourself and all knighthood? Though King Arthur is called your uncle, did he not himself beget you upon his own sister? Therefore, how may you wed your father's wife? Sir, leave this opinion, or I shall curse you with book and bell and candle.'

'Do your worst,' answered Mordred, 'I shall defy you.'

'I shall not fear me,' said the bishop, 'to do what I ought to do. Also, you say that Lord Arthur is slain. It is not so, and therefore you will make a foul work in this land.'

'Peace, false priest,' cried Sir Mordred. 'If you chafe me any more I shall strike off your head.'

So the bishop cursed Mordred in the most solemn wise. And then he fled, for Sir Mordred sought to have slain him. He went nigh unto Glastonbury, and there he lived as a hermit, in poverty and holy prayers, for well he understood that mischievous war was at hand.

Then came word that King Arthur had raised the siege of Sir Lancelot and was coming homewards with a great host to be avenged upon Sir Mordred. At this, many people drew unto Sir Mordred. It was the common voice among them that with Arthur was none other life but war and strife, and with Sir Mordred was joy and bliss. Thus evil was said of King Arthur, and many that he had made up from nought, and given them lands, said not a good word of him.

Lo, all you Englishmen, see you not what a mischief was here? Would they not hold content with he who was the most king and knight of the world? Lo, thus was the old custom and usage of this land. Have we yet lost or forgotten that custom and usage? Alas, this is a great default of we Englishmen, for nothing pleases us for long.

And so fared many people, that they were better pleased with Sir Mordred than with King Arthur. With a great host that would abide him for better or worse, Sir Mordred drew him unto Dover, to beat his own father from his lands.

After some days, when fair winds did blow, King Arthur came with a bold navy of ships. And Sir Mordred was ready waiting upon his landing. Upon the beach there was launching of boats great and small, all full of noble men of arms. And then there was much slaughter of gentle knights, and on both parties many a full bold baron was laid low.

But no knight could withstand Arthur's courage, and his men-at-arms fiercely followed him to land, where they put Sir Mordred aback so that he fled with all his people. When this battle was done, and King Arthur went about to bury the slain, he found noble Sir Gawain felled into the bottom of a boat, lying more than half dead.

Then the king took Sir Gawain in his arms, and said most sorrow-fully, 'Alas, Sir Gawain, my sister's son, here now you lie, he whom I loved most. Now is my joy gone. In Sir Lancelot and you I most had trust and joy, and now I lose you both.'

'My uncle King Arthur,' replied Sir Gawain, 'my death day is come, and all is through my own hastiness and wilfulness. Of all this unhappy war I am the causer. And now you shall miss Sir Lancelot. But, alas, I could not accord with him. Therefore, fair uncle, let me have paper, pen and ink, that I may write to Lancelot a letter with my own hands.'

With the help of the king, Sir Gawain sat up weakly, and he wrote thus:

Unto Sir Lancelot, flower of all noble knights that ever was, I, Sir Gawain, King Lot's son of Orkney, sister's son unto the noble King Arthur, send you greeting. On the tenth day of May I was smitten upon the old wound that you gave me before Benwick, and thus I am come to my death day. All the world will know that I, knight of the Round Table, came to death, not by your deserving, but by my own seeking. Therefore I beseech you, Sir Lancelot, to return again unto this realm, and see my tomb, and say some prayer more or less for my soul.

Sir Lancelot, for all the love that was ever betwixt us, make no tarrying, but come over the sea in all haste, to rescue our noble king, our lord Arthur. For he is full straitly beset with a false traitor, that is my half-brother Sir Mordred. This I tell you but hours before my death, written with my own hand, and so subscribed with part of my heart's blood.

Then they both wept, and the king made Sir Gawain to receive his Saviour. So, at the hour of noon, Sir Gawain yielded up the spirit and the king interred him in a chapel within Dover Castle, where yet all men may see his skull with the wound that Lancelot gave him.

While the king was in Dover, anon word came that Sir Mordred had pitched a new field upon Barham Down. On the morn, King Arthur gave chase and harried him with fierce battle, and drove him out, so that Sir Mordred fled unto Canterbury. Then the folk began once again to draw unto Arthur, saying that war upon the king was wrong. Thus the king's host increased, and King Arthur marched all his party down by the seaside, westward towards Salisbury.

Sir Mordred set out to raise much people about London, in Kent, Sussex and Surrey, and a little to the north from Essex to Norfolk. When the hosts were full and ready to do battle, a day was assigned on a Monday after Trinity Sunday when King Arthur should meet with Sir Mordred on a down beside Salisbury, so that the king might be avenged upon Sir Mordred.

On the night of Trinity Sunday, King Arthur dreamt a wonderful dream. It seemed he sat on a chair bound fast to a wheel, and under him was a hideous deep black water, all full of serpents, worms and wild beasts, foul and horrible. Of a sudden it seemed the wheel turned upsodown and the king fell among the serpents, and every beast took him by a limb, so that the king in his bed cried 'Help!'

Then knights and squires assayed to wake him, but he fell on slumbering again, neither full sleeping nor quite waking. And it seemed that Sir Gawain came to him with a number of fair ladies, all of whom the king gladly welcomed, saying, 'My sister's son, O welcome, for I weened you were dead. Fair nephew, what be these ladies come hither with you?'

'Sir,' answered Gawain, 'all these be ladies for whom I have fought in righteous quarrel when I was a living man. God has given them leave to bring me hither, to warn you of your death. For if you fight tomorrow with Sir Mordred, doubt not that you must be slain, and most of your people also, of both parties. In no wise do battle, but take a treaty for a month. Proffer you largely to gain this delay. For within a month Sir Lancelot and all his noble knights shall come and rescue you with honour, and slay Sir Mordred and those with him.'

Therewith Sir Gawain and all the ladies vanished. When the king awoke, he took counsel of noble lords. Then he commanded Sir Lucan the Butler, and his brother Sir Bedevere, with two bishops, to take a treaty for a month with Sir Mordred. 'Spare not,' said the king, 'but proffer him lands and goods as much as you think best.'

So they came to Sir Mordred with his grim host of a hundred thousand men, and they entreated him long time. At last, to make the treaty, Mordred agreed to have Cornwall and Kent in Arthur's days, and to have all England after the king's death. And to seal agreement to this end, they two, Arthur and Mordred, consented to meet betwixt the hosts, each in company with no more than fourteen persons.

As he departed unto this meeting, King Arthur warned all his people, saying to them, 'If you see any sword drawn, look that you come on fiercely and slay that traitor Mordred, for I in no wise trust him.'

And in likewise did Sir Mordred warn his own host, for he knew well that his father would be avenged on him.

So they met betwixt the hosts, and were agreed and accorded thoroughly. Wine was fetched and they drank. Right so an adder came out of a little bush of the heath, and it stung a knight on the foot. When the knight felt this sting, he drew his sword to slay the adder, and thought of no other harm. But when the hosts on both sides saw this sword drawn, then they blew bugles, trumpets and horns, and shouted most grimly. Both parties flew to arms, and dressed themselves together.

Never was seen a more doleful battle in Christian land. Thus they fought all the long day, and never stinted till the noble knights were laid to the cold earth. When night fell upon that dismal day, there were a hundred thousand dead upon the down. Then King Arthur looked about him in the shambles and saw that of all his good knights but two were left alive. One was Sir Lucan the Butler and the other was his brother Sir Bedevere, and they were both full sore wounded.

Then the king looked about the grim field again, and saw that Sir Mordred leant upon his sword among a great heap of dead men.

'Now give me my spear,' said Arthur unto Sir Lucan, 'for yonder I have espied the traitor.'

'Sir, let him be,' said Sir Lucan, 'for he is unhappy. If you pass this day, you shall be right well revenged. My good lord, remember your night's dream. God of His great goodness still preserves you. Therefore, for God's sake, leave off this. You have won the field, for here we be three alive, and with Sir Mordred is none alive. If you leave off now, this wicked day of destiny is past.'

'Come death, come life,' cried the king, 'now I see him yonder alone he shall never escape my hands, for I shall never have him at better avail.'

'God speed you well,' said Sir Bedevere.

200

So the king got his spear in both his hands and ran towards Sir Mordred, crying, 'Traitor, now is your death day come!'

When Sir Mordred heard King Arthur, he roused himself and ran at him with sword held high. As they hurtled together, the king smote Mordred under the shield, piercing him throughout the body with his spear, more than a fathom. When he felt this death wound, Sir Mordred plunged himself with all his might up to the hand-guard of his father's spear. Face-to-face, in labouring breath and out-bursting blood, Sir Mordred took his sword in both his hands and smote his father King Arthur on the side of the head, so that the sword cleaved the helmet and the brainpan. Therewith Sir Mordred could do no more and fell stark dead, while noble Arthur swooned away to the earth.

In haste, Sir Lucan and Sir Bedevere heaved up Arthur and weakly bore him betwixt them to a little chapel not far from the sea. As the king waked, and eased himself there, they heard behind them the cry of folk in the field. Then, at the king's asking, Sir Lucan went, though he was grievously wounded in many places, to see what betokened that noise.

He hearkened by moonlight, and heard and saw how pillagers and robbers were come into the field to pillage and rob many a full noble knight. And if there were poor knights not yet dead, there they slew them for their harness and riches. When Sir Lucan understood this work, he judged it most safe that the king should be taken from thence.

'I would it were so,' said the king, 'but I may not stand, my head works so.'

Betwixt them, Lucan and Bedevere strove to lift the swooning king. But Sir Lucan fell with the lift, and part of his guts came out of his body, and therewith this noble knight's heart burst. Then the king was conscious that Sir Lucan lay foaming at the mouth, and a part of his guts lay at his feet.

'This is a full heavy sight,' lamented Arthur, 'to see this noble duke so to die for my sake. Alas, he would not complain, his heart was so set to help me. Now Jesu have mercy upon his soul.'

Then Sir Bedevere wept for the death of his brother.

'Leave this mourning and weeping,' said the king. 'If I might live myself, the death of Sir Lucan would grieve me ever more. But my time hies fast. Therefore take you Excalibur, my good sword, and go with it to yonder waterside, and there I charge you throw my sword in the water, and come again and tell me what you see there.'

201

As Sir Bedevere departed, he beheld that the pommel and haft of that noble sword were all of precious stones. He said to himself, 'No good will come if I throw this rich sword in the water, but only harm and loss.' So he hid Excalibur under a tree.

When he came again to the king, Arthur said, 'What saw you there?'

'Sir, I saw nothing but waves and wind.'

'That is untruly said. Therefore go lightly again, and do my command.'

Sir Bedevere went again, with the sword in his hand. But still he thought it sin and shame to throw away so noble a sword. So again he hid the sword, and returned again to the king.

'What saw you there?' asked the king once more.

'Sir, I saw nothing but the waters lap and the waves grow wan.'

'Ah, traitor untrue,' said King Arthur, 'now have you betrayed me twice. Who would have thought that so dear and noble a knight would betray me for the riches of a sword? Now go lightly, for your long tarrying puts me in great jeopardy of my life. My wound takes cold. Would you, for my rich sword, see me dead?'

Then Sir Bedevere went a third time to the waterside. He took the sword, and bound the girdle about the hilt, and threw it as far into the water as he might. An arm and a hand rose above the water and caught the sword, and shook it thrice and brandished it. Then the hand vanished away with the sword into the water. With that, Sir Bedevere returned again to Arthur and told him what he saw.

Then Sir Bedevere took the king upon his back and carried him to the waterside. Fast by the bank, there hoved a little barge with many fair ladies in it. They all had black hoods, and they wept and shrieked when they saw King Arthur.

'Now put me into the barge,' said the king.

Softly they did so, and three queens received him there with great mourning. So he lay him down, and his head was in a queen's lap.

'Ah, dear brother,' said that queen, 'why have you tarried so long from me? Alas, this wound on your head has caught overmuch cold.'

Then they rowed slowly from the land. And as Sir Bedevere beheld them all go from him, he cried out, 'My lord Arthur, what shall become of me, now you go from me, and leave me here alone among my enemies?'

'Comfort yourself,' said the king, 'and do as well as you may, for in me you may trust no further. I will go into the Vale of Avilion to heal me of my grievous wound. If you hear never more of me, pray for my soul.'

As they went, ever the queens and ladies wept loud, that it was pity to hear, till soon Sir Bedevere lost sight of the barge. Then he wept and wailed and took the way into the forest, and so he went on all that night. In the morn, he saw a chapel and a hermitage betwixt two steep grey woods. When he came into the chapel, he saw a hermit grovelling on all fours, fast by a new-dug tomb. Sir Bedevere knew this hermit well, for but a little before he was the Bishop of Canterbury, whom Sir Mordred had made to flee.

'What man is here interred,' asked Bedevere, 'that you pray so fast for him?'

'Fair son,' replied the hermit, 'I know not verily. This night, at midnight, there came a number of ladies and brought hither a dead corpse. They prayed me to bury him, and offered here a hundred tapers, and they gave me a hundred bezants.'

'Alas,' cried Sir Bedevere, 'that was my lord King Arthur.'

So there abode Sir Bedevere, with the hermit that was before Bishop of Canterbury. He put upon him poor clothes, and served the hermit full lowly in fasting and prayers.

When all this battle was done, word came anon to Queen Guenevere, and she understood that all were slain. King Arthur was slain, and all the noble knights, and Sir Mordred, and all the remnant. Then the queen stole away, with five ladies, and so she went to Almesbury. There she became a nun, and wore clothes white and black. She took great penance, as ever did sinful lady in this land, and no creature could make her merry, but she lived in fasting, prayers and alms-deeds, so that all manner of people marvelled how virtuously she was changed. Thus in Almesbury she was a nun, in white and black, until she became abbess and ruler there.

Meanwhile, in France, it had been told Sir Lancelot how Sir Mordred was crowned king in England, and how he laid siege to Queen Guenevere in the Tower of London because she would not wed him. Then was Sir Lancelot angry out of measure, and spoke unto his kinsmen.

'Alas, that double traitor Sir Mordred,' he lamented. 'Now I repent me that he ever escaped my hands, for much shame has he done unto my lord Arthur. And by this doleful letter that my lord Gawain has sent me, on whose soul Jesu have mercy, I see my lord Arthur is hard beset. Know you well that Sir Gawain's doleful words, praying me to see his tomb, shall never go from my heart. For he was as full noble a knight as ever was born. O unhappy hour of my birth, that ever I should slay first Sir Gawain, then Gaheris the good knight, and my own true friend, noble Sir Gareth. And yet I could not slay that traitor Sir Mordred.'

'Enough complaints,' replied Sir Bors. 'First avenge the death of Sir Gawain, and it will be well done that you see his tomb. Then avenge you my lord Arthur and my lady Queen Guenevere.'

'I thank you,' said Sir Lancelot humbly to Bors, 'for ever you think of my honour.'

So Sir Lancelot landed at Dover with seven kings, and the number of his army was hideous to behold. And the people of the town took Sir Lancelot to the Castle of Dover and showed him Sir Gawain's tomb.

At the tomb Sir Lancelot knelt down and wept, and prayed heartily for the soul of Sir Gawain. Then he put on a mourning gown and with his own hand dealt his money, so that all who asked had as much flesh, fish, wine and ale as they wished, and every man and woman had twelve pence, come who would. On the morn the priests and clerks sang a Mass of requiem, and there was great offering. Sir Lancelot offered a hundred pounds, and the seven kings offered forty pounds apiece, and each of a thousand knights offered a pound. And this offering lasted from morn to night. Sir Lancelot lay two nights on the tomb weeping and praying, and on the third day he spoke to all the barons.

'Fair lords,' said he, 'I thank you all of your coming, but we came too late. Against death, alas, may no man rebel. I will myself ride and seek my lady Queen Guenevere, for as I hear she has had great pain and much disease. Abide me here and if I come not within fifteen days, take your ships and your fellowship and depart into your country.'

'My lord Lancelot,' said Sir Bors, 'what shall you do, now riding in this realm? You shall find few friends.'

'Be as be may,' replied Lancelot, 'keep you still here. I will forth on my journey, and no man nor child shall go with me.'

So he departed and rode westerly. In those countries he searched seven or eight days, and at last he came to a nunnery. And of a sudden Queen Guenevere saw Sir Lancelot as he walked in the cloister. At this, all her ladies and gentlewomen had work enough to hold the queen up. After a time, when she might speak, she said to them, 'You marvel, fair ladies, why I make this fare. Truly, it is for the sight of the knight that stands yonder. I pray you all, call him to me.'

Sir Lancelot was brought to her, and again she said to her ladies, 'Through this man and me has all this war been wrought, and the death of the most noble knights of the world. And through our love together is my most noble lord Arthur slain. Sir Lancelot, know you well that I am set to get my soul's health. After my death, I trust through God's grace to see the blessed face of Christ, and at Doomsday to sit at His right side. For sinful as I ever was, even so were saints in heaven. Therefore, Sir Lancelot, I require and beseech you heartily, for all the love that was ever betwixt us, that you never see me more face to face. I command you, forsake my company and turn to your kingdom again, and keep well your realm from war and wrack. Take there a wife, and live with her in joy and bliss. And pray for me to Our Lord that I may amend my misliving.'

'How now, sweet madam,' said Sir Lancelot, 'wed a lady? Nay, madam, that shall I never do, for I shall never be so false to you. But the same destiny that you have taken, I also will take me unto, to please Jesu, and ever for you I cast me specially to pray.'

'If you will do so,' replied the queen, 'hold your promise. But I may never believe except that you will turn to the world again.'

'Well, madam, you never knew me false of my promise. In the name of God I shall forsake the world. For in the quest of the Sangrail I would have forsaken the vanities of the world had it not been for your love. Therefore, lady, since you have taken you to perfection, I must needs do likewise, of right. For I take record of God, in you have I had my earthly joy, and if I had found you now so disposed, I would gladly have placed you in my own realm. But since I find you as you are, I ensure you faithfully that I will ever take me to penance, and pray while my life lasts. Wherefore, madam, I pray you kiss me and never no more.'

'Nay,' said the queen, 'that shall I never do. But abstain you from such works.'

Now there was lamentation as if they had been stung with spears. The ladies bore the queen to her chamber, and Sir Lancelot took his horse and rode weeping all that day and all night in a forest.

On the morn he came to a chapel betwixt two cliffs, and he heard a little bell ring for Mass. He alighted and tied his horse to the gate, and heard Mass. And he saw that the priest that sang Mass was the Bishop of Canterbury. Sir Bedevere was there also, upon his knees, and after Mass they all spake together. Sir Bedevere told his tale all whole, and Sir Lancelot's heart almost burst for sorrow when he heard of Arthur's battle upon the heath. He threw his arms open wide and cried, 'Alas, who may trust this world?'

Then the good bishop shrived Sir Lancelot and absolved him, and put a religious habit on him. So there Sir Lancelot remained, serving God day and night with prayers and fastings.

In the meantime, the great host from France abode at Dover. After the appointed time for Sir Lancelot's return, Sir Lionel went with fifteen lords and rode to London to seek him. There he was unkindly met by men-at-arms who slew him and many of his lords. At this, Sir Bors ordained that the host should go home again, as Sir Lancelot had wished it. But Sir Bors, Sir Ector, Sir Blamor and Sir Bleoberis, with some other of Lancelot's kin, took on them to ride all England across and along to seek Sir Lancelot.

By fortune, after much travel, Sir Bors came to that same chapel where Sir Lancelot was. He saw him at Mass in the religious clothing, and then Bors also prayed the bishop that he might be in the same suit. A habit was put upon him, and he lived there in most religious wise.

Within half a year, seven more noble knights came there and abode. When they saw that Sir Lancelot had taken him to such perfection, they had no lust to depart, but took a habit as he had. For six years they endured in great penance, and then Sir Lancelot took the clothing of priesthood from the bishop, and a twelvemonth he sang Mass. And all of those noble knights read in holy books and helped to sing Mass, and rang bells, and did all manner of lowly service. So their horses went wildly where they would, for the masters took no regard of worldly riches.

Then upon a night there came a vision to Sir Lancelot that charged him, in remission of his sins, to haste him unto Almesbury. Sir Lancelot took his seven followers and on foot they went from Glastonbury to Almesbury, which is little more than thirty miles. Thither they came within two days, for they were weak and feeble and walked but slowly. They came at last within the nunnery at Almesbury, and they found that Queen Guenevere had died but half an hour before.

The queen had told her ladies, before she passed, that Sir Lancelot was priest. 'Hither he shall come,' she told them, 'as fast as he may to fetch my corpse. Then he shall bury me beside my lord King Arthur.'

206

When Sir Lancelot saw the queen's dead face, he wept not greatly, but sighed. Then he did all the observance of the service himself, both the dirge and the sung Mass. With a hundred torches ever burning about the corpse of the queen, Sir Lancelot and his good fellows went about the horse bier, singing and reading many a holy orison, and sprinkled frankincense upon the corpse. Then they retraced their way from Almesbury to Glastonbury.

In the chapel of Glastonbury the queen had a dirge. Then she was wrapped in waxed cloth of Rennes, from top to toe, in thirtyfold. And after she was put in a web of lead, and then in a coffin of marble. They carried her unto the earth, and then Sir Lancelot swooned and lay long still, until the hermit waked him and said, 'You are to blame, for you displease God with such manner of sorrow.'

'Truly,' Lancelot replied, 'I trust I do not displease God, for He knows my intent. My sorrow was not for any rejoicing of sin, but it may never have an end. When I remember her beauty and her noblesse, that was both with her king and with her, and when I saw his corpse and her corpse so lie together, truly my heart would not serve to sustain my careworn body. And when I remember how by my default and pride they were both laid full low, those two peerless Christian people, then my heart sank so that I might not sustain myself.'

Thus Sir Lancelot spoke, and ever after he ate but little meat, nor drank, till he was dead. Neither his bishop nor his fellows might make him eat, so that he waxed a cubit shorter than he was, and the people knew him not. For he sickened more and more, and dried and dwindled away. And ever he lay grovelling on the tomb of King Arthur and Queen Guenevere.

Within six weeks after, Sir Lancelot fell so sick that he lay in his bed. In weak and dreary voice he said to the hermit, 'Sir bishop, I pray you give me all the rites of a Christian man.'

'Nay,' said the hermit, 'you shall not need it. It is but heaviness of your blood. Tomorrow you shall be well mended, by the grace of God.'

'Fair lords,' Lancelot replied wearily, 'know well that my careworn body will into the earth. I have warning of it more than now I will say. Therefore give me my rites.'

So he took the sacrament and was anointed, and had all that a Christian man ought to have. Then he prayed all his fellows that they might bear his body to Joyous Gard. Some men say it was Alnwick, and some say it was Bamburgh.

Then, with weeping and wringing of hands, all his fellows went to their beds in one chamber. After midnight, against the day, the bishop began a great laughter as he lay in his bed asleep. Therewith the fellowship awoke and cried to him, 'Good bishop, what ails you?'

'Jesu mercy,' said he, 'why did you awake me? I was never in my life so merry and so well at ease. Truly, here was Sir Lancelot with me, with more angels than ever I saw men in one day. I saw the angels heave up Sir Lancelot into Heaven, and the gates of Heaven opened against him.

'It is but the disturbance of dreams,' said Sir Bors, 'for I doubt not Sir Lancelot ails nothing but good.'

'It may well be,' said the bishop. 'Go to his bed, and then shall you prove the truth.'

So his fellows came to his bed, and they found him stark dead. He lay as he had smiled, and had the sweetest savour about him that ever they felt.

On the morn, the bishop did the Mass of requiem. Then Sir Lancelot was put in the horse bier and all his fellowship went with his corpse for fifteen days until they came to Joyous Gard. There they laid him in the choir, and sang and read over him and about him. And ever his face was laid open and naked, that all the people might behold him.

Right so, as they were at their service, unto Joyous Gard there came Sir Ector de Maris, that had seven years sought all the realm for his brother Sir Lancelot. When Sir Ector heard such noise and saw light in the choir of Joyous Gard, he alighted and beheld that men did sing and weep. And all these good men knew Sir Ector, but he knew not them, for they were in religious habit.

Then Sir Bors went unto Sir Ector and took him by the hand, and said most gently, 'Sir, look there. It is your brother Sir Lancelot that lies dead.'

Sir Ector beheld his brother's face. Then he threw his shield, sword and helm from him. And hardly any tongue can tell the doleful complaints he made for his brother.

'Ah, Lancelot,' he cried, 'you were head of all Christian knights, and I daresay you were never matched by hand of earthly knight. And you were the most courteous knight that ever bore shield. And you were the truest friend of your lover that ever bestrode horse. And you were the truest lover of a sinful man that ever loved woman.

And you were the kindest man that ever struck with sword. And you were the goodliest person that ever came among press of knights. And you were the meekest man and the gentlest that ever ate in hall among ladies. And you were the sternest knight to your mortal foe that ever put spear in the rest.'

Thus he finished, and there was weeping and dolour out of measure. And they kept Sir Lancelot's corpse aloft full fifteen days, for all folk to see. Then they put him in the earth, the most noble knight of the world, dead and gone.

✠ Knighthood's End ✠

he long mental journey was over, and he was tired. He wrote slowly in laborious longhand:

Here is the end of the whole book of King Arthur, and of his noble knights of the Round Table. And here is the end of the death of Arthur. I pray you all, pray for my soul. For this book was ended the ninth year of the reign of King Edward the Fourth, by Sir Thomas Malory, knight.

As he turned the last leaf of the manuscript face down, he wondered about that phrase 'the whole book'. Perhaps there was more to be said, things he could not quite comprehend? Certainly the story was obscure, rich and complicated, stretching back into the childhood of many peoples. With honest endeavour he had scoured all the texts he could find from several nations. But in all of them there was a sense of the incomplete, something left unsaid about the death of Arthur. It seemed as if it were a necessary mystery. Three queens had led King Arthur away to death: one was his sister, the sorceress Morgan le Fay; the second was the Queen of Northgales; and the third was the Queen of the Waste Lands. All these were queens of enchantment. They bore the body of the dying king to their ship, and sailed from the shores of storytelling onto the insubstantial waters of myth.

Yet, as Malory knew well, many throughout England believed that King Arthur was not dead. God had translated him into another place, and he would come again when faith and nation needed him. He was here, hidden in our world, awaiting the call. Even his supposed tomb, the sombre sign of his passing, was said to carry this hopeful message: *Hic jacet Arthurus, Rex quondam Rexque futurus.* That is to say, 'Here lies Arthur, the once and future King'.

In his cell in the year 1469, watching autumnal evening light strain through the bars of his window, Malory sighed. His task, now finished, had served its purpose. His spirit had been beguiled while the prison took a toll on his body. But the more he had written, the more keenly he felt the mismatch between the old chivalry and the new practices of men and nations. The history of King Arthur was nothing if not a celebration of love, and of honour in war. But love nowadays! A question of lust and financial calculation. 'So it fares,' Malory lamented to himself. 'Men cannot love seven nights but they must have all their desires. Soon hot, soon cold. There's no stability. The old love was not like this. That was love, truth and faithfulness, and thus it was in King Arthur's days.'

As for noble deeds of arms and honour in war, in 1453 the flower of English knighthood, those who gloried in their descent from the fellowship of the Round Table, finally limped home from the hundred years of the French Wars with their tails between their legs after untold many acts of squalor and outrage. Two years later, in England, these same knights further disgraced themselves in the Wars of the Roses. Fraternal knights cut one another's throats for the small advantage of a Lancastrian nod or a Yorkist smile. Knights became murderers, left mouldering on rotting biers by the aloof and disgusted folk of the land.

Malory sighed again. The sigh turned into a cough that he could not quiet until it had left him gasping and wretched. He saw, as his contemporaries so often saw, the skull beneath the skin. This world he lived in was no chivalrous land, no Arthurian realm of Logris, still less the holy country of Sarras. In the course of his reading, he had come across these lines in some old German volume:

> The world is fair to look on, white and green and red,
> But inly it is black of hue, and dismal as the dead.

That, he thought, was the very truth.

In 1471 Sir Thomas Malory, knight and prisoner of Newgate, was carried off by a pulmonary collapse. He was buried just down the road, in the chapel of St Francis at Greyfriars. On the tomb of this indicted rapist, cattle-stealer, robber and all-round bandit was written the legend: 'Sir Thomas Malory, Valiant Knight'.

✤ Index ✤